CRITICISM AND CULTURE

CRITICISM AND CULTURE:
The Role of Critique in Modern Literary Theory

Robert Con Davis and Ronald Schleifer

LONGMAN

Longman Group UK Limited
Longman House, Burnt Mill, Harlow,
Essex CM20 2JE, England
and Associated Companies throughout the world.

First published 1991

BRITISH LIBRARY CATALOGUING-IN-PUBLICATION DATA
Davis, Robert Con
    Criticism and culture: The role of critique in
    modern literary theory
    I. Title   II. Schleifer, Ronald
    801

    ISBN 0–582–05081–2
    ISBN 0–582–05082–0 pbk

LIBRARY OF CONGRESS CATALOGING-IN-PUBLICATION DATA
Davis, Robert Con. 1948–
    Criticism and culture: the role of critique in modern literary
theory / Robert Con Davis and Robert Schleifer.
        p.   cm.
    Includes bibliographical references and index.
    ISBN 0–582–05081–2. – ISBN 0–582–05082–0 (pbk.)
    1. Criticism.   2. Culture.   I. Schleifer, Ronald.   II. Title.
PN81.D375   1991
801'.95 – dc20   91–13609
                                                          CIP

Set in Linotron 202 10/12 Bembo

Produced by Longman Singapore Publishers (Pte) Ltd.
Printed in Singapore

Contents

Contents

Preface

We started writing this book two years ago to answer a question that we had formulated in the writing of previous books. Simply put, the question amounted to asking *what* criticism is. How does criticism come about, how does it change, and how does it interact with and reflect culture? We had finished books with cultural-studies orientations – *Rhetoric and Death* (Schleifer, Illinois 1990), *The Paternal Romance* (Davis, Illinois 1992) and a book we had written with Nancy Mergler entitled *Culture and Cognition* (Cornell 1992). These projects followed our anthology, *Contemporary Literary Criticism: Literary and Cultural Studies* (Longman, 1989). In writing these books we found ourselves noticing something almost too simple to discuss – the common reliance in literary studies on the concepts of 'criticism' and 'critique' with little regard for what they mean, have meant, or could mean in reconstituted English departments and cultural-studies programmes. In an era of hypercritical activity and incessant theoretical reconfiguration, we saw it as strange that there should be communal silence about the nature of those fundamental concepts – that there was little or no expressed need to define, redefine, or clarify them. We began exploring these concepts, particularly their relation to each other, in the developments of modern literary studies.

We also wanted to address the odd absence or relative neglect of discussion in the literary community about the difference between 'criticism' and 'critique'. This led the book – inevitably we now see – to a study of the ways of establishing new grounds for critical practice, the way modern criticism is both undone and advanced through the continual erosion of critical presuppositions and grounds. We ended up writing a book about modern literary criticism in relation to the idea of criticism as a social and cultural practice in the

vii

twentieth century. Our discussion in *Criticism and Culture*, in other words, concerns both what criticism is and how it operates in culture and through social relations.

The importance of thinking about criticism in the post-semiotic and post-deconstructive era of cultural criticism can hardly be over-stated. Currently there is tremendous pressure on students and teachers alike to read and interpret unfamiliar and difficult texts – including many of the critical texts and cultural analyses we explore in this volume. An 'English' education, now less a tour of the familiar 'monuments' of Western culture and more a confrontation with live and exotic (and unpredictable) beasts, is defined increasingly by the proliferation of reconstructed canons of study in the academy, includ-ing the texts of the 'new' Anglo-American studies and the steady importation of African and other Third-World texts, from the explorations of nation and narration to the diversity of transnational cultural schemes and texts.

The task of 'English' – both as a body of professional knowledge and as a collection of texts – has come to be no less than a global redefinition of literary studies according to the 'critical' element in literary criticism. Such a task includes examining the role and significance of 'critique' in philosophy from the eighteenth-century through to the present. We explore this model of critique as it is realized in literary study to show a clear and yet helpfully complex sense of criticism and critique as analytical and quite different but related strategies for understanding texts. To this end, we survey twentieth-century literary studies to demonstrate the common, if sometimes unacknowledged, purpose of situating literature in relation to culture. This situating is often apparent within larger cultural formations; at other times it takes the form of a global definition of 'culture' found in and through the study of literature. In this way *Criticism and Culture* attempts to offer a new understanding of what we do when we read, teach, and write about literary texts.

The immediate aim of this book is threefold. (1) It develops a history (or genealogy) of the concept of philosophical critique from the Enlightenment through to the present. (2) It examines this concept in relation to literary studies to show a more or less self-conscious pursuit of a 'critical' definition of culture. In this examination of criticism and critique we focus on particular 'critiques' of cultural assumptions and institutions that are pursued in literary studies – large modes of assumption and inquiry. (3) In doing so, we present a revised understanding of literary criticism as consisting of modes of cultural critique and suggest a selective 'history' of twentieth-century literary studies within the broad areas of psychological criticism, structuralism and semiotics, philosophical criticism (particularly deconstruction and post-structuralism), historical criticism (Marxist and Foucauldian), and feminism and other more or less self-conscious forms of cultural criticism. We hope in pursuing this complex aim, *Criticism and Culture* will make clear the link between literary criticism and critique and the fact that critique cannot proceed without an engagement with cultural analysis.

ORGANIZATION OF THE BOOK

This book is divided between two chapters that introduce the nature of our inquiry and five subsequent chapters that explore criticism and critique across the twentieth-century. The first two chapters create theoretical and historical contexts for thinking about criticism and critique, setting the stage with attempts to understand the nature of the critical enterprise as both an epistemological and a social activity. The last five chapters explore major portions of the critical terrain from the mid-nineteenth-century through to comprehensive twentieth-century projects to redefine critical activity and engage in effective cultural critique.

The first chapter, 'Terrible Learning: Critique and Culture', presents a historical and functional definition of critique as a mode of inquiry. Beginning with Enlightenment definitions of critique, we contrast critique with criticism, noting that the 'method' of critique is to subject a mode of understanding to a thorough interrogation of its procedures and conclusions from the viewpoint of its own presuppositions. We analyse models for critiques elaborated by Kant, Hegel, Nietzsche, Freud, Saussure, Marx, and the Frankfurt School that emphasize the close relationship between critical practice and cultural analysis. The chapter also closely examines texts by Lévi-Strauss, Todorov, Lacan, Jean-François Lyotard, Jacques Derrida, Hillis Miller, and Raymond Williams. In examining these latter figures, we are centrally concerned with developing a conception of critique in relation to the prospects for modern literary studies. We end with a discussion of the history of the concept of 'culture', contrasting anthropological and literary uses of critique in E.B. Tylor, Matthew Arnold, Clifford Geertz, Lévi-Strauss, and Williams.

In the second chapter, 'The Function of Criticism: Humanism and Critique,' we examine the humanistic and pedagogical (as opposed to 'critical') study of literature in the early twentieth-century, especially descriptions of the function of literary studies from Matthew Arnold through to British and American New Criticism. Northrop Frye described the work of the New Criticism as a form of 'delicate learning' – the opposite of the 'terrible learning' of critique we describe in the first chapter – and this chapter develops the argument of Chapter 1 by showing the limitations of the 'humanistic' tradition in literary criticism while at the same time demonstrating its necessary engagement with critique, the 'terrifying' element within its intricate and humane analyses. In doing so, we examine the description of the function of criticism as the transmission of culture rather than the critique of culture in the work of Irving Babbitt, T.S. Eliot, F.R. Leavis, I.A. Richards, and American New Criticism. Such transmission, we believe, describes the 'delicate' tradition of a humanistic study of literature in the twentieth-century as it interacts with attempts to provide alternatives to the critical tradition the rest of the book examines.

In the next five chapters we examine schools of literary criticism divided into four large categories, not so much schools or movements as fields of inquiry. The purpose of these chapters is not merely to survey literary criticism in the twentieth-century, even though they accomplish that. Rather, our aim is to examine attempts to create different definitions of culture in relation to the reading of literature. We foreground implicit delimitations of literary value, making them explicit, in order to examine to what extent such values respond to their cultural and social setting. These chapters, in sum, examine the ways in which criticism has gone about situating 'literature' as an object of knowledge by defining culture in relation to literary texts. In such inquiries it is often not clear whether literature is an example or a model for the idea of culture, and the difficulty in making such distinctions will be our concern in the interrogation of different forms of literary study.

In Chapter 3, 'The Critique of the Subject', we examine literary studies that assume culture itself is best understood in relation to the idea of the individual subject, the person who reads or writes. In literary studies this strategy includes criticism that assumes literary works to be governed by a particular author's or particular reader's intentions, taking the concept of intention to include unconscious as well as conscious motives. More specifically, it examines both expressive conceptions of literature and conceptions which are bound to the definition of the subject of discourse as an individual agent in the act of reading, even if this individualism is sometimes conceived in the context of social forces and collective archetypes. To this end, Chapter 3 examines Freudian, archetypal, and a version of reader-response criticism within the framework of a psychoanalytic critique. The chapter also presents different versions of psychoanalytical readings – the ego psychology of Holland and the semiotic Freud of Lacan – and examines the 'pre-Lacanian' archetypal critique of Frye and 'post-Lacanian' feminist critiques that constitute an avant-garde critique of Freud and Lacan in a kind of post-Freudian psychoanalytic criticism. The major figures include Sigmund Freud, Northrop Frye, Norman Holland, Jacques Lacan, Hélène Cixous, Shoshana Felman, Luce Irigaray, Gilles Deleuze, and Felix Guattari.

In Chapter 4, 'Structuralism, Semiotics, and the Critique of Language', we examine literary studies that assume culture itself is best understood in relation to the idea of the formal structures is linguistics and other semiotic systems. In literary studies this includes criticism defined by the assumption that literary works are best conceived as formal, linguistic articulations of meaning. More specifically, we examine Saussure's formulation of structural linguistics at the turn of the century and Roman Jakobson's work in Moscow, Prague, and New York, both of which helped to define linguistics and linguistic-based criticism in the twentieth century. In this chapter we also examine 'formal' conceptions of literature in Russian Formalism (with commentary about 'New Critical' formalism), Prague Semiotics, and French Structuralism. The chapter ends with a discussion of the post-structural critique of structuralism. The major figures include Ferdinand de Saussure, Roman Jakobson, Viktor Shklovsky, Jan Mukařovský, Roland Barthes, Claude Lévi-Strauss, Jacques Derrida, and Julia Kristeva.

In Chapter 5, 'Deconstruction, Post-structuralism, and the Critique of Philosophy', we examine literary studies with the assumption that culture itself is best understood in relation to significant ontological, epistemological, and/or ethical questions. In literary studies this includes criticism that sees literary works as best conceived as articulations of the ethical questions implicit in ideas, ideology, and understanding. We examine conceptions of literature and art that Nietzsche developed in the late nineteenth century in his self-conscious 'philosophic critique' of Kantian aesthetics – what Paul de Man calls the 'aesthetic ideology' – that governs the humanistic study of literature in twentieth-century criticism. In this chapter we read Nietzsche's *Genealogy of Morals* as a critique of Kant's three critiques and show the relationship between Nietzsche's 'method' of genealogy to Derrida's procedure of 'grammatology'. We examine deconstruction by focusing on Derrida's more or less 'literary' reading of Nietzsche in *Spurs* and the ethics of reading in J. Hillis Miller. We conclude with Foucault's 'philosophical' critique of deconstruction and Shoshana Felman's 'literary' critique in *The Literary Speech Act*. The major figures in this chapter include Nietzsche, Gilles Deleuze, Derrida, Martin Heidegger, Foucault, Paul de Man, J. Hillis Miller, and Felman.

In Chapter 6, 'The Critique of Social Relations,' we examine literary studies with the assumption that culture itself is best understood in relation to the idea of the social nature of human life. In literary studies this includes criticism that takes literary works to be articulations of social and historical forces. We discuss Marx's formulation of a sociological critique in *The Eighteenth Brumaire*, *The German Ideology*, and *Capital*. We then read 'sociological' understandings of literature that follow Marx and Engel's model of base and superstructure, focusing on Raymond Williams, Fredric Jameson, Mikhail Bakhtin, and Kenneth Burke among others. From these readings we turn to Foucault's historical readings of culture in which he developed a textual or genealogical model for critique that significantly modifies the Marxist paradigm. The chapter ends with a critique of this model, as articulated by Gayatri Spivak, and then examines post-Foucauldian historicism in the New Historicism and feminism. The major figures in this chapter include Marx, Taine, Bakhtin, Williams, Jameson, Spivak, Stephen Greenblatt, Annette Kuhn, and Tania Modleski.

After the general examination of twentieth-century literary studies from the viewpoint of the definition of culture pursued in the four preceding chapters, we examine literary criticism that self-consciously pursues cultural critique in the final chapter, 'Notes Towards a Definition of Cultural Studies'. More specifically, we examine feminist critiques of literary studies and those literary critics (including many already treated within particular 'schools' of twentieth-century criticism) who attempt to define culture and situate literary criticism within cultural studies. In this chapter we attempt to give our own sense of the current directions of cultural critique and the cultural significance of contemporary cultural criticism. The major figures in this chapter include Shoshana Felman, Henry Louis Gates, Elaine Showalter, Monique Wittig, Raymond Williams, and Clifford Geertz.

In the writing of this study we have constantly reminded ourselves of the provisional and fragile nature of any assessment of cultural directions or tendencies in developments that are far from concluded – developments, in fact, that our work participates in and cannot separate itself from. Clearly we have our own critical and cultural blind spots that others will identify far better than we can. At the same time, in an era of great cultural diversity and exhilarating social and institutional change, but also of reduced educational budgets and attacks on the institution and fundamental activity of education, we have keenly felt the need to argue for the best and most productive tendencies we see in feminist critiques and the work of cultural studies generally. But as our discussion of cultural critique would suggest, the 'truth' about developments in cultural criticism lies not in any idealized middle ground that we have charted in advance in the relation of our pedagogical aims and our own *interests*. We are reminded that the union president George Meany once responded to a colleague who had proclaimed that the 'truth' of negotiation always lies in the middle of two extremes. Meany replied with some irritation that 'No, the truth is wherever you find it'. We submit this book with the hope of facilitating our readers' own discovery of a negotiated 'truth,' or at least a position, in contemporary critical discourse and cultural critique.

Acknowledgements

Several people helped us in thinking about the issues of this book and put aside their own work to help with ours, and we are happy to acknowledge them. In the early stages of formulating our ideas we were assisted by James Comas, of Syracuse University, Richard A. Barney and David S. Gross, both of the University of Oklahoma and Patrick McGee, of Louisiana State University. At a later stage, Chiara Briganti, of Carleton College, contributed significantly to our discussion of Luce Irigaray in Chapter 3. At the conclusion of the project we received valuable commentary and corrections on large portions of the manuscript from Robert Markley, Susan S. Green and Richard A. Barney. The chair of our department, Stephen Tabachnick, was of great support to us. Shelley Cadamy offered fine advice for our cover and, as ever, Melanie Wright aided our work in innumerable ways. We also received general support from our other collaborators, Nancy Mergler, Susan Green, Richard Barney, Yvonne Fonteneau, David S. Gross, Kathleen Welah, Hunter Cadzou, Geary Hobson, David Mair, and Alan R. Velie of the cultural-studies working group at Oklahoma. To all of these friends we dedicate this book.

CHAPTER ONE

Terrible Learning: Critique and Culture

Cultural analysis is intrinsically incomplete. And, worse than that, the more deeply it goes the less complete it is. It is a strange science whose most telling assertions are its most tremulously based, in which to get somewhere with the matter at hand is to intensify the suspicion, both your own and that of others, that you are not quite getting it right.

Clifford Geertz
The Interpretation of Cultures

In the winter of 1860 Matthew Arnold gave a series of lectures at Oxford, subsequently published as *On Translating Homer*, and in this work he took great exception to the recent translation of the *Iliad* by Francis Newman, the brother of the man who was to become the celebrated Cardinal. Newman responded to Arnold's attack in a pamphlet, and then Arnold again took up the issue of the translation in a lecture he subsequently published entitled *On Translating Homer: Last Words* (1862). Quoting Newman's assertion that Arnold blamed him 'for rendering the words correctly', Arnold goes on to ask:

What *is* correctness in this case? This correctness of his is the very rock on which Mr. Newman has split. He is so correct that he finds peculiarity everywhere. The true knowledge of Homer becomes at last, in his eyes, a knowledge of Homer's 'peculiarities, pleasant and unpleasant.' Learned men know these 'peculiarities,' and Homer is to be translated because the unlearned are impatient to know them too. 'That,' he exclaims, 'is just why people want to read an English Homer – *to know all his oddities, just as learned men do.*' Here I am obliged to shake my head, and to declare that, in spite of all my respect for Mr. Newman, I cannot go these lengths with him. He talks of my 'monomaniac fancy that there is nothing quaint or antique in Homer.' Terrible learning, – I cannot help in my turn exclaiming, – terrible learning, which discovers so much!
Here, then, I take my leave of Mr. Newman, retaining my opinion that

1

his version of Homer is spoiled by his making Homer odd and
ignoble. . . . (184–5)

In this lecture, Arnold defines terrible learning as that which makes
the familiar odd and uncomfortable, which transforms the self-evident
into the questionable and what seems to be natural and universal,
such as the 'truth' of Homer's poetry, into quaint institutions marked
by historical time. Still, this description of Arnold is too one-sided
and fails to acknowledge the positivism of Newman's antiquarian
reading of Homer – the 'quaintness' of isolated fact. Arnold is offering
a critique in his sarcasm – what is 'terrible' about Newman's writing
is its very facticity. Yet Arnold is also offering, as he does throughout
his career, self-evident humanism as the opposite of terrible learning,
which we examine in the next chapter.

We have taken 'Terrible Learning' for the title of our examination
of the relationship between criticism and critique precisely to capture
the double sense of the *learning* of critique, which terrorizes received
ideas and, at the same time, resists the traditionlessness of rational
positivism. Swift figured such positivism in Gulliver, whose gullibil-
ity allowed him to elaborately deny charges that he committed
adultery with a Lilliputian woman and never to notice that he might
have some responsibility in the shipwreck of the *Antelope*, whose
crew was reduced and weakened by disease and immoderate labour
while he was its surgeon. Gulliver's learning – his naive dependence
on his individual powers – was terrible in its own way just because it
imagined no *cultural* component to understanding. For this reason, he
quotes Sinon as a figure for truth telling. But Swift himself, like
Arnold after him, also imagined that the received truths of culture –
its sweetness and light – could fully resist the terrible learning, not
only of positivism, but of cultural critique.

Critique, we will argue, situates itself between the learning of
positivism and the received ideas – what Northrop Frye calls the
'delicate learning' (1957: 72) – of 'culture'. In this way, it makes
positivism's 'reason' and culture's honeyed sweetness and light subject
to the terror of basic questions, the terrible imagining of things being
different from what they are, which ask what Terry Eagleton calls
'the most impossibly fundamental questions' that 'press perversely on
to interrogate the whole form of social life' (1986: 171). As such,
critique is *always* questioning culture: it is neither the reasoned critique
of positivism that imagines itself free from culture nor the resistance
to critique that 'culture,' described in terms of necessity, tradition,
human nature, often manifests. Such cultural critique, we will argue,

inhabits literary studies in the twentieth-century when it is most powerful – when it situates literature as a *cultural* phenomenon which calls for the terrible learning of critique. This 'situating,' we believe, makes literature important as well as powerful in our understanding and analysis of ourselves, the relations among ourselves, and the culture that we participate in, share, and can imagine transformed. The combination of understanding and transformation of cultural critique creates a kind of 'terrible learning' different from yet related to the terrible learning Arnold describes and Swift enacts. It is such a conception of critique in relation to literary criticism conceived as cultural critique that we will explore in this chapter and in this book.

PHILOSOPHICAL CRITIQUE

The concept of critique is central to post-Enlightenment philosophy and to the study of culture and cultural institutions such as literature. The word itself is derived from the Greek term *krinein*, which means to separate and discern and from which the term 'crisis' also derives. Its classical usage referred principally to three spheres of activity: it was applied in the administration of justice to describe the re-establishment of order in a legal dispute; in medicine to describe the turning point of an illness; and later, in Hellenistic Greece, as a more general cultural term to describe the study of literary texts. It was with the background connotations of law, medicine and philology that the Latin articulation of *krinein*, the term 'critique', became part of the modern European languages during the seventeenth century. (For a more extensive description of this etymology, see Connerton 1980, Ch. 1.)

This widespread adoption in the seventeenth century makes sense, because 'critique' was a term especially appropriate for the Enlightenment. While in the Renaissance it bore as its primary significance the classical connotation of the activity of the grammarian/philologist, by the late seventeenth century it took on wider and more modern significance in the great theological disputes raging throughout Europe that were the most turbulent symptoms of 'modernization'. 'If any particular turning-point [in the history of the concept of 'critique'] can be singled out,' Paul Connerton (1980) points out,

> it is the publication of Bayle's *Dictionnaire historique et critique* in 1697. From then onwards the concepts of 'reason' and 'critique' were

indivisible. Critique came to be seen no longer as a symptom of the sharpening opposition between reason and revelation. It was viewed as itself the activity which separated the two spheres. It was the essential activity of reason. (18)

If critique and reason came to be seen as 'indivisible', it is because the concept of reason had also changed in the course of time. The aim of the traditional or classical conception of reason was to discover and describe first principles, universal truths that governed phenomena under consideration by providing them with 'sufficient reason'. In this way the reasonable was the 'fitting' and 'proper', and Aristotle, for instance, could equate the law with 'order' or 'reason' and assert that reason was the highest of men's faculties because it allowed them to understand the order of the cosmos and to pursue their lives accordingly. (It is significant that by 'man' Aristotle meant the free males of Athens.)

In the early eighteenth century Leibniz subtly altered Aristotle's conception when he asserted in the *Monadology* that the 'principle of sufficient reason' is one of the two great founding principles of reason (the other being 'the principle of contradiction'). By virtue of the 'principle of sufficient reason', Leibniz writes, 'we hold that no fact can be true or existing and no statement truthful without a sufficient reason for its being so and not different; albeit these reasons most frequently must remain unknown to us' (1714: 153). Reason in this conception, as in that of Aristotle, is an understanding in a positive way of what is. But if Leibnizian understanding led, inevitably, to 'givens' about the world, to 'revelations' and 'self-evident' truths in the same way that Aristotle's 'reason' led to self-evident truths, for Leibniz, unlike Aristotle, reason could be opposed to 'facts'. 'There are two kinds of *truths*,' Leibniz wrote: 'those of *reason*, which are necessary and of which the opposite is impossible, and those of *fact*, which are contingent and of which the opposite is possible. When a truth is necessary, the reasons for it can be found through analysis, that is, by resolving it into simpler ideas and truths until one comes to primitives'. Fact, like reason, must have 'sufficient reason', but for the contingent world of fact 'the resolution into particular reasons could be continued without limit' (153).

In the great theological disputes of the seventeenth century, Aristotelian 'reason' took its place in the debates, especially in the form of the 'Right Reason' of the churches. But this 'reasoning' was opposed to the new kinds of reasoning and rationality that arose in the Renaissance. Thus reason no longer took cultural or traditional norms as its limit, but rather broke with the classical tradition. In these disputes, reason no longer was solely what Raymond Williams has called the 'faculty of connected thought and understanding' (1985: 253). Instead, the 'new' reasoning came to be opposed to revelation in the very limitlessness of its analyses, as Leibniz describes, so that Bayle could write that 'human reason . . . is a principle of destruction, not of edification' (cited in Connerton 1980: 19). Connerton argues that Bayle's assertion is a decisive transformation in the concept of reason. With it, he suggests, reason came to see itself as 'certainly committed to the task of seeking truth; but to a truth which has yet to be established' (19). In other words, reason came to see itself as critique. It no longer simply accounted for what exists in terms of general and universal given truths, in terms of a natural order, but it attempted to understand 'facts' in relation to what could be, on the basis of first principles (such as Leibniz's 'founding principles'), apprehended by human reason itself as opposed to the supernatural revelations (or the social and traditional inheritance) of first principles. Reason questioned and judged the world – including the reasonable orderliness of the cosmos, which seems so self-evidently true to Aristotle – on the basis of its own sovereign power.

In his metaphysics Aristotle describes the actual as always also a part of the potential so that reason can discover that actuality, in Leibniz's terms, is 'so and not different' because of certain universally evident truths about the world rather than any possibility of arbitrary and contingent accidents. By the eighteenth century, however, reason came to be the function of subjecting the actual – the 'facts' of the world Leibniz describes – to relentless questioning and judging. In the Preface to the first edition of The *Critique of Pure Reason* (1781), Immanuel Kant wrote that

> our age is, in especial degree, the age of criticism, and to criticism everything must submit. Religion through its sanctity, and law-giving through its majesty, may seek to exempt themselves from it. But they then awaken just suspicion, and cannot claim the sincere respect which reason accords only to that which has been able to sustain the test of free and open examination. (7)

Kant is describing the negative 'destructive' function of reason, and certainly this sense of the power of 'critique' was a function of the politicization of thought from Bayle to Voltaire and Diderot, to which Kant alludes in reference to the church and state in his Preface.

But the next major development in the concept of critique was Kant's own use of the term in his great 'Critiques' beginning with the *Critique of Pure Reason*. In this work he transforms critique from the reasoned 'criticism' of existing institutions (both public and private) to a search for the conditions governing that reasoned criticism altogether. In the *Critique of Pure Reason* Kant effects what he calls a 'Copernican revolution' in philosophy by turning critique from its focus on external dogmas governing understanding and social institutions to a focus on the inner workings of understanding and the procedure of critique itself. As he says in the Preface to *Critique of Pure Reason*, his critique 'is a call to reason to undertake anew the most difficult of all its tasks, namely, that of self-knowledge, and to institute a tribunal which will assure to reason its lawful claims, and dismiss all groundless pretensions, not by despotic decrees, but in accordance with its own eternal and unalterable laws' (7). In this task can be seen the double sense of Kant's title *Critique of Pure Reason*: pure reason will be the *agent* of critique and, at the same time, it will be the *object* of critique.

This complexity of critique situates it in opposition to mere 'criticism'. Seyla Benhabib (1986) writes:

> While criticism . . . stands outside the object it criticizes, asserting norms against facts, and the dictates of reason against the unreasonableness of the world, critique refuses to stand outside its object and instead juxtaposes the immanent, normative self-understanding of its object to the material actuality of this object. Criticism privileges an Archimedean standpoint, be it freedom or reason, and proceeds to show the unfreedom or unreasonableness of the world when measured against this ideal paradigm. By privileging this Archimedean standpoint, criticism becomes dogmatism: it leaves its own standpoint unexplained, or it assumes the validity of its standpoint prior to engaging in the task of criticism. (32–3)

In this description, we believe, can be seen the Enlightenment conception of reason as a faculty which does not need the support of Archimedean truths and assumptions that more or less 'transcend' its powerful functioning. Reason, in this conception, is sovereign and self-sufficient. In Kant's important phrase, reason is 'disinterested', simply the more or less sufficient servant of truth.

THE CRITIQUE OF LANGUAGE

A clear and instructive contemporary example of the contrast between criticism and critique can be seen in Claude Lévi-Strauss's important critique of Russian Formalism, 'Structure and Form: Reflections on a Work by Vladimir Propp' (1960) and Tzvetan

Todorov's later application of this argument to literary criticism in his critique of Northrop Frye's 'formalism' in the first chapter of his structuralist study of Gothic fantasy, *The Fantastic*. (This example should also clarify the Enlightenment conception of reason we have discussed.) This is all the more apt an example because Lévi-Strauss himself has characterized structuralism as 'Kantianism without a transcendental subject' (cited in Connerton 1980: 23). In 'Structure and Form' Lévi-Strauss contrasts structuralism and formalism by noting that opposed to *form*, '*structure* has no distinct content; it is content itself, and the logical organization in which it is arrested is conceived as a property of the real' (1960: 167). That is, the 'structures' of structuralism – the 'logical organization' of understanding – are *immanent* in human apprehension of phenomena just as the a priori categories of Kant's critique of pure reason are immanent in human apprehension. The model Lévi-Strauss is using is that of linguistics. As he says in 'Structure and Form': 'we define a "universe of the tale," analyzable in pairs of oppositions interlocked within each character who – far from constituting a single entity – forms a bundle of distinctive features like the phoneme in Roman Jakobson's theory' (1960: 182). In this argument, Lévi-Strauss gives a powerful example of the way that Kant's critique turns philosophy in the twentieth century towards linguistic analysis.

In this essay, Lévi-Strauss critiques Propp's formalist analysis of the Russian wondertale in *Morphology of the Folktale* (1928; Lévi-Strauss responded to the English translation, 1959). The problem with Propp's *Morphology*, he argues, is that it absolutely separates form and content in analysing the pattern of narrative in Russian folktales. Structuralism, on the other hand, asserts that 'form and content are of the same nature, amenable to the same type of analysis. Content receives its reality from its structure, and what is called form is a way of organizing the local structures that make up this content' (1960: 179). For Lévi-Strauss, as for Jakobson in his linguistic analyses, the opposition between form and content does not exist: the very 'content' of linguistic entities – phonemes, morphemes, words – is indistinguishable from their 'form'. A word, for instance, is a formal entity so that there is no 'content' except what is formed and structured. In these terms, the opposition between formalism and structuralism, as Lévi-Strauss sees it, is an example of the opposition between criticism and critique. Propp's remarkable analysis of the narrative structures of folktales (see Schleifer 1987: 110–26) offers Lévi-Strauss the opportunity to define structuralism and to clarify his own activity as cultural critique. It is precisely part of his point, in

'Structure and Form', to situate both folktales and myths as cultural activity, as part of the great cultural activity of language and semiosis. Tales are different only in degree from myths, he argues. 'The former,' he writes, 'are not cosmological, metaphysical, or natural, but, more often, local, social, and moral. In addition – precisely because the tale is a weakened transposition of the theme whose stronger realization is the property of myth – the former is less strictly subjected than the latter to the triple consideration of logical coherence, religious orthodoxy, and collective pressure' (1960: 176). What marks both folktales and myths – and he explicitly distinguishes them from 'literature' in the 'stability' with which they maintain their structures – is that they are, in fact, 'local' manifestations of universal, 'logical' structures of organization – the very self-sufficient reason of Kantian critique. In this, they manifest *culture* and, in a sense, transmit it.

Lévi-Strauss's structuralism is a major influence in twentieth-century *cultural* anthropology, and it presents an alternative definition of *culture* to that of Raymond Williams, which we will examine later in this chapter (see Hall 1980). Anthropology defines culture as 'that complex whole which includes knowledge, belief, art, morals, law, custom, and any other capabilities and habits acquired by man as a member of society' (cited in Stocking 1968: 73). Lévi-Strauss certainly assumes this definition but modifies it by the additional assumption that universal human capacities govern all the particular manifestations of culture. That is, his overriding assumption is not the Hegelian one that the real is rational, but the closely related Enlightenment assumption – perhaps a version of Kant's – that human *experience* is rational. Accordingly, for Lévi-Strauss, human 'experiences' – including experiences as seemingly immediate as the smell of perfume or the taste of chocolate – are *forms of meaning* (semiosis) and, like all forms of meaning, are 'effects' of universal intellectual structures of apprehension. For this reason, experience is susceptible to rational analysis.

Throughout all of Lévi-Strauss's work, as Edmund Leach has noted, the 'general object of analysis' is the 'human mind' which is objectively 'an attribute of human brains' (Leach 1970: 40). The mind itself is the locus of what we are calling the intellectual structures of human apprehension, and those structures themselves are *human*, or universal, in that they enable the distinction between human and other life forms. They distinguish *culture* from *nature*. Moreover, the distinguishing feature of culture as opposed to nature is that culture is everywhere *meaningful*, everywhere imbued with signification, and meaning itself is an *effect* of logical, intellectual structures by which mind orders experience.

Those structures, as we will argue in Chapter 4, are based upon the logic of binary opposition that governs twentieth-century linguistics. This is the logic of combinations (or of a 'combinatory') – the isolation of units or elements that distinguish themselves from other units and also combine to form 'higher-level' units – through which meaningful language is structured. That such a 'structural' arrangement governs meanings beyond the sentence of traditional linguistics – that it governs the meaningful apprehensions of reality within social formations and 'cultures' just as it governs the narratives found universally in all human cultures – is Lévi-Strauss's great contribution to twentieth-century thought that allows him not only to shape, in many ways, cultural anthropology as a discipline but also to help transform linguistics into semiotics. As he says in the Introduction to *The Raw and the Cooked* (1964):

> I had tried to transcend the contrast between the tangible and the intelligible by operating from the outset from the sign level. The function of signs is, precisely, to express the one by means of the other. Even when very restricted in number, they lend themselves to rigorously organized combinations which can translate even the finest shades of the whole range of sense experience. We can thus hope to reach a plane where logical properties, as attributes of things, will be manifested as directly as flavors or perfumes; perfumes are unmistakably identifiable, yet we know that they result from combinations of elements which, if subjected to a different selection and organization, would have created awareness of a different perfume.   (14)

The aim of Lévi-Strauss's analysis of cultural artifacts – rituals and kinship organization and narratives – is to demonstrate that the 'forms of judgment' Kant attempts to understand as the *condition* for reason, moral judgment and aesthetic experience are best understood on the 'sign level', which is to say in relation to the *structures* rather than to the *subject* (or agent) of those 'forms', now conceived as fully *discursive*.

The attention to discourse demonstrates how easy it is to move from Lévi-Strauss's structural anthropology to a structural analysis of literature. In fact, Lévi-Strauss's dependence on linguistics as the model for his cultural analysis, implicitly at least, privileges explicitly discursive formations as 'representative' cultural artifacts. All culture, Lévi-Strauss argues, is made up of artifacts whose logic of organization is that of discourse, and so explicit discourses – especially myth and, to a lesser degree, folktales, whose 'authors', collectively, can be seen as a culture taken as a whole – are actually the major focus of

9

Lévi-Strauss's life work. Tzvetan Todorov, among others, has appropriated Lévi-Strauss's methods of narrative analysis to study literature, and his critique of Northrop Frye's work helps to demonstrate the distinction between criticism and critique we are pursuing here.

In *The Fantastic* Todorov (1970) attempts to define the genre of the 'fantastic' in structural terms. To do so, he creates a 'combinatory' of possible interpretations of literary plots. A story, even when it narrates unbelievable events, can be understood as having a naturalistic explanation, so that what appears to be unbelievable can be integrated into a pre-existing category of understanding. However, the (binary) opposite of this naturalistic explanation is *logically* possible: the events of a story will call for the abandonment of a naturalistic explanation in favour of a supernatural explanation. In the context of this simple binary logic, Todorov describes the 'very heart of the fantastic'.

> In a world which is indeed our world, the one we know, a world without devils, sylphides, or vampires, there occurs an event which cannot be explained by the laws of this same familiar world. The person who experiences the event must opt for one of two possible solutions: either he is the victim of an illusion of the senses, of a product of the imagination – and the laws of the world then remain what they are; or else the event has indeed taken place, it is an integral part of reality – but then this reality is controlled by laws unknown to us. . . .
>
> The fantastic occupies the duration of this uncertainty. Once we choose one answer or the other, we leave the fantastic for a neighboring genre, the uncanny or the marvelous.   (25)

In this simple example we can see the ways reason attempts to deal with something as complex as the cultural phenomenon of literature. In its sovereignty, reason pursues three goals or methods (all of which are articulated by Leibniz): it is (1) logical (that is, non-contradictory), (2) true to the facts (that is, explanations of existing phenomena), and (3) as simple as possible (that is, explanations that are *sufficient* for accounting for the facts in a logical way). In his analysis, as in Kant's goal for the *Critique of Pure Reason*, Todorov is presenting the *conditions* for the existence of a particular literary genre. He is doing so, moreover, by means of the *spatial* figuring of experience which, as we shall see in Chapter 4, structuralism favours.

Of greater interest to us here, however, are the ways in which Todorov distinguishes his enterprise from Northrop Frye's similar categorizations of literary genres in *Anatomy of Criticism* (1957). Like linguistics itself, Todorov is attempting to make sense of the fact that literature produces repeatable effects in such a way that they can be analysed in terms of the general category of literary genre. For Todorov, genre is analogous to an element of grammar just as for Lévi-Strauss myth is a part of cultural grammar: it is the means by which unique discursive events can be apprehended. In other words, as with linguistics, Todorov imagines that the best model for literary criticism is *science*, which is, as Louis Hjelmslev (1943) notes in defining the 'science' of linguistics, 'systematic, exact, and generalizing' – the three goals of reason just mentioned. Science pursues these goals by assuming that

> for every *process* there is a corresponding *system*, by which the process can be analyzed and described by means of a limited number of premises. It must be assumed that any process can be analyzed into a limited number of elements recurring in various combinations. Then, on the basis of this analysis, it should be possible to order these elements into classes according to their possibilities of combination. And it should be further possible to set up a general and exhaustive calculus of the possible combinations. (8–9)

While Frye attempts to set up a 'scientific' criticism in the *Anatomy*, he does so, according to Todorov, on the level of analysis which does not allow for the *generalizing* power of science, just as Lévi-Strauss claims that Propp's morphology, by rigidly distinguishing between the general form of folktales and the specific content of particular narratives, remains too close to the accidental surface of the narratives he analyses.

That is, Frye does not establish his 'calculus' of genres on the basis of the 'logical organization' that Lévi-Strauss as well as Todorov sees as necessary to rigorous 'objective' analysis. For Frye, as Todorov describes his work, 'the *structures* formed by literary phenomena *manifest themselves at the level of these phenomena* – i.e. those structures are directly observable'. Todorov, however, follows and quotes Lévi-Strauss in arguing that 'the fundamental principle is that the notion of social structure is not related to empirical reality but to the model constructed according to that reality' (1970: 17). In other words, Frye analyses literature not in terms of the 'model' of its 'logical organization', but in terms of its manifest content. 'To return to our example,' Todorov says, '. . . the forest and the sea *can* often be found in opposition, thus forming a 'structure'; but they do not *have to*; while the static and the dynamic necessarily form an opposition, which can be manifested in that of the forest and the sea' (1970: 18). In the analysis of the fantastic Todorov, like Lévi-Strauss, is not attempting the critical interpretation of a particular meaning based upon norms which judge the facts at hand. Rather, he is attempting a more or less Kantian critique of the 'grounds' of literary meaning, of generic structures, and is willing to apply the same criteria to his own procedures and assumptions which his critique brings to the texts it studies: the ground of *logical organization*. Todorov begins *The Fantastic* with a general discussion of genre and structuralism, in other words, because the *method* of analysis is as important as the analysis itself. In the same way that Lévi-Strauss says form and content are indistinguishable, method becomes an object of analysis because it participates in the same discursive formations – the same universal meaning-formation, the same 'textuality' – as the texts being analysed. In this way, criticism shades into critique.

KANT AND HEGEL

It is Kant, then, in a Copernican revolution in philosophy, who effects a transformation of criticism to critique. Richard Rorty has argued that the aim of Kant's work is to transform philosophy from scholastic dogmatism to critical inquiry modelled on the emerging new science of the eighteenth century. Kant, he writes, 'takes scientific truth as the center of philosophical concern' (1982: 92). 'Philosophy since Kant,' Rorty argues, 'has purported to be a science which could sit in judgment on all the other sciences. As the science of knowledge, the science of science, *Wissenschaftslehre, Erkenntnistheorie*, it claimed to discover those general principles which made scientific discourse scientific, and thus to 'ground' both the other sciences and itself' (1982: 141).

Rorty opposes this tradition in philosophy to that of Hegel, and although Hegel rarely uses the term 'critique' in his work, this opposition nevertheless helps to delineate two conceptions of critique that are crucial to understanding literary and cultural studies in the twentieth century. Rorty argues that the opposition between Kant and Hegel is best understood as an opposition between two radically different conceptions of what philosophy does. If Kantian philosophy is 'scientific' – if it regards 'the truth, goodness, and beauty,' as Rorty says, 'as eternal objects which we try to locate and reveal' – then the Hegelian philosophy is essentially discursive, 'regarding [truth, goodness and beauty] as artifacts whose fundamental design we often have to alter'. Kantian philosophy 'takes scientific truth as the center of philosophical concern' and 'asks how well other fields . . . conform to the model of science'. The Hegelian tradition 'takes science as one (not especially privileged nor interesting) sector of culture, a sector which, like all the other sectors, only makes sense when viewed historically' (1982: 92). In this description, the opposition between Kant and Hegel is the opposition between truth conceived as 'eternal' and 'transcendental' – truth, to use an important Kantian word, that is 'grounded' in the 'eternal and unalterable laws' of reason – and truth conceived as 'historical' and 'material'.

The opposition between truth conceived transcendentally and historically can be seen in Hegel's implicit critique of Kant. The 'ground' of Kant's critiques – the Archimedean point upon which he establishes his critiques – is the sovereign *subject of reason*. If reason is sovereign and self-sufficient, it is so because it corresponds, not to the 'nature of things' – this is Aristotle's view – but to the harmonious and 'natural' foundation of its agent and subject. Kant's Copernican revolution in philosophy, as he himself says in the Preface to the 1787 edition of the *Critique of Pure Reason*, transforms philosophy from ontology to epistemology. It moves the centre of philosophic attention from objects in the world to the subject of understanding. 'Hitherto,' he writes, 'it has been assumed that all our knowledge must conform to objects.' Now, however, Kant wants to explore the possibility that experience itself may be 'a species of knowledge which involves understanding; and understanding has rules which I must presuppose as being in me prior to objects being given to me' (1781: 16–17).

In other words, if the dogmatic scholastic philosophy which Kant critiques asserts a 'pre-established harmony between subject and object', then Kant substitutes 'the principle of a necessary submission of the object to the subject itself' (Deleuze 1963: 23; see also Eagleton 1990: 85). For Kant this submission, Gilles Deleuze has argued, is governed by the harmony of the human faculties implicit in the universal participation in 'common sense'. That is, *knowledge* itself is possible even when it 'involves' subjective understanding because such 'subjective' understanding exists in harmony with other subjective faculties – the harmony of reason, judgment, imagination – universally across individual subjects. Deleuze (1963) writes:

> From this point of view, common sense appears not as a psychological given but as the subjective condition of all 'communicability.' Knowledge implies a common sense, without which it would not be communicable and could not claim universality. Kant will never give up the subjective principle of a common sense of this type, that is to say, the idea of a good nature of the faculties, of a healthy and upright nature which allows them to harmonize with one another and to form harmonious proportions. . . .

13

> *Even reason,* from the speculative point of view, possesses a good nature
> which allows it to be in agreement with the other faculties: the Ideas
> [Kant writes in the *Critique of Pure Reason*] 'arise from the very nature of
> reason; and it is impossible that this highest tribunal of all the rights and
> claims of speculation should itself be the source of deceptions and
> illusions.' (21–2)

Throughout his work, Kant universalizes the subject of knowledge
even while he submits the objects of knowledge to his critiques. In
this way the truth, goodness and beauty which constitute the objects
of knowledge can be 'eternal'. Kant asserts here, dogmatically, that
'it is impossible' that reason can fool itself; that is, he asserts that it
must be impossible that the subject of reason, which is also the subject
of the other faculties, could be a self-divided subject of warring and
'dissonant' faculties. Were the subject of reason self-divided – were it
subject to contingencies of deceptions and illusions and the accidents
to which they give rise – there could be no ground for knowledge or
its 'understanding'.

It is precisely this transcendent subject of knowledge in Kant that
Hegel subjects to critique. Hegel – and the tradition of 'critique'
beginning with Hegel and running through the unlikely grouping of
Marx, Nietzsche, Freud, Dewey, Heidegger, Horkheimer, Adorno,
Lévi-Strauss, Derrida, Foucault, Kristeva, and many of the contemporary approaches to literary study we will examine in this book –
submits the disembodied ahistorical and asocial epistemic, moral and
aesthetic *subject* in Kant to the same kind of critique to which Kant
submits reason and knowledge. If Kant calls reason to undertake the
most difficult of all its tasks in undertaking the task of 'self-
knowledge', then Hegel focuses upon the subject of this knowledge.
That is, as Seyla Benhabib (1986) notes:

> Hegel interprets the 'self-knowledge' of reason more radically than Kant,
> to mean the self-reflection of reason upon all its presuppositions, and
> among them the faculty and the act of critique itself. The radical self-
> reflection of reason cannot be restricted to an analysis of the
> presuppositions which constitute the objectivity of experience alone. Such
> self-reflection must be extended to the presuppositions which underlie the
> constitution of subjectivity, or of the subject of knowledge, as well.
> Precisely because the 'Copernican turn' initiated by Kant places the
> activity of the knowing subject at the center of the process of knowledge,
> Hegel's analysis of the constitution of subjectivity and objectivity cannot
> dispense with the turn to the subject. Hegel must show that a radical
> critique of knowledge, or of the subjective moment, necessarily leads to
> an analysis whereby the unity of subjectivity and objectivity and their
> reciprocal relationship is revealed. (45)

The 'unity' of subjectivity and objectivity is, for Hegel, *historical*. Both subject and object are determined by historical forces so that each can be understood as a particular 'moment' within this process. In this, knowledge and morality and aesthetic experience – the 'truth, goodness and beauty' Rorty enumerates and Kant submits to analysis in the *Critique of Pure Reason*, the *Critique of Practical Reason* and the *Critique of Judgment* – occur as historical phenomena with histories that can be traced through time and whose effects can be configured at particular moments. Rorty offers the general term 'culture' to describe these configurations, and their analysis along with the historical tracings of their development constitute critiques of Kant's transcendental categories.

THE CRITIQUE OF THE SUBJECT

The first of Kant's transcendental categories to be examined is the category of the subject. Hegel does so in his examination of the master–slave relationship in the *Phenomenology of Mind* (1807). There he analyses the subject not in isolation – not as *transcendent* – but as precisely realizing himself or herself in relation to other people. 'Self-consciousness,' Hegel writes, 'exists in itself and for itself, in that, and by the fact that it exists for another self-consciousness; that is to say, it *is* only by being acknowledged or "recognized"' (229). In this analysis, Hegel implicitly critiques the subject as a self-consistent entity that *has always* existed in and for itself with a simple and direct relationship to 'external' experience. That is, while the subject does exist, phenomenally, in and for itself and even has the (phenomenal) sense of its own sovereignty in relation to the world of experience – after all, it is the *subject* of experience – it exists only in a reciprocal (rather than direct or unidirectional) relationship to the world of other subjects. What is most striking about this analysis is that it places the subject in relation to others in history. Acknowledgement and recognition, as Stanley Cavell (1976) notes, are functions of situated, historically occasioned events (254; see also Schleifer 1990, Ch. 7). 'Hegel,' Eagleton notes, 'projects Kant's aesthetic fiction into the very structure of the real, thus rescuing the subject at once from the *hubris* of subjectivism and the miseries of estrangement' (1990: 122).

This historicization of the subject – the critique of the subject, as found in Freud and his followers as well as Hegel – attempts to see the subject not as a 'harmony' of faculties, working towards a self-identical end, as in Kant, but as the strife of warring parts at odds with one another. For this reason Jacques Lacan, in his self-proclaimed 'return' to Freud, focuses on the 'split' subject – the wars among need, demand and desire. Such a split is readily seen in the discourse of psychoanalysis – in its existence as a 'talking cure' – which constitutes a critique of the very nature of 'subjective experience'. 'In psychoanalytic anamnesis,' Lacan writes, 'it is not a question of reality, but of truth, because the effect of full speech is to reorder past contingencies by conferring on them the sense of necessities to come, such as they are constituted by the little freedom through which the subject makes them present' (1966: 48).

In psychoanalysis, Lacan argues, language transforms the contingency of accidental events that simply 'happen' to someone into necessary causes by articulating events in a discursive frame on the 'stage' of narrative. In this way, language and discourse confer upon experience the consistency of reason. But more than this – in order to do this – discourse also subjects the speaking subject to its own impersonal logic and laws. In other words, the 'talking cure' achieves its reasoned understanding of experience by revealing the subject of experience emerging in time and language. It shows that discourse *posits* the subject (rather than expressing a pre-existing subject) in the same way syntax creates the conditions for the emergence of the 'subject' of a sentence and, in this sense, posits the grammatical subject.

The positing of the subject, in the psychoanalytic critique of the subject, is also a *positioning* of the subject similar to Hegel's positioning of the subject in relation to other subjects. Thus, in Lacan's elaboration of psychoanalysis the 'ego' is no longer a central concept. In its place is what Lacan calls the 'subject', the whole mechanism of conscious and unconscious operations. The subject is not a personal identity at all but a construct, in much the way a character in a narrative is a semiotic construct for Lévi-Strauss. The subject, in this respect, is a way of organizing and understanding the discourse that relates individual people to culture. Lacan specifically thinks of positions in language corresponding to family roles (father, mother, child), which are then conceived on the order of grammatical 'persons', that is, markers for structural positions.

In the 'Seminar on "The Purloined Letter"' (1966a), for instance, Lacan analyses Edgar Allan Poe's story as a parable describing psychoanalysis. That parable describes psychoanalysis as the study of subjectivity as patterned by 'truths', as he says, that are independent of the subject (the ego) and, indeed, independent of 'reality'. He writes:

> If what Freud discovered and rediscovers with a perpetually increasing sense of shock has a meaning, it is that the displacement of the signifier determines the subjects in their acts, in their destiny, in their refusals, in their blindnesses, in their end and in their fate, their innate gifts and social acquisitions notwithstanding, without regard for character or sex, and that, willing or not, everything that might be considered the stuff of psychology, kit and caboodle, will follow the path of the signifier. (60)

The central term here is 'signifier' which Lacan takes up from the linguistic and semiotic tradition established by the linguist Ferdinand de Saussure. The signifier is the 'logical' arrangement of material substances in a sign which, for Saussure, is made of a signifier and a signified. For both Saussure and Lacan the signifier is purely *relational*: it exists only insofar as it exists in its difference from something or things not itself. In this analysis, 'truth' in Lacan's language is 'logical consistency', truth as the coherence of relational parts to one another.

It is precisely such relationality that governs the psychoanalytic critique of the subject. The ego is but one 'position' – designated as the 'speaking subject' or the 'I' – in the subject's discourse, and it has no controlling influence on the overall function of the discourse. This paradigm suggests a psychology (and, in Kantian terms, an epistemology) in which neither the ego nor the 'subject' is taken as naturally meaningful and possessed of an identity. The achieved effects of ego and subjectivity belong essentially to the operation Lacan calls the 'discourse of the Other'. In the 'Seminar on "The Purloined Letter"' (1966a) Lacan describes such positions in relation to seeing – to the 'glance' – which are filled by different characters at different moments in the story.

> The first is a glance that sees nothing: the King and the police.
>   The second, a glance which sees that the first sees nothing and deludes itself as to the secrecy of what it hides: the Queen, then the Minister.
>   The third sees that the first two glances leave what should be hidden exposed to whomever would seize it: the Minister, and finally Dupin. (44)

What is most exposed is the signifier itself: the material object which, bearing meaning, seems to disappear into transparency. It is precisely *this*, before our eyes yet not 'seen' – of which we remain unconscious – to which Lacan (and psychoanalysis) draws attention. In terms of critique, the signifier replaces the 'hidden' causes of conscious and unconscious motives within a horizon of possible actions and determination beyond the ken of the subject. In this analysis, 'reason' is one possible action among the many activities of a subject with no particularly privileged position in the heterogeneous life of historically and culturally determined needs, demands and desires.

Such a conception of the subject – of reading as well as of 'reason' – implies a reconception of literature, one which implies, as we are suggesting in this book, that criticism be conceived as a form of *cultural* critique. An example of this conception of criticism can be seen in Jean-François Lyotard's (1970) psychoanalytical reading of the relationship between *Oedipus* and *Hamlet* in 'The Jewish Oedipus'. In this essay, Lyotard explores the function of staging in culture and in psychoanalysis, and he does so in order both to understand *staging* as such – how representation works in art and in psychoanalysis – and also to read such stagings as functions of cultural representation. Thus, the implicit question of this essay concerns the relationship between art and culture. Specifically, he questions the relationship between Greek and Jew: 'Oedipus,' he writes, 'fulfills his fate of desire; the fate of Hamlet is the non-fulfillment of desire: this chiasmus is the one that extends between what is Greek and what is Jewish, between the tragic and the ethical' (401).

Staging for Lyotard, like psychoanalysis itself for Lacan, is best understood in terms of positions through which characters pass. *Hamlet* offers stage upon stage. The play-within-the-play in Shakespeare, Lyotard notes, fulfils 'on the stage the function comparable to that in *Oedipus* filled by the prophet Tiresias' (407). But Shakespeare also multiplies the 'stage' of the family, presenting the family constellations of Polonius as well as those of Hamlet in order to enact 'the function assigned to representation', that of 'recognition', within a drama of relationships. The aim of recognition is to stage the constitution of the subject – of desire, of guilt, of 'subjectivity' itself. Lyotard notes:

> This principle, applied by Hamlet on the stage [in the play-within-the-play], obtains the expected effect on the spectator Claudius. But Hamlet himself, spectator of the other stage . . . does not recognize his fate, his non-recognition, except negatively, as his own coldness of feeling, slowness, inertia, his own lag behind the time prescribed for vengeance, compared to the violence of Laertes. (409)

Hamlet, that is, *acts out* his symptoms in the psychoanalytical definition of 'acting out' that Lyotard presents. Acting out 'effectuates desire without fulfilling it, off its stage, on an alibi stage set up by derivation and without representation' (410).

In this analysis Lyotard defines representation in a way that describes its cultural power and suggests its function within a critique of culture. The theatre in our culture, he argues, like *culture* in its narrower sense of 'art' and 'art objects', makes desire appear 'in order to make it be seen, in order to make of it a work'. Such desire is not a 'faculty' or a possession of a subject; rather, it is 'unconscious' in the way the positions subjects occupy – precisely those that make subjectivity itself possible – are beyond the apprehension of those so positioned. In this way, the theatre stages the unconscious, which is not a function of a person but a cultural configuration, a horizon of possibilities which, like language and syntax, are socially constituted and inherited. 'The unconscious process is not masterable,' Lyotard says. 'The theatre, on the contrary, shows that it is our master; it shows us dispossessed; it manifests cognition's lack of recognition, the delusion of whoever inquires in order to know' (397). Psychoanalysis's great contribution to the understanding of culture is thus the critique of the sovereign subject: it demonstrates that, in Lyotard's words, the 'disorders' of cognition and knowledge – disorders in the 'harmonious' subject of Kant's critical philosophy – are paths to understanding. 'Freud's genius,' Lyotard notes, 'is to treat these disorders not as obstacles, but as revelations' (395).

THE CRITIQUE OF REASON

A second and explicitly more radical contemporary example of the post-Kantian critique of the *subject of reason* can be seen in Jacques Derrida's discussion of reason itself in relation to institutions of higher education, 'The Principle of Reason: The University in the Eyes of its Pupils' (1983), and in J. Hillis Miller's application of insights gained from Derrida in his earlier essay, 'Stevens' Rock and Criticism as Cure' (1976). In 'The Principle of Reason' Derrida explicitly addresses the Kantian conception of 'reason' as the ground of the university as an institution. As we have done, Derrida turns to Leibniz's formulation of the 'principle of reason' in order to 'plunge into the history of reason, its words and concepts, into the puzzling scene of translation which has shifted *logos* to *raison*, reason, *Grund*, ground, *Vernunft*, and so on' (7). Such a plunge raises a bewildering array of questions. He asks:

> Are we obeying the principle of reason when we ask what grounds this principle which is itself a principle of grounding? We are not – which does not mean that we are disobeying it, either. Are we dealing here with a circle or with an abyss? The circle would consist in seeking to account for reason by reason, to render reason to the principle of reason, in

> appealing to the principle in order to make it speak of itself at the very
> point where, according to Heidegger, the principle of reason says nothing
> about reason itself. The abyss, the hole, the *Abgrund*, the empty 'gorge'
> would be the impossibility for a principle of grounding to ground
> itself. . . . Are we to use reason to account for the principle of reason? Is
> the reason for reason rational? Is it rational to worry about reason and its
> principle? (9)

Such a whirl of questions, as Rorty says of the Hegelian tradition in
philosophy, aims less at answering an argument with a counter
argument than at answering an argument with discourse (1982: 90–5),
with the situated, historical *enunciations* of language.

In articulating such questions, Derrida *situates* reason historically by
giving it a moment in time at which it came to be what it is now: 'the
modern dominance of the principle of reason had to go hand in hand
with the interpretation of the essence of beings as objects, an object
present as representation [*Vorstellung*], an object placed and positioned
before a subject' (1983: 9–10). This is the 'moment' of Leibniz and
Kant. Derrida goes on to link the rise of the principle of reason with
certain Kantian categories and oppositions, such as 'the essential and
noble ends of reason that give rise to fundamental science versus the
incidental and empirical ends which can be systematized only in terms
of technical schemas and necessities' (12). Chief among these, however (though Derrida does not mention it), is the Kantian category of
the sublime itself, and the irrational and overwhelming power that,
in the eighteenth century, Kant included within his thinking as its
opposite, its 'other'. 'Irrationalism, like nihilism,' Derrida adds, 'is a
posture that is completely symmetrical to, thus dependent upon, the
principle of reason' and dates 'from the period when the principle of
reason was being formulated' (14–15). In these terms, Derrida
answers the assertion of the transcendental and universal nature of
reason with its history and its other. Even reason, in this critique, the
apparent guiding principle of critique altogether, can be subject to a
historicizing analysis – which is to say, an analysis which questions
its sovereignty even as the 'ground' of critique itself. Equally important, in this critique philosophy becomes (as psychology becomes in
Lacanian psychoanalysis) a form of *cultural* analysis.

In literary criticism J. Hillis Miller has extended Derrida's critique
in his influential survey of contemporary literary studies published in
1976, 'Stevens' Rock and Criticism as Cure'. In that essay Miller
examines two seemingly contradictory approaches to literature in
contemporary discourse, what he calls (following Nietzsche and
Freud) 'canny' and 'uncanny' criticism. The former possesses faith in

reason – Leibniz's assumption that there is a reasonable explanation for all phenomena – and 'the possibility of a structuralist-inspired criticism as a rational and rationalizable activity' (335), while the latter, even while following the logical procedures of reason, arrives 'into regions which are alogical, absurd' (336). The practitioners of such 'uncanny' criticism, he argues, are 'not able by any "method" or strategy of analysis to "reduce" the language of the work to clear and distinct ideas.' Instead, they are 'forced at best to repeat the work's contradictions in a different form' (333).

Miller ends his essay by erasing the distinction between canny and uncanny understanding in a 'deconstructive' gesture (which we will examine in Chapter 5) that articulates the kind of sublime 'metaphysical' experience that he has always discovered in literature and literary studies – a kind of *sublime* of reading – which represents a chief motivating factor in his experience of literature. 'The work of the uncanny critics,' he writes, 'however reasonable or sane their apparent procedure, reaches a point . . . [of] encounter with an "aporia" or impasse. . . . In fact the moment when logic fails in their work is the moment of their deepest penetration into the actual nature of literary language, or of language itself' (338). In discovering such 'aporetic', self-contradictory moments in reason itself, Miller, like Derrida, is denying the *harmony* in Leibniz's description of reason: that reason is logically self-consistent and can simply account for all aspects of phenomena. Miller's language of 'deep' penetration, unlike Derrida's whirl of questions, seems to mark a recuperation of an 'actual nature' that criticism, as opposed to critique, attempts to recover. Still, in respect to the self-contradictions in reason itself they both are exploding the 'reason' that has governed scientific inquiry since the seventeenth century: that scientific understanding is consistent, exhaustive and parsimonious so that it produces knowledge which does not contradict itself, is not contradicted by the phenomena it is examining, and offers the simplest and most elegant description/explanation possible. For Derrida, phenomena are not necessarily 'reasonable' in this way. This can be seen in his very discourse, which constantly asserts, in its loquacity, its puns, its digressions and its non-seriousness that phenomena are 'irreducibly nonsimple' (1972: 13). And it can be seen in Miller, for whom the *power* of literature (as opposed to its 'actual nature') lies in the ways it explodes the self-sufficiencies of self and reason.

MODES OF CRITIQUE

The opposition between Kant and Hegel, or in broad terms between Lévi-Strauss and Derrida, suggests two different modes of critique – two different conceptions of critical analysis – and two different strands of cultural history. They could be distinguished, perhaps, by whether or not they believe that harmony exists among the elements of reason. For instance, there is just such a lack of harmony in the work of Paul de Man. In his criticism de Man pursues a critique by means of reason that leads to impasses precisely because the *logical* reasonableness of language does not comport with the absence of *empirical* 'reason', as he sees it, in what language describes. In de Man, in other words, there is dissonance between reason's aim at consistency (logical non-contradiction) and its aim at exhaustiveness (accounting for empirical phenomena). But in this contradiction there is little question of the faculties of reason Kant describes. Instead, it articulates the opposition between two conceptions of critique we will describe – *institutional* critique and *transformative* critique – in relation to the third aspect of reason, its *universalizing* power, its 'parsimoniousness'. The 'simplicity' of reason assumes that one explanation is better than two, and if there are two or more competing explanations, the one which accounts for more phenomena – the one whose reason is more 'sufficient' – is the 'best'. (This aspect of reason was articulated by William of Occam, and thus it has come to be called 'Occam's razor', an implement which cuts away unnecessary explanations.) One result of this assumption is the constant gesture of reason to generalize, to abstract invariant elements from the wealth of phenomena and attempt to account for phenomena in terms of these more or less universal and 'trans-historical' (i.e. invariant) first principles.

Critique, however, can focus on these abstracting and dehistoricizing aspects of understanding, as opposed to basing (or 'instituting') its judgments upon them. Doing this, however, it abandons the parsimony of generalization for the loquacity of a series of particular historical events whose very particularity is a function of the specificity of 'variants'. This historicization defines another important function of critique. With the appropriation of Kant by language-based philosophers and the appropriation of Hegel by Marxian philosophers in the nineteenth century, the distinction between critique's attempt to account for existing institutions in terms of 'simple' universal principles and its attempt to question those very principles themselves, in their particular, historically determined applications, has been crucial in the historical development of the concept of critique. Rather than Kantian ontological and epistemological approaches to philosophy, psychology and linguistics – approaches which are abstract and universalizing – the 'transformative' critique we are describing presents variousness as the object of analysis and thus explodes simplicity as a goal of science.

Paul Connerton describes these two different modes of critique under the terms 'reconstruction' and 'criticism', while Seyla Benhabib variously describes them as 'immanent' and 'defetishizing' critiques and as critiques that aim at 'the politics of fulfillment' and 'the politics of transformation'. We will describe these two modes of critique as institutional critique and transformative critique. We will do so in order to suggest that the very opposition we will present is not absolute or absolutely parsimonious in its application. Rather, each form of critique is a version of or analogous to the other, different 'takes' of critical activity depending upon the *ends* pursued in the analysis. Thus, we are calling Benhabib's 'immanent' critique 'institutional' because the immanently existing phenomena that come under the scrutiny of 'institutional' critique – phenomena such as the psychological subject, linguistic forms, self-evident concepts, even the seemingly 'natural' social relationships that arise among human beings – are, in fact, cultural institutions that have historical occasions and, for this reason, are subject to 'transformation'. We are calling Connerton's 'criticism' – a term he uses to mark the relationship of this form of critique with the political analyses of the 'critical theory' of the Frankfurt School in Germany between the wars – 'transformative' to mark more fully than his term does the *political* programme implicit in such critique, its aim at changing cultural practice and phenomena.

Institutional critique attempts to discover, as does Kant, the invariant conditions that govern the existence of any phenomena. It subjects the actual to relentless questioning in order to discover sufficient reason why it should be so and not otherwise, to discover how phenomena 'make sense'. Reconstructive critique, Connerton (1980) says,

> (as proposed for instance by Kant or Chomsky) tries to understand anonymous systems of rules which can be followed by any subject, provided he has the requisite competences. . . .
>
> [It] is based on data which are considered to be objective, like sentences, actions, or cognitive insights; these are the conscious operations of the human actor. . . .
>
> [It] explains what is considered to be 'correct' knowledge; for instance

> the knowledge we must acquire if we are to operate rules
> competently. (25–6)

Such critique focuses on existing conditions, existing institutions. It attempts to understand the conditions or 'grounds' for the functioning of phenomena. As Connerton's yoking of Kant and Chomsky suggests, it can be seen in the development of metaphysics – especially in Anglo-American philosophy – from a concern with transcendental Kantian categories to a concern with linguistic structures, to what Connerton calls the 'intensified interest in language' in the twentieth century which 'has led to reformulations of Kant's model' (25). 'During the hundred years following the publication of his *Critique of Pure Reason*,' Allan Janik and Stephen Toulmin (1973) argue in *Wittgenstein's Vienna*, '. . . the problems of language were brought into the center of the philosophical picture' (120). Kant's emphasis on the 'forms of judgment', they argue, introduced the standard forms of logical grammar as central concerns of philosophy. 'Between 1800 and 1920,' they assert, 'the problem of defining the essential scope and limits of the *reason* was twice transformed: first, into the problem of defining the essential scope and limits of representation and, subsequently, into that of doing the same for language' (121).

Also brought into the centre of the philosophical picture during the nineteenth century was the Hegelian project of historicizing reason and understanding – the project, implicit from the introduction of 'critique' into the intellectual life of the West, of the *negative* of reason. 'The negative' in Hegel, Connerton suggests,

> connotes those historical forces which are incompatible with a certain
> form of social life and which act upon it destructively: but forces which
> nonetheless arise inevitably out of the particular social structure which
> they negate and surpass. Human rationality has a history which consists
> in the criticism in life and in thought of the constraints imposed by each
> of its specific historical forms. Hence this understanding of critique
> implies a particular narrative structure in which the potentialities for
> development of a given mode of thought or a given social condition are
> latent within the very structure of the initial terms. (25)

The particularity of narrative is crucial in understanding transformative critique. Its narrative component can be clearly delineated in the contention that 'in contrast to both positivism and idealism, a genuinely negative dialectics acknowledges what Adorno called "the preponderance of the object" irreducible to . . . active subjectivity' (Jay 1984: 63). In other words, negative transformative critique can never simply or wholly attend to the 'ideas' of anonymous systems, objective data and correct knowledge, even while it does not, like positivism, simply take self-evidence as the sole criterion for 'truth'. Rather, transformative critique aims at criticizing 'positive' existing phenomena but not, as Kantian idealist critique does, simply to understand and make explicit the conditions and grounds that govern those phenomena and understanding itself. Instead, it aims to make something happen: to assert that things could be otherwise, that what exists is not necessary (in contrast to Aristotle's suggestion that what exists *is* necessary), and that critique can allow us to imagine and to articulate a *narrative* in which things would be different from what they are.

To do this, transformative critique focuses on particular phenomena rather than anonymous systems, phenomena whose very 'objectivity' is called into question by the powerful negative forces of history. Secondly, it aims at 'changing or even removing the conditions of what is considered to be a false or distorted consciousness' (Connerton 1980: 26). In other words, if Kantian critique leads, over the course of the nineteenth century, to the study of the anonymous logical and linguistics systems that condition and govern abstract 'understanding', then Hegelian critique leads to the study of *particular* situations of understanding – discursive, psychological and philosophical – that condition and govern understanding. In this way, Hegel 'leads to' not only Marx's works, all of which have the word 'critique' as part of their titles (*Capital*, for instance, is subtitled *A Critique of Political Economy*), but also Freud's project of discovering 'unconscious' determinants for the experience of subjectivity and Nietzsche's project of 'deconstructing' the seeming whole (discursive) cloth of philosophic systematization. Freud's 'unconscious' and Nietzsche's 'revaluation' function like Hegel's (and Adorno's) 'negative'. They subject the 'actual' – in Freud's case the apodictic, self-evident truth of subjective (phenomenal) experience, in Nietzsche's the simple consistency of reason's understanding of the world – to the relentless questionings of critique. It is for this reason that Rorty asserts as strongly as he does that the Kantian and Hegelian traditions governing twentieth-century philosophical inquiry are simply not able to address one another. Unlike Kantian and neo-Kantian philosophers in the twentieth century, he writes, 'non-Kantian philosophers like Heidegger and Derrida are emblematic figures who not only do not solve problems, they do not *have* arguments or theses. They are connected with their predecessors not by common subjects or methods but in the "family resemblance" way in which latecomers in a sequence or commentators on commentators are connected with older members of the same sequence' (1982: 93).

If Kantian philosophy institutes understanding the way science does, then Hegelian philosophy frames its analyses in terms of what Nietzsche and others call genealogy, the examination of the specific conditions governing the institution of cultural phenomena. Still, Connerton's description of Hegel's project in terms of 'false or distorted consciousness', like Miller's 'actual nature' of literature we cited earlier, reveals an abstract idealism within Hegelian historicization, a version of Kant 'haunting' Hegel. Such a haunting marks the non-parsimonious relationship between the two modes of critique we are examining, the possibility that 'sufficient reason' understood as both empirical and logical understanding is not a 'single' phenomenon. In this context, Rorty's distinction between two modes of discourse, argumentative and emblematic, like the modes of constative and performative discourse in J.L. Austin, are not so much absolute oppositions as different 'takes' on language determined by different questions being posed and different ends being sought. In any instance discourse is constative or performative, just as in any instance critique will be institutional or transformative. But set to different ends, the distinction breaks down without one being reduced to an example or instance of the other. Such instances are not 'moments' in a larger hierarchical order, as Hegel's analyses suggest, but rather 'alternative' understandings and undertakings.

THE GROUNDS OF CRITIQUE

In this discussion of critique we have attempted to describe categories that will help to understand the focus and function of twentieth-century literary studies, criticism as cultural critique. Later in this chapter, following Raymond Williams, we will turn to the 'idea' of culture as it develops in the nineteenth and twentieth centuries. But first we want to set forth, 'synchronically', four fields of understanding that are implicit in the concept of critique as it has been presented here and that govern the exposition of this book.

Critique, we have argued, seeks in both its Kantian and Hegelian manifestations to account, relentlessly, for existing phenomena in terms of 'sufficient reason'. Critique stipulates that nothing should be accepted simply as given, and that, in Kant's words, reason accords its sincere respect 'only to that which has been able to sustain the test of free and open examination' (1781: 7). Nevertheless, reason needs an Archimedean standpoint: otherwise, it collapses into a *mise-en-*

abyme, a set of multiplying contexts that go on and on and on. Even the '*mise-en-abyme*' standpoint of the 'non-Kantian, dialectical tradition' Rorty describes, in which 'writing always leads to more writing, and more, and still more – just as history does not lead to Absolute Knowledge or the Final Struggle, but to more history, and more, and still more' (1982: 94, 95) – even this particularized, historicized standpoint remains an Archimedean 'ground' for the understanding of critique.

One way to describe this problem is to see that reason (even negative reason) always creates hierarchic relationships among the phenomena it 'understands'. As Roman Jakobson notes, the essence of language (and of understanding more generally) is synecdochic in that some part of a phenomenon, in *any* understanding, can be seen as being its essence, as standing for the whole (1932: 459; see Schleifer 1990, Ch. 5). To posit 'history' or 'writing' as *particular* phenomena which call for other particularities still generalizes and institutionalizes the particular: it makes particularity the general 'ground' of understanding. Here, then, is one 'ground' for the understanding of cultural critique: the concept and critique of 'culture' is based upon the assumption that cultural phenomena, as opposed to 'biological' or 'physical' or whatever we might call 'non-cultural' phenomena, can be understood only as unique and non-repeatable events – particularities that can never be subject to anonymous, objective analysis that can be 'correct' for all time. Derrida suggests a version of this view when he asserts that the 'sacred' exists beyond the 'reserve' of Hegel's dialectic. The 'reserve' of language, Derrida argues in a discussion of Hegel, is that ability of language and discourse to use everything in, to appropriate everything to, its signifying force 'by means of which philosophy . . . could both include within itself and anticipate all the figures of its beyond' (1967a: 252). Against this reserve – which is the reserve of reason and 'sufficient reason' itself – is the possibility of non-assimilable phenomena, phenomena which do not possess an abstractable 'essence' by which reason can distinguish between the invariants and variants, its 'inside' and 'outside'. Julia Kristeva suggests a similar, negative 'ground' which she calls 'the fourth 'term' of Hegel's dialectic: 'what the dialectic represents as negativity . . . is precisely that which remains outside logic . . . what remains heterogeneous to logic even while producing it through a movement of separation or rejection' (1974: 112).

But even in Kristeva's account we have a version of Kant's transcendental philosophizing. If Kant transforms ontology to epistemology (as he claims to have done), his 'epistemology' nevertheless remains, at least from one vantage, dogmatic ontological philosophizing, and the same can be said of the various versions of the negative dialectics of critique – Hegel's, Marx's, Heidegger's, Adorno's, Derrida's, and so forth – that we will encounter in this book. This contention may be clearer if we examine the other 'grounds' besides the ontological (or 'philosophical') our discussion of critique has set forth governing the opposition between essence and accident, the general and the particular, invariants and variants.

We have already mentioned three developments of critique: its turn to linguistics (as in the example of Lévi-Strauss), to psychology (as in Lacan) and to metaphysics (as in Derrida) to establish the basis (or ground) of its operations. In a moment we will examine a fourth development of critique, its turn to the social life of history and sociology (in the cultural studies of Raymond Williams) in order to ground its activities. Although we are presenting these in order, each in fact claims to 'ground' the others. Linguistic analysis claims that critiques based upon sociological or psychological analyses are ultimately reducible to 'forms of judgment' which are, essentially and invariably, linguistic in nature. Sociology claims that the groundings of individual psychology and private and public utterances are, in fact, socially determined so that social analysis will produce the sufficient reasons for psychological or linguistic effects. Psychology claims that all experience is ultimately subjective (in whatever condition the 'subject' is conceived) and that language and society reflect the deeper 'ground' of subjectivity. Philosophical ontology claims that each of these is simply a version of what uniquely is best understood in terms of the remarkable experience of 'being'.

The grounding of cultural studies in philosophy, psychology, sociology or linguistics seems to exhaust the logic of possibilities (even if, as our discussion as a whole attempts to suggest, such a logic need not exhaust possibilities of understanding and of grounding the transformative power of critique). They offer, as structuralism might suggest, a 'combinatory' that spells out 'objective' and 'subjective' modes of explanation against personal (human) and impersonal grounds: psychology = /personal/ + /subjective/; linguistics = /impersonal/ + /subjective/; sociology = /personal/ + /objective/; philosophy = /impersonal/ + /objective/. J. Hillis Miller (1985) has made this argument in 'The Search for Grounds in Literary Study'. Beginning with a Kantian notion of 'ground', he argues that

> current criticism tends to propose one or another of the three following grounds on the basis of which the anomalies of literature may be made lawful, the unaccountable accountable: society, the more or less hidden

social or ideological pressures which impose themselves on literature and reveal themselves in oddnesses; individual psychology, the more or less hidden psychic pressures which impose themselves on a work of literature and make it odd, unaccountable; language, the more or less hidden rhetorical pressures, or pressures from some torsion within language itself as such, which impose themselves on the writer and make it impossible for his work to maintain itself as an absolutely lucid and reasonable account. (21)

Miller adds to these three grounds a 'fourth possibility for the disturber of narrative sanity and coherence, a disruptive energy neither society nor individual psychology nor language itself', one which is 'properly religious, metaphysical, or ontological, though hardly in a traditional or conventional way' (21). Although he does not say so, this 'last' possibility is that of the sacred and 'uncanny' in experience, perhaps best captured in Kant's description of the sublimity of existence, a version of the 'preponderance of the object' Adorno describes.

Our point, though, in beginning with the category or ground with which Miller ends is to suggest that the very narrative technique he follows in presenting three categories and then a fourth which, in an important way, *negates* the others, privileges the last ground over the others. Following Blanchot, Miller tries to describe the 'philosophical' category as 'an ontology without ontology', not quite a 'negative theology', and the very fact that he presents it last seems to transform this last, most narrativized ground into one which is somehow more basically 'mysterious' than the others. Our point is to demonstrate the *power* of more or less 'accidental' and more or less 'unconscious' discursive formations. In other words, Miller is right when he argues that each of these 'grounds' is exclusive or imperialistic, that each claims to ground the others. But this imperialism correlates with the doubling of critique into two modes that we are describing. Discourse manifests (or does it 'produce' and 'ground'?) such doubling. It imposes diachronic development upon the synchronic schema Miller describes, even upon those things which we tend to think are without history.

NINETEENTH-CENTURY CULTURAL CRITIQUE

The grounds of literary study Miller describes – Archimedean standpoints for criticism and institutional critique when they are understood as imperialistic bases for all understanding, even while they also describe fields for the practice of transformative critique – present in their very complexity our inheritance of the great 'humanistic' achievements of the nineteenth century (an inheritance we will trace through literary criticism in the twentieth century in the next chapter in terms of its pedagogic imperative). Each of these grounds is articulated by a nineteenth-century thinker who has, as W.H. Auden says in his elegy for Freud, become 'no more a person / Now but a whole climate of opinion'. We are thinking of the work of people we have already mentioned in our discussion: Marx in social analysis, Nietzsche in the 'revaluation' of philosophy, Saussure in his reconception of linguistic science, and Freud in his psychological studies. We are leaving out the work of others we could have mentioned, for instance that of Weber, Darwin, Peirce, and nineteenth-century psychological novelists of England and France, among others. We are also leaving out the great political struggle of Western women in the nineteenth century, a struggle, as we will suggest in the final chapter, which cuts across the logic of exposition we are pursuing here and inhabits all these fields. In any case, we do not want to privilege the psychology of individuals over the social forces that produced them, or the linguistic constraints that focused their attention, or the conceptual frameworks they inherited and transformed, in this exposition of 'representative' people. We chose Marx, Nietzsche, Saussure and Freud because they produced what we might call 'signal texts' that literally transformed how we experience and understand the world and created new ways of conceiving the horizons and limits of possibility. Moreover, each of them created a form of what we are calling 'cultural critique', and in each we can find a positive and negative moment – institutional critique in which existing institutions and ideologies are realized and fulfilled, and transformative critique in which they are done away with.

Sigmund Freud – who among these four representative thinkers perhaps most fully maintains a faith in reason as logical consistency, its attempt to achieve (in Lacan's words) 'truth' rather than 'reality' – articulates these moments in two related assertions. In a famous, positive description of psychoanalysis, he asserts that 'where the id is, there shall the ego come to be'. Psychoanalysis, this dictum suggests, is the fulfilment of the Enlightenment dream of reason so that even the darkest powers with which psychoanalysis traffics can come to be governed by consciousness and knowledge. In a second statement, though, Freud articulates the negative, transformative critique of psychoanalysis. The aim of psychoanalysis, he claims repeatedly, is the transformation of hysterical misery into common unhappiness.

Here psychoanalysis denegates the Enlightenment faith and hope in the goodness and harmony of humanity and human life and asserts that life, after all, is simply and ordinarily unhappy.

If Freud most fully maintains a faith in reason as logic, then Friedrich Nietzsche most fully maintains a faith in reason as an exhaustive accounting of particulars. It is for this reason that he transformed the discourse of philosophy from system to aphorisms and distrusted as fully as he did generalizing universals. In his work he also articulates the two moments of critique we are describing. In a famous dictum that voices the global humanist goal of the Enlightenment, he declares that 'God is dead'. The death of God makes humanity itself the measure of all things. As he says in *The Gay Science* (1882), 'must not we ourselves become gods simply to seem worthy of it?' (181). All things – all the minute particulars of existence (Yeats describes Nietzsche as the writer he felt to be most close to William Blake) – are possible in a world without transcendental, universal meanings. As Gilles Deleuze notes (1962), 'the phrase "God is dead" is not a speculative proposition but a dramatic proposition, *the* dramatic proposition *par excellence*. God cannot be made the object of synthetic knowledge without death entering into him' (152). But the other side of this critique, this freedom from universals, is the transformation of the significance of experience into universal meaninglessness. 'Knowledge,' Nietzsche writes, is 'the making possible of *experience* by tremendous simplification of real events. . . . *Knowledge is falsification of the manifold and uncountable into the identical, the similar, the countable.* Thus *life* is possible only through such an *apparatus of falsification*. Thinking is a falsifying re-shaping; willing is a falsifying re-shaping' (cited in Stambaugh 1972: 71). For Nietzsche all thought and knowledge are particular moments of will-power.

Karl Marx, finally, most fully embodies a faith in reason as elegantly simple, a faith in Occam's razor that finds the most simplified and unified explanations most convincing (see Eagleton 1990: 209, 227). This is clear, perhaps, in his insistence in *Capital* that profits should not be understood as value more or less 'added' to commodities, but as a direct result of understanding the genesis of wealth through the labour theory of value and the 'surplus value' created when labour is commodified. In this argument, the major concepts – 'commodity', 'value', 'labour' – provide 'sufficient reason' for a complex array of social and cultural phenomena without multiplying causes.

In the positive moment of his critique of political economy – that is, of contemporary social life – Marx sees the modes of production created by capitalism as the great fulfilment of the Enlightenment dream of human mastery over the world. He writes in *The Communist Manifesto* (1848):

> The bourgeoisie, during its rule of scarce one hundred years, has created more massive and more colossal productive forces than have all preceding generations together. Subjection of nature's forces to man, machinery, application of chemistry to industry and agriculture, steam navigation, railways, electric telegraphs, clearing of whole continents for cultivation . . . what earlier century had even a presentiment that such productive forces slumbered in the lap of social labor? (12)

In this description, as Marshall Berman has pointed out (1982), Marx is less interested in the material products of bourgeois, capitalist civilization than in 'the processes, the powers, the expressions of human life and energy: men working, moving . . . organizing and reorganizing nature and themselves' (93). Moreover, Marx's elegant and powerful theory collecting together all these elements of bourgeois civilization, participates in the mastery it describes.

The negative moment of this critique, however, transforms the inherent *humanism* of this institutional critique into an analysis that questions the very 'energy' Marx sees and transforms it into crisis and chaos. 'Constant revolutionizing of production,' Marx also writes in the *Manifesto*, 'uninterrupted disturbance of all social conditions, everlasting uncertainty and agitation, distinguish the bourgeois epoch from all earlier times. . . . All that is .solid melts into air, all that is holy is profaned, and man at last is compelled to face with sober senses his real conditions of life and his relations with his kind' (10). Here, Marx offers the other dimension of the energy of capitalism as strongly as Freud offers the other side of psychoanalytic 'cure' and Nietzsche offers the other side of knowledge and will.

The final figure who articulates the nineteenth-century heritage that informs twentieth-century cultural critique is the Swiss linguist Ferdinand de Saussure. Saussure does not stand for a particular 'faith' in one or another aspect of reason. In fact, the schematization we have followed with Freud, Nietzsche and Marx is, at best, an approximation. Rather, Saussure is a special case because, more than any of these others, he pursues the logical, exhaustive, and simplifying aims of scientific reason in his linguistic research. He addresses all of these areas early in his *Course in General Linguistics* (1916), attempting to define a 'new' science of language by offering the logic of a generalizing system that can account for the 'confused mass of heterogeneous and unrelated things' of which language seems comprised (9)

in terms of a small number of homologous assumptions and procedures. He does so by fulfilling the *positive* (and positivist) aim of
nineteenth-century science by critiquing its grounding notion of 'fact'.
In Saussure, as Emile Benveniste has noted, 'the positivist notion of
the linguistic *fact* has been replaced by that of *relationship*' (1966: 20).
As Saussure puts it, 'although both the signified and the signifier are
purely differential and negative when considered separately, their
combination is a positive fact; it is even the sole type of facts that
language has, for maintaining the parallelism between the two classes
of differences is the distinctive function of the linguistic institution'
(1916: 120–1).

Yet the negation of his critique of linguistics as he found it – its
empirical bias, its racism, its assumption that effects were sufficiently
explained by historical 'causes' – is his perception of the overwhelming *arbitrariness* of meaning. This negation is best seen not as a
different 'moment' in his reasoned critique but as its constant 'other'.
Throughout his career, as he developed and taught many of the
seminal concepts that have governed the way we understand language
and, indeed, other phenomena in the twentieth century, he worked
concurrently on a lifelong study of possible anagrams inscribed
silently in late Latin poetry. More specifically, as he records in one of
his notebooks, the presence of coded *parts* of proper names in poetry
might, in fact, constitute the power of poetry: 'the reason [for the
presence of anagrams in Latin lyrics],' he writes, '*might have originated*
in the religious idea that an invocation, prayer, or hymn would have
power only if the syllables of the divine name were worked into the
text' (Starobinski 1971: 42). In other words, Saussure's life work to
discover the 'sufficient reason' for the existence of *meaningful* language
exists concurrently with his life work to discover patterns in the more
or less meaningless sound patterns of language.

For this latter project he devised intricate systems of analysis to
'discover' codes, hidden for millennia, that presented proper names
within these texts. Proper names are the most arbitrary and least
systematic aspect of linguistics – both Lévi-Strauss and Derrida have
strenuously argued the *impossibility* of 'pure' proper names in
language, and Lacan takes some trouble to inscribe his general
category, 'name-of-the-father' (*nom-du-père*), within the Symbolic
order itself (see Lévi-Strauss 1962; Derrida 1967; Lacan 1966). In this
study Saussure pursued the negative of his positive linguistic science.
Of such a pursuit he was quite self-conscious. In one notebook he
explicitly addresses the 'other' of the Enlightenment dream of
reason, arbitrary chance, as the negative 'other' to his great quest for

reason. 'Can the materiality of the fact be a matter of chance?' he asks.

> Are not the laws of the 'hypogram' sufficiently spacious that inevitably, and without surprise, one finds within them every proper name? We accept that as the immediate problem, and the principal object of this book, because this discussion of chance – for anyone who has given any measure of attention to the material fact – becomes the inevitable foundation of everything.   (Starobinski 1971: 101)

For Saussure, the constant underside of reason is chance, contingency, the arbitrary. In the *Course in General Linguistics* (1916) he even argues that the form of ancient Hebrew, the language of Adam and Eve, 'persists only through sheer luck' and 'blind evolution' (229, 231; Schleifer 1990: 69–71). In his negative or transformative critique – as in those of Freud, Nietzsche and Marx – the dream of reason itself is subject to the negativity of reason: its single-minded pursuit of logical consistency no matter where (into what despair) that logic may lead; its urge not to ignore any existing fact of phenomena even when that 'fact' contradicts and undermines its own most powerful tools and assumptions; its attempt to construct the simplest explanation of phenomena even when that explanation reduces itself to the anti-rationalism of chance rather than sufficient reason.

The legacy of the intellectual life of the nineteenth century (which we will trace in twentieth-century criticism in the next chapter) was, in its most powerful spokesmen, the articulation of questions about the most 'self-evident' truths of human life: the self-evidence of subjective control (at least over the inner life), the self-evidence of basic conceptual truisms, the self-evidence of social ideologies, the self-evidence of scientific discourse as a good that would enhance the fulfilment of human life. Freud, Nietzsche, Marx and Saussure subjected these self-evident truths – these 'grounds' of understanding and well-being – to both institutional and transformative critique, and precisely because they challenged these truths, they encountered (and still encounter) remarkable opposition. Each ground of under-standing, as Miller argues, generates strong opposition and dismissal – 'resistance' in Freudian terms – whose emotional affect seems somehow out of proportion to the intellectual discourse of sufficient reason. Not only do some people find one or another of these grounds of explanation literally unintelligible, they also find themselves *angry* that these grounds are proposed. What they are resisting, in part, is the historical contingency of the ground to which they subscribe – the fact that things could have been otherwise than the self-evident truths they perceive. They resist also the realization that critique is transformative as well as institutional, a call for action as well as a reasoned understanding.

THE CRITIQUE OF SOCIETY

It is the Marxian legacy of critique that has met the greatest resistance in Anglo-American literary studies, perhaps because of its political content, perhaps because a professional and conservative academy favoured Kant's institutional critique, perhaps because of the very Arnoldian concept of culture as 'disinterested' criticism which was so important to the establishment of the study of modern literature in the nineteenth century, perhaps because these 'reasons' in various combinations seem to make Marxian readings of literature suspect. But it is precisely such 'resistant' attachment to the self-evident that critique aims at questioning and understanding, and here, finally, is the importance of joining critique to the study of literature. Literature offers an object which can be subject to all three of Kant's critiques, of reason, morality and aesthetics. Moreover, it does so by offering a conception of 'culture' to a polity that needs such a conception precisely because the more or less unconscious assumptions and grounds that have held that society together no longer seem operative in nineteenth- and twentieth-century Western culture. Such a conception, as Raymond Williams has examined over the course of his career, is closely connected to the idea and activity of critique we have been examining, and this conception situates critique, criticism and the development of 'literature' itself as agencies in human affairs and as objects of study within concrete historical and ideological contexts. ('Ideology' here, as in Bakhtin, includes the 'ideas' instituted by language, by working conceptions of the psychological subject, and by philosophical conceptualization. See Bakhtin 1927, 1929.) The development of the concept of literature narrowly understood as a fine art (as opposed to simply what can be read by the literate) arises along with the professionalization of literary studies in the late nineteenth century. This professionalization, often despite itself, almost necessarily posits reading as critique, just as it transforms the 'cultural' artifacts of the polity into objects of professional study.

In his description of the concept of 'culture', Williams (1977) describes it and its history in ways similar to our narration of the concept of 'critique'.

> The complexity of the concept of 'culture' is remarkable. It became a
> noun of 'inner' process, specialized to its presumed agencies in
> 'intellectual life' and 'the arts.' It became also a noun of general process,
> specialized to its presumed configurations in 'whole ways of life.' It
> played a crucial role in definitions of 'the arts' and 'the humanities,' from
> the first sense. It played an equally crucial role in definitions of the
> 'human sciences' and the 'social sciences,' in the second sense. Each
> tendency is ready to deny any proper use of the concept to the other, in
> spite of many attempts at reconciliation.   (17)

'Culture', like the opposition between Kantian critique and Hegelian
critique, encompasses the possession of an individual subject's 'inner'
world and of a society of individuals conceived as a whole greater
than the sum of its parts. It describes the ways in which societies
make sense of the common experience of their members, situating
'culture' within the domain of 'ideas', and, in Williams' repeated
phrase, it describes social practices as 'a whole way of living of a
people' (1958: 83; see Hall 1980: 58–9). In both conceptions, to add to
the complexity of 'culture', it can be understood in terms of what
Paul de Man has called the 'aesthetic ideology' of *disinterested* contemplation (in the Kantian tradition) – that is, subject to institutional
critique – or it can be understood as a concept that makes something
happen, subject to the transformative critique that conceives of
understanding as historically and functionally *effective*. Culture, as
Matthew Arnold argues in *Culture and Anarchy* (1869), is 'not solely
the endeavor to see things as they are, to draw towards a knowledge
of the universal order which seems to be intended and aimed at in the
world . . . but as the endeavor, also, to make it *prevail*, the moral,
social, and beneficent character of culture becomes manifest' (207).

Equally important to understanding the complex concept of culture, even in Arnold, is the way in which it responds to particular
historical events. Throughout *Culture and Society* (1958) Williams
argues that the 'idea' of culture, beginning with Burke in the
eighteenth century, is a response to the growing industrialism of
Britain, and more specifically to the fragmented individualism of
laissez–faire capitalism. In Arnold's terms again (1869), any idea of
culture suggests that 'men are all members of one great whole, and
the sympathy which is in human nature will not allow one member
to be indifferent to the rest or to have a perfect welfare independent
of the rest' (208). In this way, the conception of culture developed
over the course of two hundred years in opposition to the fragmentation of society into warring classes, and in its explicit articulation in
the nineteenth century its theological function is emphasized. For this
reason, Cornel West argues that Arnold is the harbinger of modern-

ism precisely because he felt so acutely the breakdown of 'the whole and unified life of man' in Britain (Williams 1958: 30). Arnold, West argues (1988), is one of the first to recognize that the traditional ideology of the Occident – and especially the religious ideology that sustained the great 'centring' of world political and social power in Europe from 1492 until the triumph of liberal capitalism in the nineteenth century – no longer authoritatively sustains the European polity as a whole. This is why Arnold argues at such length – and with such uncharacteristic sarcasm in *Culture and Anarchy* – against the low-church affiliations of the liberal middle classes of his time, and it is for this reason that he asserts, remarkably, that 'culture goes beyond religion, as religion is generally conceived by us' (208).

This tracing of the function of the idea of culture can be seen in the great nineteenth-century articulation of culture as a concept that Williams traces in *Culture and Society*. In fact, Williams makes Arnold's definition of culture – both the explicit definition of culture in *Culture and Anarchy* we have been discussing and the implicit definition of culture in 'The Function of Criticism at the Present Time' (1865) which we will examine in the next chapter – the silent 'centre' of his great examination of the genealogy of the concept of culture and 'cultural studies'. In *Culture and Society* Williams quotes Arnold's famous definition of culture as the 'great help out of our present difficulties; culture being a pursuit of our total perfection by means of getting to know, on all the matters which most concern us, the best which has been thought and said in the world; and, through this knowledge, turning a stream of fresh and free thought upon our stock notions and habits' (Arnold 1865: 142, cited by Williams 1958: 115).

Here, 'culture' is both a body of knowledge and a mode of behaviour. Like George Eliot's earlier description of 'a really cultured woman' in terms of behaviour – 'a really cultured woman, like a really cultured man, will be ready to yield in trifles' (1855: 1643) – Arnold sees as part of culture the pursuit of making the best which has been thought and said in the world prevail.

Arnold's concept of culture, like that of Werner Jaeger in our century, eschews the more relative sense of 'culture' developed by anthropology (which, as we have seen, Lévi-Strauss both uses and modifies). 'Culture,' Jaeger argues in the Introduction to *Paideia*, has come to possess the 'trivial and general sense [of denoting] something inherent in every nation of the world, even the most primitive. We use it for the entire complex of all the ways and expressions of life which characterize any one nation. Thus the word has sunk to mean a simple anthropological concept, not a concept of value, a con-

37

sciously pursued *ideal*' (1933: xvii). In a famous definition of culture, the anthropologist E.B. Tylor articulated in 1871 what came to be considered the first 'scientific' anthropological use of the term Jaeger is describing. 'Culture or Civilization,' he wrote in *Primitive Cultures*, 'taken in its wide ethnographic sense, is that complex whole which includes knowledge, belief, art, morals, law, custom, and any other capabilities and habits acquired by man as a member of society' (cited in Stocking 1968: 73; see also MacDonald 1986). The difference between this definition and Arnold's is that it creates the possibility of a plurality of cultures. Culture does not aim at the universal 'perfection' and the adherence to the will of God Arnold describes in *Culture and Anarchy*. Rather, it is a relative and local concept representing a particular culture at a particular moment. In fact, George Stocking has argued quite persuasively that Tylor's concept of culture depends precisely on the currency of the less 'scientific' description Arnold offers. Tylor, he suggests in a fully *cultural-anthropological* argument, chooses the word 'culture' and links it to what in Arnold is its antithesis, 'civilization', precisely because Tylor subscribed to the ideology of laissez-faire individualism Arnold is attacking in *Culture and Anarchy* (1968: 69–90).

In this debate we can see another version of the opposition between Kantian universalizing and Hegelian historicizing. That is, Stocking, like Williams, is offering a *critique* as well as an exposition of the concept of 'culture'. He is attempting to *situate* historically what seems, in the Arnoldian tradition, to be a universal and transcendent idea. Even in Arnold, however, the concept of culture carries the burden of transformative critique: 'culture', as Williams describes Arnold's use of the term, 'is both study and pursuit. It is not merely the development of "literary culture," but of "all sides of our humanity." Nor is it an activity concerning individuals alone, or some part or section of society; it is, and must be, essentially *general*' (1958: 115). That is, 'culture', in Arnold's use of the term, is above all *normative*, and such a value-laden use of the word exemplifies the problem we have described in the unstable, radical negativity of transformative cultural critique more generally. Arnold, Williams (1958) concludes,

> was caught between two worlds. He had admitted reason as the critic and destroyer of institutions, and so could not rest on the traditional society which nourished Burke. He had admitted reason – 'human thought' – as the maker of institutions, and thus could not see the progress of civil society as the working of a divine intention. His way of thinking about institutions was in fact relativist, as indeed a reliance on 'the best that had

been thought and written in the world' (and on that alone) must always
be. Yet at the last moment he not only holds to this, but snatches also
towards an absolute: and *both are Culture*. Culture became the final critic
of institutions, and the process of replacement and betterment, yet it was
also, at root, beyond institutions. This confusion of attachment was to be
masked by the emphasis of a word.   (p. 128)

Here Williams is offering his own critique of Arnold's and most of
the other conceptions of culture examined in *Culture and Society*. His
understanding of Arnoldian 'culture' participates in both modes of
critique we have examined, positing a conception of culture as both
the *fulfilment* and the *transformation* of existing institutions.

But most importantly, his critique is based upon the *socio-historical*
investigation pursued throughout that book, its study of the *genealogy*
of the concept in Nietzsche's sense of genealogy as the tracings of
transformations rather than the pursuit of authoritative 'causes'. (We
will examine this more closely in Chapter 5.) Genealogy, as Michel
Foucault (1971) has understood Nietzsche's conception, is a 'patiently
documentary' enterprise that does not assume that words have kept
their ('invariant') meanings. Rather, it attempts to

> record the singularity of events outside any monotonous finality; it must
> seek them in the most unpromising places, in what we tend to feel is
> without history – in sentiments, love, conscience, instinct; it must be
> sensitive to their recurrence, not in order to trace the gradual course of
> their evolution, but to isolate the different scenes where they engaged in
> different roles.
>   Genealogy, consequently . . . does not oppose itself to history as the
> lofty and profound gaze of the philosopher might compare to the
> molelike perspective of the scholar; on the contrary, it rejects the meta-
> historical deployment of ideal significations and indefinite teleologies. It
> opposes itself to the search for 'origins.'   (pp. 139–40)

Cultural studies attempt to bring historical consciousness – including
the history of conceptual, psychological and linguistic formations as
well as social formations – to 'what we tend to feel is without history'.
In Nietzsche's and Foucault's understanding of genealogy we can see
the rationale for Williams' recurrent tracings of what he describes as
'key points' in 'the general pattern of change' of words in his earliest
book (1958: xiii), a procedure which he follows in many later works,
most noticeably in *Keywords* (1976). Williams traces the *genealogy* of
these words in order to isolate the different scenes in which they
engage in different roles. Thus, his study of culture in *Culture and
Society* is the study of the genealogy of this word in English, just as
in *Marxism and Literature* he offers a short genealogy of 'literature' as
well as 'culture'.

Williams' socio-historical genealogy of culture is also an etymology. It also participates in a kind of *linguistic* critique of Arnold, and of culture in general, in its recognition of the linguistic foundation of the word. Williams describes such a foundation (although he is not quite aware of it in linguistic terms) in *Marxism and Literature* in the tendency of language to convert 'experience into finished products', a tendency which takes 'terms of analysis as terms of substance' (1977: 128, 129). In this tendency, Williams sees what he calls in the conclusion of *Culture and Society* the 'barrier in the mind . . . a refusal to accept the creative capacities of life' so that 'a habit of thinking' governs the possibilities of thought. In other words, he writes, 'we project our old images into the future, and take hold of ourselves and others to force energy towards that substantiation' (1958: 336). Earlier he made a similar argument when he described 'the tendency of function to turn into property' (1958: 236), the 'fetishizing' of culture in Arnold (1958: 126).

All of these instances, like the instances of genealogy and etymology, participate in the 'tendency' of language to 'substantiate' and, in the technical term of A.J. Greimas, to 'substantify' the dynamism of relational terms – in the context of Williams' critique of Arnold, to substantify the *process* of culture Arnold describes – into linguistic substantives (Schleifer 1987: 41). Such 'substantification' is part of the doubling of critique we have already mentioned and the very doubling of culture as particular objects within social life and as a whole way of life. It is just such 'substantification' which governs Saussure's turn from the diachronic study of language in the nineteenth century to the synchronic study of linguistic systems he inaugurated; this very turn 'substantifies' the relational systems of language and cultural formations into the universals of logic and 'mind'.

In his explicit historical analysis and the more or less implicit genealogical and linguistic analysis, Williams is participating in the complexity not only of 'culture' as he describes it but also of 'critique' as we have described it. This is perhaps clearest in the conclusion of *Culture and Society*. Williams concludes:

> The development of the idea of culture has, throughout, been a criticism of what has been called the bourgeois idea of society. The contributors to its meaning have started from widely different positions, and have reached widely various attachments and loyalties. But they have been alike in this, that they have been unable to think of society as a merely neutral area, or as an abstract regulating mechanism. The stress has fallen on the positive function of society, on the fact that the values of individual men are rooted in society, and on the need to think and feel in

those common terms. This was, indeed, a profound and necessary
response to the disintegrating pressures which were faced.   (p. 328)

Here Williams is arguing that the concept of culture arose precisely in
opposition to a 'bourgeois' conception of human life as *essentially*
individual, as best conceived, as Rousseau and Richardson conceived
it, in terms of a single individual existing alone on the blank tablet of
a neutral and *unresponsive* world. If such a conception described the
forms of consciousness created in the world of interchangeable parts
(which Jean Baudrillard calls the reigning scheme of 'production' in
the industrial era (1976: 83)) or the world of etymological authority
(in which the 'origin' of a word somehow was interchangeable with
its 'essence' (see Attridge 1988: 103–4)), then the concept of culture
offers a critique of that understanding of human experience.

It is a critique in which the concept of the *unconscious* is particularly
operative, not a personal unconsciousness but a sense of a more
general unconsciousness concerning what seems most 'natural' about
experience – what Fredric Jameson calls the 'political unconscious'.
Such a critique would understand 'natural' experience as 'institutional'
in precisely the way that Williams argues that culture itself is
institutional beyond Arnold's understanding, in precisely the way a
'word', so self-evidently bearing its meaning to a native speaker, is
institutional (its 'content' being its instituted 'form'), or a 'feeling' is.
In all of these instances – and in the final instance of 'history' itself,
whose 'genealogies' seem so natural rather than instituted even when
we 'know', on some level, how determined genealogy is by *instituted*
patriarchal lineation – what is 'unconscious' is precisely the arbitrariness and contingency of self-evident truths. We have already examined three of these institutions in the concept and word *culture* and in
Williams' socio-historical genealogical examination of both the word
and the concept, but a final area to explore the possible unconscious
and 'institutional' nature of understanding is in what seems to us (in
late twentieth-century Western culture) most self-evident, the area of
psychological 'feeling' itself. With this, we will have examined culture
from that vantage of the four 'grounds' – philosophical, linguistic,
social and psychological – that govern the expositions of this chapter.

LITERATURE AND CRITIQUE

We can explore the *institution* of 'feeling' – that is, of subjective
experience – by examining two further concepts in Williams'

exploration of cultural studies, 'structures of feeling' and the idea of 'literature' itself. In the phrase 'structure of feeling' Williams self-consciously brings together two categories of understanding – the logical abstraction of 'structure', the felt immediacy of 'feeling' – which are usually strictly separated. In this phrase we can see the juxtaposition – not (or not necessarily) the reconciliation – of Kantian abstraction and Hegelian particularity. (See Holenstein's description of Roman Jakobson's linguistics as 'phenomenological structuralism' [1974] for a different version of this conjunction.) Williams coins this phrase in order to emphasize the social and communal nature or 'institution' of what is usually held to be private and personal. 'What we are defining' in the term, Williams writes, 'is a particular quality of social experience and relationship, historically distinct from other particular qualities, which gives the sense of a generation or of a period' (1977: 131). The object of inquiry, he writes in *The Long Revolution*, is the 'felt sense of the quality of life at a particular place and time: a sense of the ways in which the particular activities [of life] combined into a way of thinking and feeling' (1961: 63). Such a 'community of experience' hardly needs expression (1961: 64) – this is the sense of 'unconscious' we are using – and, Williams suggests, this communal experience is best seen in the fact that generations 'never talk quite "the same language" (1961: 64), a fact recoverable in precisely the genealogical studies Williams pursues. The structure of feeling, he writes, 'is the culture of a period', and 'it is in this respect that the arts of a period, taking these to include characteristic approaches and tones in argument, are of major importance' (1961: 64–5).

Such 'feelings', like the genealogical meanings of words, are *discontinuous*. They are not passed on from generation to generation but rather arise within the social relations and patterns of a particular time. They develop because they manifest themselves in the least self-conscious attitudes of people: in 'style' or, as Williams argues, in the *process* of living before phenomena are even considered objects of attention. For this reason, such phenomenal experiences are often 'not yet recognized as social but taken to be private, idiosyncratic, and even isolating' experiences (1977: 132). In this focus on 'feeling', as in his focus on history, ideas and language, the study of culture aims to understand and situate aspects of human life which living individuals have rare occasion to question. We all imagine that our experience is simply 'human experience': self-evident, natural, universal. In this, we take 'private' individual experience as the 'ground' of our understanding.

As Williams suggests, however, the study of literary art allows us to see around the self-evident truths we 'experience' in encounters with structures of feeling other than our own. 'Literature' itself is a key word that, like 'culture', suggests self-evident truths by suppressing its own genesis 'within the social and formal properties of language' so that literature is taken to be equivalent to 'immediate living experience' (1977: 46). As such, literature in the sense of creative linguistic art (Williams offers a panoply of other, historically determined usages of 'literature' in *Marxism and Literature* and *Keywords*) participates in the two *kinds* of culture we have examined. It is a particularly elaborate way in which a society makes sense of the common experience of its members by narrating more or less 'representative' examples of that experience; and, in the very 'style' of its narration, it participates in the complex structure of feeling of its own generation and time.

THE DIFFICULTY OF CRITIQUE

To see around the self-evident truths we experience, like overcoming 'resistances' in psychoanalysis, entails enormous difficulties for thought and feeling. Theodor Adorno articulates aspects of these difficulties when he notes that the culture critic 'is necessarily the same essence of that to which he fancies himself superior' (1967: 19). This is another way of describing the relationship between institutional and transformative critique as different 'takes' on the same phenomena. Thus, as we shall see in this book, the reconception of the study of literature as forms of cultural critique entails the great difficulties in language and thought of situating and resituating reason, canons of appropriateness and persuasiveness in argument, and the relationship between truth and beauty in apprehension. In other words, these self-evident categories that Kant gives in his critiques of reason, morality and aesthetics and that govern the definition of scientific knowledge we have presented (its reasonable self-consistency, its appropriate regulation by empirical fact, and the elegance of its simplicity) are time and again explored in criticism aspiring to cultural critique. For this reason, many of the critical texts we discuss in this book are obscure in their density and at times difficult to read. But what does it mean exactly for a critical text or argument or 'take' to be difficult? For one thing, because they do not write in the tradition of *explication du texte*, or 'close reading', or in the formalist mode that dominated the humanist literary tradition discussed in the next chapter, many twentieth-century literary and cultural critics often seem maddeningly elliptical, especially in word play. As George Steiner remarks about such 'difficult' writers, it can seem as though 'at certain levels, we are not meant to understand at all, and our interpretation, indeed our reading itself, is an intrusion'. 'For whom' – and here Steiner could be referring to many contemporary critical texts – are they 'composing [their] cryptograms?' (1978: 45).

Steiner describes four types of difficulty – *contingent, modal, tactical* and above all *ontological* – that are relevant to the task of reading literary and cultural studies. In brief, he describes *contingent* difficulties as those problems we have with the obscurity of a particular text – its exotic or unclear allusions or its use of deconstructive, psychoanalytic, linguistic and philosophical terms that we, as Steiner said, need 'to look up' (1978: 27). Either we look up 'trace', 'aporia', 'aphanisis', 'metonymy', and 'metaphor' and understand them, or they simply mystify us. Next, *modal* difficulty, rather than being an obscurity in the text, is the reader's resistance to a text's presentation and the reader's misunderstanding or possibly dislike of its mode (its genre or form). Because literary criticism aspiring to cultural critique is interdisciplinary and steeped in the debates of philosophy, psychoanalysis, linguistics and twentieth-century thought generally, the difficulty here can be formidable. Third, *tactical* difficulty is created by discursive strategies for dislocating the reader and inhibiting any usual or conventional response to a text. Steiner identifies this difficulty (and the next) with the strategies of modernist literature – the difficulty, for instance, in simply following the 'narrative line' of *The Waste Land*, or the play of ideas and sounds in Wallace Stevens' poetry. When Kristeva, for example, splits her voice into competing double columns in 'Stabat Mater', the reader is prevented from following a linear reading pattern. The text, in effect, intentionally dislocates a customary and stable orientation in order to establish a 'deconstructive' one, and the competition within the text for the reader's attention helps to accomplish this end. Similarly, Lacan's constant word play and his refusal to pursue a clear analysis of either Poe's story or the analytic practice he is simultaneously describing in 'Seminar on "The Purloined Letter"' present the same tactical difficulty. The reader is intentionally dislocated, just as, one could argue, psychoanalysis itself strategically attempts to dislocate and disorientate the patient/reader.

These difficulties in time are 'naturalized', as the structuralists say, and become formal and familiar aspects of a text's structure and orientation just as critique institutes itself as criticism (not simply because time passes but also because of the 'substantifying' nature we have mentioned of language, concepts, agents and social tactics). The fourth difficulty of literary and cultural critique is *ontological*: the difficulty, Steiner writes, that breaks 'the contract of ultimate or preponderant intelligibility between poet and reader, between text and meaning'. 'Difficulties of this category cannot be looked up,' he continues, because 'they confront us with blank questions about the nature of human speech [and] about the status of significance' (1978: 41). That is, they confront us with blank questions about the self-evident necessity of reason, tact and form in the articulation of any 'significance' – any meaning – whatsoever. It is here that the 'complexity' of critique – its existence in relation to both knowledge of instituted phenomena and the power of transforming institutions – does violence to pure reason, practical reason, and the reasoned activity of feeling and judgment that seem the 'grounds' of understanding and purposeful activity.

An *ontological* difficulty, in other words, arises when the contract is breached between writer and reader, or text and meaning, because the text is positing a new ontology, a new paradigm of understanding, a new relationship between part and whole (such as example and generalization or literature and culture). This shift requires a new grasp of phenomena, of their relations, of the horizon of human possibility behind them, and, most difficultly, a new mode of grasping. This difficulty is insurmountable except through a transformation of understanding into the mode of the new paradigm – through a change in the sense of what is 'real'. In this difficulty the opposition between transformative and institutional critique blurs. The scandal of this difficulty can be described as the 'devastating experience' Miller narrates in 'The Search for Grounds', 'of a transformation of the scene which leaves it nevertheless exactly the same' (1985: 20). This 'nevertheless' both is and is not right: it is both an idealization of the (instituted) scene and its historical transformation, its genealogical multiplication through time. Feminism, for instance, with the instituted experience women bring to understanding that is very different from Miller's, articulates a description of the doubleness of experience significantly less melodramatically than Miller or Steiner.

Still, critique is pervaded by the figure of 'split' experience of one sort or another. Most current theories of textuality, for example, do not emphasize literary reading as an attempt at a unified 'reading' or even see a text as defined by 'meaning' or 'content'. They see, instead, a process that swings back and forth between textual 'product' and 'production', between meaning/content and reading activity – and never reaches stability or wholeness: the very doubling of critique we have noted and the questioning of the (self-evident) oppositions between content and form, subject and object, assertions and method we have mentioned. This interpretive model, encompassing order and a large measure of disorder, poses a serious threat to the empirically based tradition of interpretation as a transparent and focusable lens, the model implicit in the humanistic criticism described in the next chapter. It also poses a threat to the Kantian idealist model of an open subjectivity through which a detached critical investigator peers into a stable text. From the viewpoint of much literary and cultural studies, in fact, the notion of a detached observer – an epistemological innocent bystander – no longer exists. Rather, contemporary criticism posits strong involvement between critic and text and believes that time itself runs through and creates a radical split in all knowledge, making 'subjectivity' (both what we know and how we know it) irrevocably problematic. Contemporary criticism, in this regard, is difficult because it promotes a new paradigm and a new mode of comprehension for the study of cultural phenomena that is fundamentally inhabited by the complexity of critique. This difficulty, more than any other, explains both the challenge, the excitement and also the occasional hostility towards the conception and practice of literary criticism as cultural critique.

In the next chapter we will examine the 'other' to the conceptions of critique and culture we have presented by examining the twentieth-century inheritors of Arnold's ideas of culture and, with those ideas, literary and even cultural criticism as modes of pedagogy. In subsequent chapters we will examine the fields of the subject, language, philosophical concepts and social relations that have been traversed by critique in attempts to establish literary study as the study of cultural phenomena. In conclusion we will offer a brief description of a definition of cultural studies in relation to literary criticism.

CHAPTER TWO
The Function of Criticism: Humanism and Critique

> [Romantic poetry] did not know enough.
>
> Matthew Arnold
> 'The Function of Criticism at the Present Time'

> Arnold was not Dryden or Johnson; he was an Inspector of Schools and
> he became Professor of Poetry. He was an educator.
>
> T.S. Eliot
> 'Matthew Arnold'

THE FUNCTION OF CRITICISM

In the context of the history – the genealogy – of the concept of
critique we have been discussing, it can be argued that the critical
study of literature is a form, more or less self-conscious, of cultural
critique. Literary criticism articulates and examines particular cultural
norms. Like 'literature' (within the category of which criticism is
often included), criticism articulates and makes sense of complex
cultural phenomena. Such a 'critical' programme for criticism, however, is often at odds with the humbler, pedagogic imperative that
literary studies, as Matthew Arnold argues, should attempt 'to see the
object as in itself it really is' and simply to present to students
literature itself, 'the best that is known and thought in the world, and
. . . making this known, to create a current of true and fresh ideas'
(1865: 134, 142). In other words, literary study has two not altogether
compatible programmes: to disseminate what is already known and
to critique the already known. For this reason, it should not surprise
any reader, especially in the context of the concept of critique we

have examined, that the pursuit of literary criticism should provoke defensiveness and apology. In fact, Arnold established the genre of the *apologia critica* when, in specifically discussing the achievement of culture in 'The Function of Criticism at the Present Time,' he began by mentioning the 'many objections' to a previous 'proposition about criticism, and its importance for the present day' (1865: 130). He had erred, he quoted his detractors as saying, in that the 'importance . . . [he] assigned to criticism . . . was excessive' (1865: 131). Arnold then pointed out that there is creativity in criticism as well as in literature. 'If it were not so,' he said, 'all but a very few men would be shut out from the true happiness of all men' (1865: 132).

In his work, Arnold began a tradition of criticism that, as Gerald Graff has shown, helped to establish literary studies as a legitimate academic discipline – as something to be taught. The heart of Arnold's definition of criticism, like his definition of culture as the achievement of 'perfection,' is its *disinterestedness*, 'keeping aloof from what is called "the practical view of things;" [and] resolutely following the law of its own nature, which is to be a free play of the mind on all subjects which it touches' (1865: 142). Such disinterestedness seems to eschew precisely the 'grounds' of understanding – social, psychology, philosophical, even linguistic – that we examined in the last chapter. That is, such disinterestedness eschews the critique of its own procedures in favour of a *pedagogic imperative* of disseminating what is self-evidently the best that has been thought and said. T.S. Eliot also articulates this view when he argues in 'The Function of Criticism' that the 'end' of criticism 'roughly speaking, appears to be the elucidation of works of art and the correction of taste' (1923: 69). Allen Tate, in his apology for criticism, 'The Present Function of Criticism' makes the same point, even if his crankiness and bitterness are far beyond anything found in Arnold's (if not Eliot's) published writings. 'The function of criticism should have been, in our time, as in all times,' Tate writes, 'to maintain and to demonstrate the special, unique, and complete knowledge which the great forms of literature afford us. And I mean quite simply, *knowledge*, not historical documentation and information' (1941: 9). Such an attitude, Terry Eagleton has argued in *The Function of Criticism*, 'lacks all substantial social function' (1984: 7). The hypostatization of 'knowledge,' he argues, like that of 'disinterestedness,' ultimately is 'vacuous' (1984: 61).

Eagleton's description of the emptiness of assertions of disinterestedness leaves out the imperative to disinterested objectivity which is part of the pedagogic project of literary studies. (It is easy to do so, we think, in the face of Tate's strident assertions.) This imperative is perhaps clearest in the apologetic stance grounded in the disinterest-edness of criticism Northrop Frye assumed in his essay (later included as the introduction to *Anatomy of Criticism*), 'The Function of Criticism at the Present Time' (1949). In that essay Frye more precisely explains 'disinterestedness' (which in Arnold, Eliot and Tate seems very 'interested' indeed in maintaining the status quo). Frye defines poetry, not criticism, as disinterested: 'poetry is a *disinterested* use of words', he writes: 'it does not address the reader directly' (1949: 248). The aim of criticism, then, is to speak for literature: to give it a 'conceptual framework' which belongs to criticism alone, just as the other sciences (including the human sciences) create such frameworks for themselves. In this way, then, the disinterestedness of criticism is not, as Arnold implies, based on the fact that criticism is a 'second-hand imitation of creative power' (1949: 247). Rather, it is based on the fact that the *function* of criticism is to organize a universe of meanings (what Frye calls a 'verbal universe') in which other 'disciplines' or approaches to experience – such as sociological, psychological, linguistic, or philosophical – take their place.

> Just as mathematics exists in a mathematical universe which is at the
> circumference of the common field of experience, so literature exists in a
> verbal universe, which is not a commentary on life or reality, but
> contains life and reality in a system of verbal relationships. This
> conception of a verbal universe, in which life and reality are inside
> literature, and not outside it and being described or represented or
> approached or symbolized by it, seems to me the first postulate of a
> properly organized criticism.   (p. 262)

This programme, as Derrida notes in his discussion of Kant's *Conflict of the Faculties* in which Kant understands the organization of university faculties in terms of 'what is presently teachable' (1983: 6), assumes that the experience of literature finally is subject to rational analysis. It assumes that literature, in fact, offers transcendental and transmittable knowledge. For this reason, it is a small step from these Kantian assumptions within his essay to a sense of cultural critique – and Frye himself ends his essay by suggesting that 'the consolidation of literature by criticism into the verbal universe was one of the things that Matthew Arnold meant by culture' (1949: 265). While we are not suggesting that Frye (or Williams or Derrida or Lévi-Strauss or Lacan for that matter) is presenting a definitive description of criticism as critique, he is offering a sense of criticism beyond the narrow conception of criticism as commentary and hermeneutic guide.

Still, the organized disciplinarity of criticism Frye calls for (and works out in *Anatomy of Criticism*) achieves its justification in the pedagogic imperative – the imperative to transmit knowledge, but also to build upon existing knowledge. In a field of 'knowledge' that focuses on discourse, however, criticism's own discourse on discourse seems to call for explanation and apology. Thus, more recently, Geoffrey Hartman wrote his own version of the *apologia critica* in *Criticism in the Wilderness* (1980), the epigraph for which he took from Arnold's 'Function of Criticism' essay. Beginning with T.S. Eliot's assurance that 'criticism is as inevitable as breathing', Hartman explores 'the gulf between philosophic criticism [in Continental Europe] and *practical criticism* [in England and the United States]', repeatedly assuring us that 'criticism' must be accorded its status as 'a genre, or a primary text', too (1980: 6). In this argument Hartman is making the anxiety generated by the difference between the transmitted knowledge of literature and the systematic knowledge of criticism more apparent.

This anxiety is occasioned by the possibility that criticism might be more than just commentary, more, in fact, than 'just' pedagogic. It is occasioned by the possibility that criticism can effect the same kind of vision and critique of the world that literature does. Along this line, in 'The Search for Grounds in Literary Study' Miller focuses his discussion around Arnold and the fact that, beginning in the eighteenth century at least, literary criticism – as well as 'contemplating' and 'explaining' literary works – has attempted to address wider areas of cultural practice beyond literature. As well as pursuing the disinterested contemplation of works of art, Miller says, the study of literature 'has been weighted down in our culture with the burden of carrying from generation to generation the whole freight of the values of that culture, what Matthew Arnold called "the best that is known and thought in the world"' (1985: 24). Miller explicitly raises the questions of why this should be – what historical events in the eighteenth and nineteenth centuries might have contributed to this practice, and what implications it has for the study of literature. But whatever its implications – and in this chapter we will argue that it implies for the humanist legacy in the twentieth century that the pedagogic impulse of criticism take precedence over the more rigorous incompletions of critique – this phenomenon has occasioned repeated apologies for criticism, numerous discussions and much anxiety about the nature and goals of literary study.

Despite the wide practice of criticism and formulation of theory, the conflict within critical practice that Arnold articulates and Miller describes gives rise to great anxiety and intellectual debate. This conflict, as we have said, is the contradiction between the modest activity of creating a situation in which the best that is known and thought can have wide currency (Frye's description of the job of criticism, echoing Arnold, is 'to get as many people in contact with the best that has been and is being thought and said' [1949: 247]) and the 'burden' of maintaining cultural values in general (Frye's description of the 'verbal universe, in which life and reality are inside literature' and which only the methods of criticism can help us to understand). In fact, as Eagleton has suggested, the very function of criticism has changed or become more self-reflective in recent time. Literary criticism in the twentieth century, as we will see throughout this book, has expanded its horizon to include a vast array of questions (Miller's 'freight') that heretofore seemed outside, or only implicit within, its purview. These include questions of politics, semantics, the philosophy of language, sexual and social relations, along with questions concerning the nature of literary study, its responsibilities, and its very objects of study.

The contrary view, however, also present in the early nineteenth century and pursued in many of the descriptions of the 'function' of criticism we have presented here, says that criticism merely supplements art and, at worst, is a parasite draining away its lifeblood. (It is precisely to charges of parasitism that Frye is responding, and, as we have seen, Arnold also is responding to the charge that his conception of criticism is 'excessive'.) At best, this contrary view suggests, criticism is a pedagogical 'hermeneutics' whose aim is to recover the intentional meanings of the artist and then, mission accomplished, quietly to disappear. Only on occasion, in this view, does criticism marginally increase our appreciation of artistic form, thereby giving support to art in a limited way. This separation of criticism from art is also implicit in Frank Kermode's idea of genre as a 'consensus, a set of foreunderstandings exterior to a text which enable us to follow that text' (1979: 163). Kermode, thus, believes that criticism is totally dependent on literature, and he therefore has little sympathy for the conflicts, and convolutions, of current theory. Criticism is merely an adjunct to literature, and the two – as Kermode believes – belong in different areas of culture anyway.

PEDAGOGY AND CRITICISM

Implicit in this discussion is a definition of pedagogy that aims at the dissemination of what is known rather than its critique. In this definition, as Paul de Man says, 'teaching is not primarily an intersubjective relationship between people but a cognitive process in which self and other are only tangentially and contiguously involved'. Pedagogy, de Man continues, is a matter of 'scholarship' which must be 'eminently teachable', though 'the long and complicated history of literary and linguistic instruction' suggests that such a pedagogic imperative is complicated by the tension 'between methods of understanding and the knowledge which those methods allow one to reach' (1986: 4). Such tension, as we suggested in the last chapter, is itself the *object* of critique, which aims precisely to examine the assumptions which allow particular 'truths' to be apprehended – to examine, that is, the very processes of knowledge. In the instance of criticism as pedagogy, which govern many of the definitions of the function of criticism we have surveyed, criticism posits particular 'Archimedean' vantage points outside (undergirding) its work: the 'meaning' of literature independent of its reader/critic, the 'genius' of its subject/ author independent of the psychological and historical occasions for writing and utterance, the 'truth' of literature independent of the discourse that articulates it which the teacher passes on. These hierarchical oppositions – giving precedence to text over reader, author over text, truth over discourse – form the substance, as we shall see, of nineteenth-century humanism. Moreover, their very institution as self-evident and 'natural' helps to establish the opposition we are discussing between pedagogy and critique.

Another aspect of literary study ·generated by the opposition between pedagogical and critical definitions of criticism is the nature of humanistic study in general and the 'disciplinary' practice of literary criticism. In a sense, this opposition embodies the debate between the scientism of Kant and the discursiveness of Hegel we described in the preceding chapter. The traditional view is that the 'humanities' have been areas of knowledge which examined unique human events. Every 'object' of humanistic study – Chaucer's *Canterbury Tales*, the Battle of Waterloo, Locke's *Treatise on Human Nature*, Picasso's *Guernica*, Mozart's *Hunt Quartet*, even Newton's *Principia* and Darwin's *Origin of Species* – is a unique event that occurred only once at a particular historical and cultural moment and, consequently, can be studied only through description and paraphrase. As Louis Hjelmslev noted, according to this traditional view 'humanistic, as opposed to natural phenomena are non-recurrent and for that very reason cannot, like natural phenomena, be subjected to exact and generalizing treatment' (1943: 8). 'In the field of the humanities,' he goes on, 'consequently, there would have to be a different method [from science] – namely, mere description, which would be nearer to poetry than to exact science – or, at any event, a method that restricts itself to a discursive form of presentation in which the phenomena pass by, one by one, without being interpreted through a system' (1943: 8). This 'method', Hjelmslev suggests, is 'history' in its most chronological manifestation. Because the 'objects' of humanistic study are unique, they can be catalogued only in chronological order. For this reason, the humanities have traditionally been 'historical' studies: the history of philosophy, the history of art, history itself, the history of science, literary history, and so forth. Frye says the same thing about critical practice in his *apologia*: 'literature being as yet unorganized by criticism, it still appears as a huge aggregate or miscellaneous pile of creative efforts. The only organizing principle so far discovered in it is chronology, and when we see the miscellaneous pile strung out along a chronological line, some coherence is given to it by tradition [chronologically conceived]' (1949: 264).

Implicit in Frye and Hjelmslev – in this context, Frye's conception of culture is significantly different from the vague, humanist 'perfection' Arnold describes – is the possibility that the humanities could 'reorient' themselves and adopt a more scientific model for their study. Instead of following what Frye calls 'naive induction', the humanities could attempt, as Hjelmslev says, 'to rise above the level of mere primitive description to that of a systematic, exact, and generalizing science, in the theory of which all events (possible combinations of elements) are foreseen and the conditions for their realization established' (1943: 9). Such a discipline would attempt to account for the objects of the humanistic study in terms of systematic relationships among them rather than their chronological description. In this case, the 'humanities' could be conceived as the 'human sciences'.

In fact, such a division can be seen in the 'doubling' of critique into institutional and transformative critiques we have already described. In the *Course in General Linguistics*, Saussure specifically distinguishes between two methods of studying economics – economic history and the 'synchronic' study of the economic system at any particular moment. Most of the 'human' (or social) sciences, in contemporary practice, are divided in this fashion. Psychology, for instance, encompasses the analysis of unique case histories of 'clinical' psychology, and experimental psychology attempts to articulate the 'general' functioning of mental activity. Anthropology encompasses both the study of unique cultures and, as in Claude Lévi-Strauss's work, the 'general' functioning of aspects of culture. Even an earth science such as geology studies both the historical development and the synchronic composition of geological formations.

In this way, literary study also can be seen to offer two 'methods' of study – in Frye's terms literary history and more or less systematizing criticism, and in de Man's terms the 'scholarship' of 'historical and philological facts as the preparatory condition for understanding, and methods of reading or interpretation', the latter of which he identifies with 'literary theory' (1986: 4). What allows the systematization of criticism in Frye, however, is the common and 'recurrent' element of traditional humanistic study, the fact that, as Hjelmslev notes, all the humanities deal in the study of language and discourse. Discourse, moreover, is common to the social sciences in general, and consequently a systematic criticism could be a more general theory of discourse, a more general study of cultural (and discursive) formations. In this way, criticism can transform itself into one of the 'human sciences' which would study the functioning and creation of a host of 'discourses' within society (including, of course, 'literary' discourse). Such a human science would attempt to describe what distinguishes literature from other language uses and what literature shares with them. It would attempt, as many have already attempted, to situate literary practice within other cultural practices (including linguistics, teaching, politics, psychology, philosophy, ideology, sociology – and even the 'professional' debates within literary studies themselves), all areas, intersecting with the study of literature, that are examined in this book in the discussions of criticism as cultural critique. In this way, criticism would focus on discursive 'method' as well as 'truth', and even, as in de Man, on the question of the compatibility of truth and method and the effects that particular methods – whether linguistic, psychological, philosophical or historical – have on the 'truths' they reveal.

We are suggesting, then, that the study of criticism can profitably be situated as a part – and a leading part – of the study of culture and within it can be seen the same generative forces that have governed the philosophical debates concerning critique. In this way, literary study conceived as a systematized critical activity – a criticism that studies 'signifying systems' in a more or less systematic, exact and generalizing way – is in a position to direct its methods and observations to the widest area of the production of meanings, to cultural activities as specific signifying practices and as a general area of inquiry, just as criticism as pedagogy aspires to the transmission of a fully formed cultural heritage – fully formed truths. Raymond Williams, as we have seen, offers a strong argument that the texts which we customarily call 'literature' constitute a privileged site where the most important social, psychological and cultural forces combine and contend. T.S. Eliot also sees literary art as a site of contention, but, directly opposite to Williams, he believes it to be a privileged area where humanity reveals its essence, if only it can be properly seen. 'Criticism,' he says, 'by definition, is *about* something other than itself' (1923: 74): it is about autotelic works of art. But more than this, it is about 'civilization', 'tradition', 'the mind of Europe', above all *about*, as Eliot says, 'arriving at something outside of ourselves, which may provisionally be called truth' (1923: 76). In this way, then, as a humanistic alternative to the study of literature as a 'human science', literary study can be seen ultimately as a subject for pedagogy, the best that is already known and already thought. This humanist tradition in the twentieth century – in which 'tradition' itself is a central term – will be the focus of the rest of this chapter: the pedagogic and humanistic 'other' to the critique of tradition, humanism, and pedagogy we examine in the rest of this book.

CRITICISM AND HUMANISM

The conception of truth 'outside' ourselves participates, albeit unconsciously, in a species of Hegelian critique of the subject we discussed in the last chapter. In the next chapter, when we turn to the critique of the psychological subject of experience in our examination of criticism as cultural critique, we will pursue the critique of the subject further. In this chapter, however, we are attempting to examine the alternative to criticism as critique – the 'other' to the great argument of this book – namely, a critique of subjectivity that does not pursue the *situating* of the human subject in relation to historical, psychological, linguistic or philosophic critiques. This alternative criticizes subjectivity from the vantage of self-evident, objective truths. For this reason, even when it attempts to articulate a criticism of culture, early twentieth-century literary criticism does so on the basis of elements of the humanistic tradition inherited from the nineteenth century which makes criticism conceive of its function as the pedagogic articulation of inherited, 'traditional' truth rather than the critical project of questioning those truths. Even when the 'modernist' criticism we are examining attacks the subjectivity of romantic readings of literature and culture, it does so not by means of a critique of subjectivity, but simply by its dogmatic rejection. Traditional humanism, as we have already suggested, posits an objective truth of humanity that transcends the historical situations in which it arises, and therefore also posits a human subjectivity that is self-identical and transcends the discourses that seem to articulate it. Above all, humanism assumes the transcendental objectivity of 'humanity' itself which can and should serve as an Archimedean vantage from which to pursue the study of literature. Twentieth-century humanism modifies romantic humanism simply by rejecting individual subjectivity in the assertion that 'objective' classicism best describes what constitutes humanity. This rejection takes two forms: a return to Greek sources of European culture in a *transpersonal* humanism, which, under the name of the 'New Humanism', was an early form of cultural critique, and an assumption of *impersonal* formalism in reading which constituted a new pedagogy under the name 'New Criticism'. In both of these impulses (though sometimes despite itself), modernist literary criticism transforms critique into a new dogmatism in its polemical anti-Romanticism.

The objectivity of modern humanism, like the Renaissance humanism at the beginning of the modern era, consistently takes the form of a new Hellenism. Constant in the disparate texts of modernism and modernist approaches to literature is a return to the Greeks – to a set of classical values thought to have supported ancient Greek culture from the eighth through to the fourth centuries BC. The values that modern culture needs to retrieve from the Greeks constitute what Benhabib describes as four complex presuppositions drawn from the Greek tradition of 'practical philosophy', a practical guide that directs a single person in his or her interaction with the larger culture. For Aristotle, Benhabib argues, 'practical philosophy was a unified teaching of ethics and politics' in relation to human activity in general (1986: 5). The first assumption governing practical philosophy is that of 'a unitary model', a totalized system, of what humans do and assume to be the case as they go about the business of their lives. This assumption encompasses the diversity of human activities within a conception that shows humans to be living for a purpose that transcends particular individuals and particular cultural moments. In these terms, individuals comprise a collective, transpersonal 'subject', namely 'humanity'. Second, history in almost all of its traditional incarnations 'is constituted by the activities of this one subject' (1986: 129–30). The totality of humans is the composite social agent and the real locus and origin of experience for individual humans in history.

Third is the suggestion, following the other two, that 'human history presents the unfolding of the capacities of this one subject'

(1986: 130). That is, humanity may be static or dynamic in its relation to the gods and to world justice as the final arbitrator of how things are and will be. But the essential nature and fate of 'humanity', classically conceived as the social totality of human beings, are what is played out and discovered in history and, in this sense, constitute history's own uniquely human purpose. Fourth is the notion that human 'good' consists ultimately in the 'emancipation' achieved within a single person's learning to act in such a way as to reiterate and revitalize the connection between human modes of knowing in the past and those in the present as naturally integrated and the same, as 'one' (1986: 130).

While the remnants of practical philosophy disappeared in the later nineteenth century during the rise of the 'modern' anthropological and social sciences, the reinvigoration of the classical philosophy of transpersonal subjectivity by humanists in the early twentieth century constitutes a large-scale programme to make up for the ethical failures of nineteenth-century culture, particularly its experiments with Romanticism and, implicitly, the kind of fragmented social world that laissez-faire capitalism produced. That is, up until the end of the nineteenth century, the traditional amalgam of ethics and politics known since the Greeks as 'practical philosophy' provided a working bridge between conceptions of selfhood and the community's own well-being (Benhabib 1986: 1). But the ontological naiveté in practical philosophy concerning 'facts' and the stable world conception underlying practical philosophy were quickly eroded with the rise of scientifically oriented studies – foregrounding systematization and impersonality – of culture and society. The early modernists intended the humanistic reinvigoration of transpersonal subjectivity explicitly to counter the forces of cultural and ethical laxity associated with Romanticism and to foreground the social mission traditionally inherent in the critical enterprise. At the same time, as we will show – and this is a great paradox of intellectual history – this programme in its various incarnations of humanism and modernism often duplicated the fundamental commitments of romantic discourse it set out to oppose and to replace.

TRANSPERSONAL HUMANISM

The commitment to a rigorously critical programme – that is, the *possibility* (if not the achievement) of cultural critique over mere criticism – is a primary preoccupation of thought about culture in the first two decades of the twentieth century that aimed at this 'transpersonal' humanism (rather than the 'impersonal' formalism of literary study we will examine later in this chapter). This is a diverse body of thought that goes under the name of humanism, New Humanism, or critical humanism. A key text for understanding the intellectual commitment to cultural criticism in this form, and a work too little consulted for its self-consciously rational probing of culture and its critical method as well as its contribution to the development of Anglo-American literary criticism even to the present day, is Irving Babbitt's *Rousseau and Romanticism*. (It is also too little consulted for its examination of ancient Greek culture.) *Rousseau and Romanticism* advances a programme for a rigorous interpretation of modern culture against the backdrop of its own reading of the Western tradition. As one of Eliot's teachers at Harvard and an influential figure in cultural debates in the early twentieth century, Babbitt formulated much of the critical tenor and even specific precepts and language that were later to underlie Eliot's own critical procedures and texts – also much that followed in Eliot's modernist criticism and even New Criticism.

Babbitt's *Rousseau and Romanticism* sets out to build a case *against* nineteenth-century culture for its inability to conceive of rigorous and rationally based critical practices in the examination of literature and culture. This failure, Babbitt maintains, enabled the social function of criticism as a cultural institution to go largely undefined and unheeded. Babbitt starts with the idea that Anglo-American Romanticism of the prior century, as well as its twentieth-century strains, were based in 'emotional naturalism' (1919: x), by which he meant the advancement of vagaries of feeling and sentiment as affective 'facts', all to the end of obscuring the unchanging and true nature of culture as it really *was* for the Romantics and as it *is* for modern culture as well – the sense in which the 'subject' of the past and present really 'are one'. From Babbitt's viewpoint, Romantic sentiment, in other words, was always a counterfeit value, a fragile overlay to culture and the signal of a failure to examine the levels of knowing that, in fact, underlie culture.

Typical of Romantic sham culture is William Wordsworth's evocation in the *Lyrical Ballads* of a romantic scene of instruction, in which

> One impulse from a vernal wood
> May teach you more of man,
> Of moral evil and of good,
> Than all the sages can.

Babbitt notes that such misplaced and adolescent trust in nature's beneficence – in the fact that instruction and pedagogy could be 'natural' in that nature fully supplants the store of cultural knowledge – would leave even Rousseau gasping and staring. The easy evocation of knowledge production in this scene, in other words, does not begin to suggest the cultural pedagogy that links past and present as 'one'. Babbitt then concludes that nineteenth-century Romanticism has been detrimental to both nineteenth- and twentieth-century culture particularly because it has caused a far-reaching erosion of critical discrimination, the ability to scrutinize and weigh literature and art – as distinct from a 'single impulse from a vernal wood' – as significant contributions to communal life. In light of the serious damage done to civilization, culture and its institutions in the nineteenth century, henceforth literary criticism must eschew all traces of Romantic influence as found in this scene and follow a new direction characterized by a reconstituted neo–classic sensibility based on evident demonstration and sufficient reason.

What we see here as Babbitt's total rejection of Romanticism was at the heart of his larger critique of Western culture. This critique, resting upon the overt idealization of classical Greek culture and the denigration of Romantic culture, advances four far-reaching propositions concerning the development of the Western tradition:

1 The first concerns the superiority of classical culture to all that follows it. This elevation of the Greeks, strongly associated by Babbitt with Matthew Arnold, is ubiquitous in the thought of those who contributed to modernism and a constant theme, in one form or another, in much criticism oriented towards modernism up to the present day. This judgment, strongly supportive of what Benhabib calls the philosophy of the transpersonal subject, permeates Babbitt's discourse and contains the germ of his complex ideas about and judgment of Romanticism at almost every turn. Finally, like scores of other post-Enlightenment historians, philosophers and critics, Babbitt claimed to see a unique quality in Greek culture in its clarity of formal thought (law, philosophy and religion) and in the social responsibility of its art. Thus, Babbitt believed the Greeks to have been culturally 'balanced' in their acceptance of their fixed place, the place of humans, in the cosmos.

Babbitt believed, further, that the Greeks found a way to embrace what could be expressed in ordinary terms about their lives, and, because of this, they judged this knowable dimension of culture to be a 'sufficient' basis for values and commitments. As this argument goes, the Greeks were not so much culturally bold and exploratory as strategically affirmative in their thought and art and eager in the way they went about knowing the world. It follows that they generally elaborated their culture within those humane limits. Their subsequent respect for human limitation and cultural boundaries (at least for Greek *men* of a certain social station), in many ways the solid basis for all of Western humanism, was what Babbitt saw as the quality of directness in Greek culture's relation to itself and to the cosmos. Friedrich and Wilhelm Schlegel had also come to these conclusions about the Greeks a century earlier, just as Arnold made similar judgments at the end of the nineteenth century. In sum, the consensus was that Greek thought and art showed great vitality in its style and spirit and felt free enough within these limits to celebrate the 'humanistic' finitude of life lived within avowedly 'natural' parameters.

2 Babbitt then advanced the significant and momentous paradox that the Greeks' forthright vitality coincides more or less exactly with the quality that writers such as Goethe, Sainte-Beuve, Renan and Arnold defined as the critical and questioning 'modern spirit'. This is modernism, of course, not as a mere recognition of 'newness' in the world but as 'the positive and critical spirit, the spirit that refuses to take things on authority' (1919: xi). That is, just as the Greeks found and embraced the limits of their world, knew the place of their culture, so the 'modern spirit' also – and potentially so in a 'positive' vein – can set out to look unflinchingly at its condition and find its own boundaries and truths and then serve the cause of elaborating culture in relation to those limits. It is this 'modern spirit' – what Benhabib calls the 'subject' of the classical world, an attitude of rational inquiry – that Arnold identified as the spirit of disinterested inquiry.

Babbitt evokes this ideal of the ancient Greek world as an index for measuring other cultures and historical moments that he wishes to admonish. He reminds his readers shrewdly that '[Arnold] explains why the Greeks of the great period seem more modern to us than the men of the Middle Ages' (1919: xi). His point is that the Greeks were uniquely healthy as a culture because of their 'critical' temperament, a quality of temperament lacking in Western culture during the Middle Ages. Others in the Western tradition along the way lost track of that quality, or so Babbitt claims, especially in the Platonizing Middle Ages, but we in the twentieth century have a unique historical opportunity to win back these values and probably stave off cultural decay and disintegration in the process.

In the same vein, Babbitt everywhere implies that the Greeks at their best were more 'modern' than, and in this way superior to, much of twentieth-century culture. Here Babbitt's idea (and Arnold's) is that the 'modern spirit', a posture representing honesty, directness and boldness in cultural expression, was once held as a supreme value of Western culture and then later was gradually lost. The question crucial to civilization, then, is whether contemporary culture can or will choose to recognize its need for this 'modern' sensibility and posture and make the changes needed to regain it.

3 Babbitt's third proposition concerns the crisis of Romanticism in nineteenth-century culture. By the early nineteenth century in Europe, he maintains, there was a near total 'repudiation of decorum as something external and artificial' to cultural life and to what humans can become within culture (1919: 105). In place of the classical ideal of the 'externality' of decorum and tradition, the Romantics focused on cultural experience as narcissistic subjectivity and posited an interior life with no real ties, certainly no significant ties, to tradition and history conceived of as a contextual discourse 'external' and 'out there' in tradition. This rejection of decorum and tradition weakened the foundation of culture, and so Romantic culture occurred at a moment of extreme cultural degeneration in which a segment of society repudiated the essence of culture as a medium of conventions and so denied its own cultural life. As such, this moment realized a fall from the high moral and cultural achievements so clearly expressed by classical culture.

The goal of this Romantic drive towards cultural solipsism, Babbitt maintains, was none other than to 'get back to the primitive and naive and unconscious, or what amounts to the same thing, to shake off the trammels of tradition and reason in favor of free and passionate self-expression' (1919: 79). When Wordsworth, for example, races ahead of Rousseau on the issue of primitivism with his claim for the 'one impulse from a vernal wood', he strongly advances a frightening naiveté that, in fact, expresses a latent but true wish for cultural destruction. Even the 'romantic rebellion against Pope's [formal, poetic] diction', Babbitt maintains, 'was part of the general rebellion against artificial [that is to say, formally 'cultural'] decorum' and, ultimately, the actual life forces of Western civilization (1919: 341).

Such solipsism is the destruction of the pedagogic imperative, the substitution, in Swift's and Arnold's figure, of a spider spinning a web from itself rather than a bee creating sweetness and light from its recovery of tradition. That is, if this rebellion had succeeded, at least theoretically, there would no longer be any compelling cultural impulses except the continued elaboration of solipsism of the kind expressed in Lord Byron's 'The Island' in which he describes 'The

61

wish – which ages have not yet subdued / In man – to have no master save his mood'. At a moment of crisis in Western culture, then, the rise of Romanticism and its touting of personal 'mood' marked the virtual collapse of the 'critical spirit', the very life of culture – a critical spirit that was once the stable scaffolding of Western culture beginning in ancient Greece and continuing during a few privileged eras afterwards.

4 Finally, Babbitt argued, while Romanticism marked a historical moment of cultural collapse because of its critical softness, the New Humanism was a strong signal of cultural 'reconstruction' – to use, or rather to misuse slightly, the Schlegels' term. The legacy of 'emotional romanticism' in the nineteenth century had invited nothing other than cultural 'bankruptcy' from its inception because Romanticism tried to deploy a 'lazy floating on the stream of mood and temperament' (1919: 333) as a substitute for the 'ethical effort' of difficult cultural work – the work of pedagogy – the always formidable tasks of establishing a sense of tradition and then extending that tradition through the substantiation of artistic and critical achievement. Babbitt's judgment here, extending Arnold's, is that the carnivalesque and Romantic escape from neo-classical ideals had run its course by the nineteenth-century's end and in its own terms was exhausted. With this collapse of nineteenth-century sham culture, all that remained was for right-thinking critics to set in motion a countercurrent of neo-classicism adjusted to the particular communal needs conceived nationally and racially in the modern European and American world.

IMPERSONAL HUMANISM

Along with this articulation of transpersonal subjectivity, *Rousseau and Romanticism* also – and somewhat inconsistently – articulates the modernist value of impersonality. 'One of man's deepest needs', as Babbitt says in phrasing reminiscent of an ethical manifesto later to come from his student T.S. Eliot, is for 'genuine communion, for a genuine escape, that is, from his ordinary self' (1919: 305). One must escape the solipsistic 'self' in order to move outwards towards a true sense of community. From there one is able to situate a particular community or culture in relation to significant developments in the Western tradition and in the 'mind of Europe', that is, the achievements of European culture such as its art, its divisions of labour, its political infrastructure, and so on. The 'escape' from self, or what Eliot calls the escape from 'personality', signals a massive repudiation of Romanticism and a step towards 'reconstructing' the neo-classical (and non-Romantic) critical spirit, the classical subject made anew.

From Babbitt's viewpoint, if this project succeeds – ironically – the cultural 'escape' from self can enable a new and broader range of human freedom. Whereas in Romanticism human freedom was conceived as emanating from a single subjective 'impulse' or 'mood', Babbitt saw true freedom as achieved 'not by throwing off but by taking on limitations' (1919: 393). True freedom comes, in other words, not from the escape from rules but from one's membership in culture. And what one should wish to limit 'above all' is 'imagination' in the specifically Romantic sense of the non-rational faculty of apprehension that needs the guidance and shaping of highly critical and rational senses of form and decorum (1919: 393).

In this shift from considerations of culture to considerations of individuals – whether that individual is a psychological subject or an aesthetic subject – Babbitt is shifting his critique of the Romantic subject from one that is based on a transpersonal 'philosophy of the subject' to one that is based upon the 'impersonal' nature of cultural experience. Babbitt thus takes as cultural facts two historical breaks that he believed to have the greatest implications for twentieth-century culture. The first is that which occasioned Romanticism, the difference between the nineteenth-century Romantic perspective and the neo-classicism that dominated European culture in the eighteenth century. This 'break' articulated itself as an epistemological crisis situated on the level of the individual rather than the polity. He argued that this break was the work of 'intellectual romanticism', which may have begun as early in the West as the European Renaissance. In this respect, Babbitt fought the tendency within the Renaissance concept of critique, as we have described it, to privilege the individually reasoning subject, the tendency of critique to take nothing on the authority of the past. The second historical break Babbitt sees is that of his own time, a break between Romantic cultural influence and the contemporaneous renewal of the critical spirit. This historical break, in effect, concludes that which was begun with the European Romantics and signals the exhaustion of the Romantic sensibility and world view, the anti-cultural stance of Romanticism. Within this historical framework for both the individual subject and culture, he argues, is the space for articulating a number of distinctions about what direction culture should be developing.

We have already traced Babbitt's cultural criticism based on Greek conceptions of transpersonal 'humanity' and practical philosophy. But in his criticism that is based on assumptions about the nature of the *individual* human subject – his criticism that is more self-consciously 'literary' – he describes his understanding of what literary and artistic experiments should be encouraged and what artistic innovations in the early twentieth century will be most harmful in light of the cultural 'work' that needs to be done. In this Babbitt more forcefully emphasizes the pedagogical aims of criticism. Like many of the modernist apologists for criticism we cited earlier, he understands the study of literature to focus upon the individual subject of reading rather than the collective subject of culture. That is, in terms of literary study he criticizes the Romantic legacy from the vantage of an 'impersonal' understanding of experience rather than a transpersonal understanding of culture. For this reason, he sees the need to encourage a modified neo-classic doctrine of expression in the arts as broadly as possible. If that step is not taken, then there is no difference between the modern spirit and romantic sentiment.

A number of contemporary critics addressed this issue along with Babbitt in specific critical terms; we might even say they were beginning to answer his call for renewed neo-classical form and for a critical spirit defined by specific tenets about the deployment of technique and aesthetics in a radically new version of neo-classic art. These writers differ from Babbitt, however, insofar as they see the task of criticism to be the articulation of an impersonal sense of literature and literary study without situating that task within the critical framework of transpersonal humanism. In this failure to situate literary studies within a framework of cultural analysis, they transform the implicit cultural critique in Babbitt's work into simple criticism based upon unexamined assumptions concerning 'classical' truth.

Strongly in league with Babbitt, as if answering his call to action, were poets (Eliot, Pound) and critics (including Ernest Fenollosa and T.E. Hulme) who proposed actual poetic systems that would express the neo-classic critical spirit in specific terms to create possibilities for precise demonstration and modulated form in art – experiments always taken by their proponents to be counters and antidotes to the Romantic notions of 'mood' and purely personal expression. These writers promulgated various figures for precise form such as 'imagism', the 'ideogram', and 'vortex', which have come to be seen as crucial to Anglo-American modernism. At the beginning of the modern era writers and artists like Eliot and Pound (and even Yeats) were conceiving of themselves and their intellectual life in opposition to received ideas of subjectivity and 'opinion' – Eliot, for instance, argues in 'Tradition and the Individual Talent' that poetry for those who understand cannot be the expression of 'personality' – but they do so to promote a transcendental idea of 'objectivity' that obviates critique as we have traced its meaning.

In other words, the modernist writers of the turn of the century saw themselves as marking simultaneously an ending and a new beginning. Ezra Pound's call to 'make it new' became the rallying cry of many in the arts, precisely because of the ambiguity of his admonition which is a call both to recover the past and to break with it. In 'Tradition and the Individual Talent', Eliot set a tone for modern criticism by asserting that 'criticism is as inevitable as breathing, and that we should be none the worse for articulating what passes in our minds when we read a book and feel an emotion about it' (1919: 37). In this statement Eliot captures the double sense of criticism as an exploration of cultural life and community and as a way of creating the so-called 'objective' (critical) response to the subjective 'effects' of cultural life. In other words, it presents the sense of 'critical theory' as a mediation of the private and public realms. Later in the twentieth century the Frankfurt School pursued such critical theory to create the possibility of the transformation of 'objective' truths, but in Eliot it seems simply a rearguard action in defence of the status quo.

Still, Eliot conceived of himself, as he did of the movement in the arts that came to be called modernism, as thoroughly against the Romantic humanism of late-Victorian England. In his essay on Arnold, for instance, he takes Arnold to task for 'putting emphasis on the poet's feelings, instead of upon the poetry' (1933: 115). In this, Eliot presents a conception of the subject which is 'impersonal' and a conception of literature as something other than 'expressive'. In his criticism of Arnold, Eliot goes even further than this in arguing that expressiveness as an idea does not work because it is based on the illusion that one can traffic in 'personal' moods and values by means of a kind of currency of poetic representation. 'Nothing in this world or the next,' he writes in his essay on Arnold, 'is a substitute for anything else; and if you find that you must do without something, such as religious faith or philosophic belief, then you must just do without it' (1933: 113). Eliot takes Arnold to task for describing poetry as a 'communication theory' in which the poet functions as 'teacher, leader, or priest' (1933: 115). For Eliot the poet sees 'beneath' the phenomena of our world and ourselves to articulate feelings which are not personal at all: 'the essential advantage for a poet is not to have a beautiful world with which to deal: it is to be able to see beneath both beauty and ugliness; to see the boredom, and the horror, and the glory' (1933: 106).

Such an 'impersonal' and 'formal' conception of poetry – one which, first of all, was anti-bourgeois – led many Anglo-American modernists (though not all: Joyce, Woolf and Auden are notable exceptions) to approve of authoritarian politics to one degree or another. Pound, for instance, promoted Italian fascism as an important social movement; Eliot proclaimed himself a royalist and conservative and, in some of his published writings, made ethnic slurs he later publicly regretted; Yeats flirted with a right-wing authoritarian Irish party. Another example is the recent discovery that Paul de Man – whose work presents one of the most rigorous and 'formal' articulations of post-structuralism – had voiced pro-Nazi sentiments in book reviews during World War II. All of these instances – there are others in Lawrence and in the racism of Stevens and the New Critics – support the contention that there is some sort of correlation between a modernist 'formal' sense of aesthetic experience and an ability to overlook (if not participate in) gross violations of human rights and dignity. It has been argued that the kind of 'impersonality' that formal conceptions of poetry – that is, formalist criticism – suggest might lead (or at least be conducive) to certain kinds of disregard for human rights. In fact, some critics (such as Frank Lentricchia in *After the New Criticism*) have suggested that proponents of structuralist and post-structuralist literary criticism share some of these attitudes with those modernist writers who wanted to ground their vision and art in something other than the narrow sense of a laissez-faire subject they inherited from their forebears. It is not clear exactly how much structuralism and modernist criticism share as intellectual movements, and even if it could be shown that both are species of modernist 'formalism' (either the New Criticism we will examine later in this chapter or the Russian Formalism examined in the next), it is clearly not the case that structuralism and post-structuralism attract people with homogeneous political views of one sort or another.

If, instead of thinking of these authoritarian political commitments in terms of their relationship to their 'formalist' content, we think of them in relation to the opposition between impersonality and trans-personality we are presenting here, the failure of modernist conceptions of literature to encompass cultural critique becomes clear. As Benhabib notes in examining the Hegelian conception of trans-personal subjectivity in opposition to human intersubjectivity, 'according to the standpoint of intersubjectivity, the perspective of human agents is constitutive of the validity and meaning of their interactions, whereas the standpoint of trans-subjectivity locates this validity and meaning in a source external to the shared perspectives of social agents, in the standpoint of a thinker–observer' (1986: 89–90). In other words, transpersonal subjectivity, to be thought at all, requires a standpoint *outside* the phenomena it is describing, an Archimedean standpoint against which the 'validity' of behaviour can be measured. This is the measure of 'humanity' – the measure of 'truth' – and it casts the 'other' of intersubjective relationships into the position of a negation. In terms of European modernism, it measures its own cultural achievements *against* what it conceives of as 'other': Yeats's Catholic middle class fumbling 'in a greasy till' (1956: 106), Eliot's Sweeney or his Bleistein, Paul de Man's description of the 'unity' of Europe and necessity of isolating Jewish intellectual life as its contaminating 'other'.

Another aspect of modernism – also articulated by Babbitt – that could lead to such politics is the sense of enormous radical changes in society and the sense of the impending end of civilization altogether that many felt to be the case in the early part of the century (without critically examining the content of privileged white male 'civiliza-tion'). 'Perhaps,' Eliot says of Arnold, 'he cared too much for civilisation, forgetting that Heaven and Earth shall pass away, and Mr. Arnold with them, and there is only one stay' (1933: 119). It is here, in fact, that art and politics seem to come together. The claims of modernism are generally not so dramatic as Virginia Woolf's claim that in 1910 'human nature changed' – or William Butler Yeats's assertion in 1922 that 'after us the Savage God' – yet such an apocalyptic sense of the twentieth century as a new beginning accurately reflects the idea that runs through most modernist criti-cism. The newness consists in what Kermode calls an 'open breach with the past', 'a reaction against the crushing weight of an artistic past which cannot be surveyed any longer by any one person' (1973: 4). Like Pound in the ambiguity of his cry 'make it new', Kermode describes a double vision of the twentieth century as empowered to step free of the past and simultaneously as suffering in its failure to encompass or even to survey that past – both of which visions suggest, as Woolf says, some shift in what it means to be human. From this shift, as the critical essays of Babbitt, Eliot and Pound testify, comes the anxiety embedded in modernism and specifically in its cultural criticism. If 'modernism strongly implies some sort of historical discontinuity . . . a liberation from inherited patterns', as

Richard Ellmann and Charles Feidelson claim (1965: vi), then it simultaneously means 'deprivation and disinheritance' – being set free and also broken off from the values of the past.

POETICS OF MODERNISM

Notwithstanding the rhetoric of loss, apocalypse and new beginnings (the rhetoric typical of modernist criticism) – and notwithstanding their politics – the modernists, including Babbitt, were involved in a serious reformulation of the limits of literary form and of the possibilities for a new critical understanding of the arts generally. If not exactly new ways of being human, this reformulation encompasses at least a new critical presentation for the products of twentieth-century culture. Henceforth, as Babbitt said most forcefully, any Romantic or sentimental tendencies in literature must be viewed as mere 'emotional naturalism', a dissolving of real-world distinctions and a glossing over of important cultural demarcations. In place of nineteenth-century Romantic 'sloppiness', Babbitt said, is the emergent 'modern spirit', 'the positive and critical spirit, the spirit that refuses to take things on authority'. Babbitt calls for a further movement away from supposedly 'soft' and 'uncritical' Romanticism to 'tough', 'critical' modernism. This is a shift, as T.E. Hulme argued, into a contemporary version of the neo-classic sensibility and its modes of precise expression and carefully modulated sentiments. In short, Babbitt and Hulme, like Eliot and Pound, call for a complete abandonment of Romanticism – the Romantic *subject* of experience and language, the Romantic *order* of a recoverable past in thought and social life – and for the development of an emergent modern, anti-Romantic critical sensibility.

This sensibility, as the criticism of this period shows, most immediately calls for a movement away from the high valuation of irrationality in criticism which British Romantic poets called *imagination*. Eliot's description, for instance, of the language of modernism does not require the reader to impose emotions on the text because the text provides its own in the *form* of its progression. Eliot calls these 'structural emotions' – the boredom, horror and glory beneath existence – and says that they are generated out of the text itself. By this he means that, in reading poetry, particular 'feelings' are elicited from the reader by the formal arrangement of the poem's images. These images, in turn, are arranged in the text as an 'objective correlative', or a particular image sequence in the poem that 'corresponds' to and provokes a human emotion. It follows that the act of reading draws forth all the 'feelings' that combine to make up a particular 'emotion', which can be said to be 'in' the text insofar as the text, by means of its form, specifically provokes that emotion. This entire operation, from the deployment of images as an objective correlative through the received effect of what we are calling a 'structural emotion', takes place as a 'textual' operation, a poetic experience that is not brought to the text as a personal experience but is generated precisely out of the text's particular patterning or structure.

Such 'objectivity', of course, lends itself to demonstration and pedagogy. It creates the possibility that poetic discourse can be analysed outside the context of the human relations and situations that occasioned it. Modernist criticism, then, as a 'formal' explanation of poetry's function, is a scheme for art that fits into the twentieth century's broader picture of culture as different from the personal humanism of Romanticism. Eliot elaborates this impersonal conception of poetry and understanding in 'Tradition and the Individual Talent' when he argues that 'past', 'present', and 'future' are not given facts or simple realities of experience but a *formal* arrangement of areas of disturbance and discontinuity in the midst of which the poet constructs art and culture like a collage. Similarly, in this period Saussure – Eliot's contemporary – proposes that the apprehension of reality itself is a linguistic arrangement of 'signifiers' and potential meanings, or 'signifieds', in a rational and formal binary arrangement that is at one level of functioning entirely arbitrary. Thus, cut off from the past, disinherited from it (this, after all, is the corollary to Babbitt's break from the immediate past), the poet, artist or even any user of language can choose to accept the imperative and responsibility 'to make it new' or else remain without any operative sense of past or present culture at all. This anti–Romantic version of poetry suggests a highly rational (nearly Augustan) practice, but it is poetic logic shown to exist in the wasteland of modern culture, where the poet toils to make (to actually *create*) connections between his or her individual and cultural life that otherwise would not exist.

One example of the formal poetics of modernism is that associated with the 'Chinese written character', the ideogram, an idea discussed by Pound but advanced most visibly by Ernest Fenollosa in *The Chinese Written Character as a Medium of Poetry* (1919). This concept exemplifies attempts in this period to conceive poetics on a rational and critical basis. Fenollosa argued that Chinese writing has the potential not only to evoke 'thought pictures' by using facsimiles of conventional signs, as is the case in any writing system, but that these pictorial 'ideograms' do their work 'more vividly and concretely' precisely because they do not gesture to an ethereal significance beyond representation which need not be textually 'present' for investigation. Whereas the Romantics had gestured towards the infinite, the ideograms present experience absolutely immediate and 'concrete', because rational in form, for the reader (1919: 140).

Like other critics in this period, Fenollosa in this formulation correlates effectiveness and precision with demonstrable and particularly visual representation. That is, whereas the Romantic poets might gesture vaguely in the direction of the infinite, as Babbitt maintained they do when he discussed Wordsworth, a writer using the Chinese ideograms theoretically *represents* ideas and feelings in a tangible medium, thus one open to rational investigation of the totality of what is being conveyed. Representation and significance in this way remain separate and 'objective' and thus subject to rational inquiry. There is no merging of representation and significance into seemingly unmediated and self-evident 'experience'. Fenollosa especially values the resistance offered by the Chinese text to the possibility of misreadings that happen when actual readers are empowered, or feel themselves to be empowered, to impose their own meanings and experience on the text, as was supposedly the case in countless Romantic readings of poetry and culture in which representation and significance were apparently conflated. .

Fenollosa believed that 'in reading Chinese', and the pictorial mode it implies, 'we do not seem to be juggling mental counters' at all, sorting through potential meanings and interpretive options. Rather, we seem 'to be watching *things* work out their own fate' in a way little subject to the contaminations of personal mood or whimsy (1919: 140). Here, reading poetry, as in de Man's definition of teaching, 'is not primarily an intersubjective relationship between people but a cognitive process in which self and other are only tangentially and contiguously involved' (1986: 4). Fenollosa's conclusion about reading an ideogram, or even an approximation of it *as a form* in another language, is that we get a renewed sense that 'poetry must render what is said, not what is merely meant' (1919: 147). And again the emphasis is on what is achieved or rendered in poetry as a rational, nearly propositional logic – in other words, through an 'external' decorum of the very sort rejected by the Romantics. This emphasis points to the value of form conceived in a linear economy wherein what is culturally significant in a text is thought to approximate what is demonstrably *conveyed* by that text. Fenollosa, in other words, imagined signification to be totally adequate to the weight of the cultural sense it is positioned to convey.

A related formulation, and still influential for its call for a new critical spirit in poetic form and rigorous interpretation, is T.E. Hulme's essay 'Romanticism and Classicism' (posthumously published in *Speculations* [1924]). Hulme, too, posited that with care and respect for the rational limits of language, signification can be made adequate to sense expressions. Writing and its interpretation, in other words, have the potential to constitute a fundamentally balanced economy. Hulme's thesis, much like Babbitt's, concerns the conflict between Romanticism and classicism in early twentieth-century culture. Calling Romanticism 'spilt religion' and associating it with misguided commitments to human perfectibility and emotional self-indulgence, Hulme sees the same historical breaks with Romantic culture that Babbitt posited and, like Babbitt, calls for a rejection of the Romantic idea of 'imagination' as overstressing individual and solipsistic, anti-cultural strategies in art.

Hulme argues forcefully that the 'modern' critical commitment should be primarily to 'fancy', to the 'hard, dry' faculty of reason and rationality, and it is ironic that this is exactly the definition that the English Romantics gave 'fancy' when they were trying to dismiss the importance of rational hierarchies in culture (1924: 113). Hulme chose *fancy* – Coleridge's term for the human capacity to reason and to make demonstrable (in this sense, 'critical') connections within and among experiences – for epistemological reasons, particularly the belief that superior art comes out of the knowledge born of reasoned discriminations and a rational perspective by a subject who links past and present experience.

Hulme, of course, does not mean 'dry' in the sense of banality in poetry, but the 'hard, dry' presentation of precise images and a modulated use of sentiment in language, what Arnold had meant earlier when he called for a modern poetry that is 'particular, precise and firm poetry' (1853: 8). The poetic line that results from this impetus, like Eliot's 'pair of ragged claws / Scuttling across the floors of silent seas', aims at a 'hard, or direct and detailed, presentation of sensory data as quite particular (and thus paradoxically 'rational') emotional evocations. Imagery should be 'dry', that is, in that it is free of dependence on the pre-existing and predetermined emotions that could be brought to or imposed on the text by the reader regardless of the text's own economies of image and theme.

It seems to us quite misleading to dismiss Hulme's interest in a neo-classical poetics, as René Wellek does, as an 'ideological super-structure' which in reality is a facade which hides – as Wellek accuses Eliot of doing, too – a real taste 'for the [merely] imagistic' with no real interest for what is meant by classical decorum and what we have been referring to as the philosophy of the subject (1986: 152). Like the other critics of a humanistic orientation, Hulme is clear in referring to Romanticism as a quite broad Western set of assumptions about humanity as perfectible and as embodying 'an infinite reservoir of possibilities', a claim easy to demonstrate in a reading of British Romantic poetry (1924: 112). By 'classicism' he clearly defines a traditional Western assumption about the extraordinarily fixed character of human beings 'whose nature is absolutely constant' – the assumptions embodied in Greek practical philosophy. It follows that the technique of imagism as Hulme and Pound conceived it was intended as a poetic practice to counter the grandiose gestures of Romanticism and thus to deflate the Romantic trafficking in easy infinities with the more modest performances of achieved effect and local sense in the immediate and ordinary reading experience.

In short, Hulme opposes classical and romantic views as directly opposite to each other and summarizes the difference between them in that 'to the one party man's nature is like a well, to the other like a bucket' (1924: 117). Assuming that human beings cannot prosper and grow *in vacuo*, caught and held in a 'bucket' – that is, outside of a cultural medium – Hulme concludes with the New Humanist credo that 'it is only by tradition and organization that anything decent can be got out of [people]' (1924: 116). While Frank Kermode rightly objects to Hulme's reductive caricature of Romantic poetics as overly simple and one-dimensional (1957: 119–37), Hulme's depiction of Romanticism's particular cultural force is not at all eccentric. What the Romantics once denigrated as external decorum, as if tradition were a mere ornamentation for culture, becomes the substance and all-important focus for a redefinition of culture.

LEAVIS AND INSTITUTIONAL CRITICISM

The New Humanism we are describing spawned two different 'critical' movements in the later twentieth century, each of which aimed at realizing its own pedagogical imperative. One major strain of modernistic and humanistic influence moved towards the intense moral view of F.R. and Q.D. Leavis and its American articulation in

Yvor Winters, a line of development that tends back towards 'criticism' as an unselfconscious promotion of a particular ideological stance. The other major direction is the criticism of T.S. Eliot and I.A. Richards which came to produce the dominant force in Anglo-American criticism at mid-century, American New Criticism. (These two 'movements' – never absolutely separate – come together in the moralistic New Critical analyses of Winters.) To use figures as a kind of shorthand, Eliot and F.R. Leavis mark quite different dimensions in the twentieth-century project to shape a literary criticism. Eliot, as we have suggested, plays a key part in advancing the rationale for aesthetic 'form' as a foundation in the understanding of modern culture. But as we turn to higher education and the academic study of literature in the twentieth century, Leavis represents a differing attitude, one in which literature is studied in terms of ethics as well as aesthetics. In each case the commitment is to a pedagogy of literature and culture, but in the most immediate institutional sense – for Eliot was not by profession an academic or teacher – it is F.R. Leavis in his role as teacher at Cambridge University, literary interpreter, and cultural theorist who helped, along with Richards, to fix the early directions of literary criticism as an institutional practice and as an approach to cultural criticism.

It has been common since the early twentieth century to characterize modernism in terms of 'multiplicity', avant-garde forms of theory, and the mythical layerings of *The Waste Land* and *Ulysses* as well as the shifting viewpoints in *The Waves* and *Absalom, Absalom!*. Leavis, however, attempts to refocus and stabilize and thus to reinstitute privileged *single* perspectives on culture based on traditionally humanistic values. His professed goal was the lofty one to save humanity by giving 'command of the art of the living' amid accelerating deterioration in the modern world (Leavis and Thompson 1933: 107). He was prepared to fight in a positive effort to advance in experience a true 'faith' rather than 'duty' (1933: 100) and to affirm 'life' humanistically conceived, which he often describes, particularly in his work on D.H. Lawrence. Moreover, whereas the diversity of texts that influenced modernist criticism, for both professed poetics and implicit critical practice, makes modernism difficult to account for as a critical discourse, Leavis presumed the existence of a precisely definable 'great tradition' of Anglo-American novelists involved in an ongoing cultural discourse about values and ethics – constituted mainly by George Eliot, Henry James, Joseph Conrad and Lawrence.

The predominant view of modernism that Leavis counters is evoked by Frank Kermode's designation of the critical sources for modernism in studies of 'exotic societies', 'classical scholarship', and 'psychiatry' (1973: 6) as well as a vast sense of the 'genuine discontinuities discovered in the [modern] world' as strongly reflected in the example of quantum theory in physics and other scientific developments fostering a wholly 'different relation of mind to objective reality' (1973: 4). By contrast, Leavis deplored the rapidly increasing multiple determinants of culture that accompanied democratic egalitarianism in education, and he thought they were disastrous for humanity because of their anti-hierarchical and socially levelling effect. While Kermode saw modernism's conception of a 'different relation' to reality as an effect produced by forces too numerous ever to be fully accounted for – 'multiplicity', in this regard, becomes a figure for a doubleness in the discourse of modernist criticism (pedagogic along with critical) as well as a trait of narrative and poetic texts – Leavis defines a counter 'good' of modern culture. He described this good in the case of higher education as simply and unambiguously producing an educated public capable of sustaining a hierarchy of social order in which the responsibilities of social class are relatively unambiguous.

Because he is not a poet/critic but a professor/critic, Leavis throughout his career seeks to theorize the social mission of the academy in a world in which he saw communal order rapidly fading. It was entirely possible, Leavis reasons, that the contemporary moral foundation could not be upheld directly by any institution *except* the university. The task at hand, therefore, was not merely to 'save' the 'essential elements' inherently valuable to the Western tradition, 'but to develop them into an autonomous culture' that would serve as a regrounding of the Western tradition. If this project succeeded, culture could then be free of the weaker and destructive Romantic strains of the Western tradition and become so strong as to be 'independent of any economic, technical or social system as none has been before' (1933: 167–8). Leavis conceived this humanistic revolution as happening through the efforts of the 'organic intellectual' (to use Antonio Gramsci's term), the critic whose cultural work advances the 'good' of his or her own community and whose work features 'a continuous consciousness and a mature directing sense of value', personal judgments in which values are neither entirely objective or scientific nor merely private (1943: 15). Such an organic critic must have a 'preoccupation' with the 'problem of making the study of literature a discipline – not a discipline of scholarly industry and academic method, but a discipline of intelligence and sensibility' (1943: 7). This 'critical function', arising in this way from the critic's own material conditions and community, 'cannot be definitely accomplished as if something done in the past, but ensues from a mind, energetic and resourceful, that will apply itself to the problems of civilization, and eagerly continue to improve its equipment and explore fresh approaches' (1943: 59).

It follows that, for Leavis, a special cultural responsibility falls on literary studies as practised within the university precisely because of the adverse circumstances of modern culture: the rise of suburban culture as it decentres values invested in traditional ideas about 'country' and 'city' and the fracturing of class organization into the micro-units of a middle class of mammoth dimensions. Whereas in the eighteenth century, as Leavis wrote, 'it never occurred to anyone to question that there were, in all things, standards above the level of the ordinary man' (1933: 89), in the twentieth century authoritative experience is always simultaneously 'elsewhere' and nowhere in relation to cultural references generally available. Leavis reasons that in light of 'democratic egalitarian' and modernist fragmentation in the twentieth century, a consensus at the level of common experience and community values and goals is unlikely and probably impossible. Therefore, as he held, there would be an 'enormous importance of literary criticism for modern civilization', as Chris Baldick writes, in that criticism alone 'presupposed and developed a "consensus" which had been lost in all other social spheres and relationships'. In this respect, 'criticism' as Leavis practised it, Baldick goes on, 'character-istically defines its own audience in an act of corroboration between minds already in substantial agreement' (1987: 227); that is, criticism is capable of creating a cultural frame (or at least Leavis and his circle thought so) in relation to which critics can put aside self-consciousness about their mission as critics – not think further about the theoretical grounding of their task – and go about the business of probing and understanding the products of culture in a productive way.

The particular pertinence of trying to assess criticism's service to an immediate community as well as the Western tradition is occasioned for Leavis and his Cambridge circle by enormous demographic shifts in British education. From 1850–1900, for instance, a large number of middle and lower-middle-class children were completing their schooling and seeking additional training. These were not children with lifelong expert tutorials in the classical languages and cultures. The government's Newcastle and Taunton Commissions in the 1860s urged educators to face the near-certain demise of classical languages and literatures in higher education as primary vehicles of humanistic education, at least for the working classes. These commissions took the revolutionary stand of recommending the study of English language and literature as replacements for formal instruction in classical language and culture. 'English' and the reading of modern English literature, in effect, would replace Greek and Latin as a foundation for what an educated and literate person should know, either the middle-class young adult or the British soldiers then back from World War I and entering British universities in record numbers.

Such recommendations were advanced for over forty years before Oxford and Cambridge began instituting 'English schools' for the study of modern authors in the early twentieth century. Cambridge instituted an Anglo-Saxon language and literature course in 1878 and by 1917 offered a Modern and Medieval Languages Tripos, or baccalaureate programme. Oxford had begun a philology and Middle English literature course in 1904. By 1917 Cambridge opened a more ambitious 'English Honours School' in which to study 'English "Literature, Life and Thought" from Chaucer onwards' (Hayman 1976: 3).

Before the 1920s in these universities it was not established that English studies was in any way an actual 'discipline' in its own right, either a body of professional knowledge or a set of professionally defined approaches or methods. It was not even really clear, as Ronald Hayman points out, that lecturers in English literature should have, or would ever need, 'any qualifications in the subject' comparable to those of other actual 'professors' (1976: 3). Lecturers in the English School were often historians with an 'appreciation' of the historical dimension of literary texts, or classical scholars with a thesis about the underlying classical foundation of all English language and literature – or something else entirely. Regardless of who lectured on English studies, in pedagogical and institutional terms it was simply not established that the reading of post-Enlightenment poetry and fiction in English, the traditional 'entertainments' of the upper and lower classes together, could in any way constitute a serious programme of study or help to establish the critical foundation of a cultural inquiry.

But while there was little or no precedent for instituting the English School in the academy, the cultural rationale for doing so was overwhelming in Leavis's assessment of the modern predicament of culture and of the university's mission in response to it. The appropriate frame for this discussion is that established by Matthew Arnold to orient literary criticism towards its social function. Arnold was Leavis's predecessor in declaring modern civilization unfit as a vehicle for transmitting Western culture into the twentieth century. Arnold thought the first line of defence for rectifying this inadequacy was criticism because of its inherently pedagogic function, its operation in showing people how to read. If at times criticism could seem like an 'unrewarding' task of cultural development, a rather sterile way when compared with poetry for enhancing the fortunes of culture, then Arnold, as Baldick notes, could point to the 'promised land' past the present era when poetry would take its central and rightful place as the primary vehicle of cultural transmission (1987: 20). The task at hand for criticism is then to prepare for poetry by first saving civilization through safeguarding Western values. Once culture has been strengthened and a degree of cultural literacy restored, modern culture will then be ready for the reinstituted reign of poetry and art.

THE NEW CRITICISM

This instrumental and pedagogical use of criticism takes a different and parallel – though even more practically oriented – course in the work of I.A. Richards and the New Criticism, especially as practised in America. Like Arnold and Leavis, in the wake of lost classical and neo-classical traditions that had fortified culture and such cultural institutions as 'education', Richards notes the erosion of critical and socially responsible practices of reading, *actual* reading in the sense of deciphering texts in a normative fashion, making 'the theory of language . . . the most neglected of all studies' (1925: 261). Yet while Arnold and Leavis attempt a broad cultural criticism that constantly tries to 'place' particular works within a rational scheme of Western forms and major cultural formulations, Richards and many of the critics that come after him focus on fundamentally linguistic concerns that could generally be placed within the category of literacy and how to read. Richards distinguished, for instance, between ideas about culture – some constituting a merely 'baseless generalization' and others 'sagacious critical principles' – and the refined application of such principles in the actual practice of reading (1929: 12). 'Everything,' as Richards writes, 'turns upon how the principles [of criticism] are applied' (1929: 12). The solution to the illiteracy impasse is to identify procedures, rules and 'protocols' of actual people's responses that in turn map the terrain of accurate and effective reading and, in this way, allow educators to address endemic weaknesses in what modern readers actually do when they read.

It is seldom recognized that while the American New Critics were

much influenced by Richards' ideas about cultural literacy and methods of reading literary texts, Richards, in his emphasis on what
readers do when reading, is closer to the reception criticism of the
1970s and 1980s than to the rarefied New Critical strategies of the
1930s through to the 1950s. While in 'The Two Uses of Language' he
formulates New Critical axioms concerning the 'emotive' and 'scientific' uses of language (1925: 261–71), a distinction that continued to
be influential through to the 1980s, his main contribution to criticism
lies in his centring critical examination on the *activity* of readers.
Referring to the habitual reactions of readers to texts as 'protocols',
he attempts to assess rationally the 'principal difficulties that may be
encountered by one reader or another in the presence of almost any
poem' (1929: 13). His list of ten such 'difficulties', ranging from
'*making out the plain sense* of poetry' (1929: 13) to the '*general critical
preconceptions* . . . made upon poetry as a result of theories' (1929: 17),
is the forerunner of George Steiner's later speculations 'on difficulty'
and for much that has been said by reader–response theorists about
the conventions and procedures followed by 'competent' readers.

Although the Americans tended to intensify every aspect of Richards' approach, there are three strong ties between his formulation of
critical activity and that of the American New Critics. These concerns
cover the ethics of reading, the objective form of literary texts, and
the need for rational procedures in deciphering texts. While Richards
saw effective reading through the attention to 'protocols' as part of
the generalized ethical response of an educated person to a modern
environment of social and cultural dislocation, the New Critics, at
times somewhat shrilly, tended to see uniform reading procedures as
the urgent means needed to keep an otherwise doomed culture from
collapsing internally. This millennialist temper is expressed most
evidently in the work of Yvor Winters. In 'The Morality of Poetry',
for example, Winters offers successful reading of poetry as a kind of
therapy and cure for a supposed modern fracturing of sensibility, 'a
means of enriching one's awareness of human experience and of so
rendering greater the possibility of intelligence in the course of future
action' (1943: 29). If instituted strongly enough, such critical reading
'should offer likewise a means of inducing certain more or less
constant habits of feeling . . . [and] the possibility of one's acting, in
a future situation, in accordance with the findings of one's improved
intelligence' (1943: 29). Winters quickly escalates personal therapy-
through-poetry to generalized patterns of 'ethical thinking' in the
culture and 'morality more widely than is commonly recognized'
(1943: 29). While Winters is a New Critic at an extreme of moral

fervour, and very possibly panicked about the fortunes of modern culture, he makes explicit the ethical aim that is occasionally voiced and almost always present in the work of the New Critics.

American New Criticism also tended to surpass the British in the degree to which it was willing to formulate the objective form of poetry. While Richards had spoken about 'principal difficulties' to be found in reading most poems, the New Critics proceeded to map an aesthetic landscape of tensions (paradoxes) between poetic images, the structure of the *imagination* (defined for them by Coleridge) in relation to poetry, and predictable ironies about 'life' being intermingled with 'death'. As a group the New Critics were greatly influenced by the ideas of Eliot (and of modernism more generally) about poetic form, the image as the foundation of form, and the relationships of images, motifs and paradoxical themes that Eliot worked out in his resurrection of the Metaphysical poets. In 'The Language of Paradox', for example, Cleanth Brooks (1947: 3–21) reads the work of a Metaphysical poet, John Donne's 'The Canonization', in exemplary New Critical fashion by first performing an inventory of its images concerned with the conflict between public and intimate life, the dependency of life on death, and the figure of the phoenix in a life cycle of self-consumption and renewal. Then he shows the paradoxical alignment of the poem's many images in an encompassing motif that itself expresses the tension of life-reliant-on-death. Finally, he conflates the irony of death as the occasion for new life and the phoenix's death as the central figure of the poem, the inevitable form for all the other tensions generated by various images in the poem. Brooks arrives at a comprehensive vision developed through the poem's structure, which is none other, as he says, than the ironic view 'of the imagination itself else "Beautie, Truth, and Raritie" remain enclosed in their cinders' (1947: 21). His strong reading of this poem demonstrates the supposed close match between the New Critical model for poetic form and the revelation through New Critical interpretation that poems are, in fact, verbal icons organized according to the tensions of paradox and irony.

Finally, in a logic of reading that goes far beyond Richards's protocols, and probably anything he ever imagined as a rational procedure for reading poetry, W.K. Wimsatt Jr and Monroe Beardsley define a highly rationalized criticism that in theory neither violates the poem's integrity as an aesthetic totality nor strays from its narrow aesthetic boundaries as a particular and highly organized 'aesthetic' experience. In 'The Intentional Fallacy' they offer an extreme example of 'impersonal humanism' in a rigorously logical critique of the assumption that a poet's personal intention actively guides the poem's expressive structure. They argue against the practical inaccessibility of personal intention when reading a poem, but, more importantly, they critique the 'romantic' assumption of the existence of a personal and extra-textual intention, intention and form somehow existing apart from the achieved effect of the poem (1946). Likewise, in 'The Affective Fallacy' they argue against the reader's unwarranted projections of his or her own intentions and emotions on to the aesthetic screen of the poem, as if the poem were otherwise blank and needed the reader's experience to fill it (1949). The reader, in fact, will have 'feelings' when reading a poem, but only as orchestrated by the achieved effects of the poem as a form. As practical measures, therefore, a New Critical reader can close off inquiry into the poet's intention and can be wary of importing emotions to the poem that are not technically produced in the patterns – what Eliot called 'objective correlatives' – created by the poem. In these two essays, Wimsatt and Beardsley push New Criticism to an extreme of aesthetic definition of the 'poem itself' as a crafted 'verbal icon' isolated on an otherwise blank page, an aesthetic monad informed and to be read according to no intention other than its own conveyed through form.

The advent of New Criticism in America can also be seen, as Gerald Graff suggests in *Professing Literature*, as a twentieth-century development of the American nineteenth-century 'German-trained cadre of scholarly "investigators" who promoted the idea of scientific research and the philological study of the modern languages' (1987: 55). Beginning with nineteenth-century philology, the new academic professional in America was an expert working from rigorous discovery models and aiming to increase the knowledge store, this professional's loyalties going, as Graff says, 'to his "field" rather than to the classroom dedication that had made the older type of college teacher seem a mere schoolmaster' (1987: 62). The new humanities professional soon became diversified in literary and historical scholarship and other closely related areas not specifically philological. Eventually, with the rise of New Criticism in the 1930s and 1940s, the new 'scientific' approach carried over – helped by Richards's influence – to speculative concerns with literary criticism. This development conflicted from the start with research-based (historical and linguistic) activities, a conflict that continues in America today as theory versus scholarship and theory versus humanism. Through its rational principles, its pragmatic and teachable methods, and the demonstrable results it achieved in classrooms and in scholarship,

New Criticism continued a move in America towards professional expertise and away from the merely appreciative or even humanistic concerns of 'English' in the earlier American academy.

This move towards professionalism is very different from Leavis's institutional concerns. In this move, New Criticism closed itself off from the historical dimension of its own activity as criticism. This is not to say that the New Critics were completely ahistorical, as is often charged, in their handling of texts. This is a common misperception about their work. Cleanth Brooks, John Crowe Ransom, Yvor Winter, Allen Tate and Caroline Gordon, all of them writers and poets, were steeped in the knowledge of classical, Renaissance and Enlightenment cultures and brought this knowledge of cultural context to good effect in their criticism of poetry from many periods. Their claim, however, for the sovereignty of the 'poem itself', the potential of every poem to yield its structure and operation in a patiently performed 'close reading', presupposes a universality of human experience and a common idiom in the global production of poetry. As if at once grounded in culture but at the same time positioned in a Kantian realm of pure expressive freedom, the 'poem itself' became for the New Critics a timeless, ahistorical Esperanto. So while they did, in fact, bring ample knowledge of historical settings to their reading of poetry, they insisted on an aesthetic authority in poetry that 'transcended', in their term – we might say ignored – the limits of culture and language, precisely the historical boundaries of criticism as a cultural activity.

CRITICISM AND CULTURE

The irony accompanying this New Critical dilemma is that the move in Richards towards a focus on language and reading attempts precisely to establish a uniquely 'modern' historical and ethical sense in an otherwise fragmented and ahistorical contemporary environment. Closely aligned with the efforts of Arnold and Leavis to institute a sense, though a belated one, of continuity in the Western tradition, Richards could de-emphasize historical continuity by focusing on the contemporary rhetoric of poetry because the project to re-historicize criticism was actively being carried out in the work of Arnold and then Leavis and many others in England. The New Critics, by contrast, focused almost entirely on instituting criticism as a demonstrable and repeatable procedure of 'close reading'. Still, they 'never fully succeeded', as Catherine Belsey notes, 'in theorizing the relationship between the poem made of words, the verbal icon, and the language within which it exists and signifies' (1980: 17). What success they did achieve was fully *pedagogical*: they produced a codifiable 'method' made readily accessible to students and teachers of varying backgrounds in an academy characterized by open access as a middleclass institution. This success was accompanied, paradoxically, by the failure to explore the relationships between language and culture and to develop a discourse about, and sensitivity to, cultural difference and the limits of criticism as a rational procedure. In the 'success' of close reading the potential for cultural critique in New Criticism was not realized, and the ethical ends of criticism as imagined by Arnold, Leavis and Richards went largely unmet.

What keeps Matthew Arnold and the modernist New Humanists and New Critics who follow him from advancing a cultural *critique*, in the manner we are defining that term, is their formal reluctance to pursue the logic of their own inquiries past a predetermined boundary. This is a failure resulting not from a lapse or weakness in presentation or the inconsistency of an argument, although Arnold has been accused of such flaws many times. Rather, as Baldick notes – and this is certainly true of the New Critics as well – Arnold advanced 'anti-theoretical tendencies' and actually chose to work against the critical view that he espoused in 'The Function of Criticism at the Present Time' (1987: 24). Arnold perceived criticism as a social institution to have a huge responsibility as pedagogy. That is, while philosophers pursue their 'terrible learning' in whatever way they must, a 'critic' is a pedagogue who must be mindful of the adequacy of his or her task in relation to the ends sought – ends which are cultural as well as pedagogical. In such reasoning Arnold privileges the form of the well-constructed inquiry over the critical pursuit of truth. This anti-critical programme is perhaps Arnold's great legacy to criticism, part of his signature on the modern critical tradition. In his critical essays Arnold even chooses to present himself explicitly as a cultural pragmatist who transcends ideological conflict and appears to be an agent who can stand above mere controversy and political squabbling so as to present himself, as Baldick argues, as occupying a 'privileged standpoint' of cultural authority (1987: 25).

While it is clear that Arnold as a literary critic is fundamentally a critic of culture, it is also clear that he chooses to define the endlessly probing function of *critique* as practical, 'well-formed' criticism, and in this sense the New Critics are his faithful heirs. But whether modernist criticism is seen as an instrument of inquiry or a system of preferred symbols, it at best partially succeeds in advancing a critique of Western culture that queried how the West has developed and what cultural ends it served. The enduring importance of modernist criticism as both an articulation of and a response to the cultural forces that conditioned it is contained in the potential for critique in its practices. Modernist discourse, after all, self-consciously promulgates 'guides to kulchur', as Pound said, and systematic investigations of Western civilization according to the indices of cultural criticism.

In this light, we are emphasizing the possibility of taking the modernist and modern 'humanist' critics in their capacity as cultural critics, writers of guides to 'reading', 'kulchur', and 'notes toward a definition of culture'. For unmistakable in the diversity of critical thought that comes from these twentieth-century projects is a programme for a rational critique of culture – for what Freud called the task of finding 'reason in the wasteland' – that runs through diverse texts that could all claim to be 'humanistic'. In these terms, we are arguing that the humanist movement *in toto* – which is well exemplified by the work of Babbitt, Fenollosa, Hulme, Leavis and the New Critics – conceived as a counter to nineteenth-century Romanticism, is a principal intellectual force in the movement towards cultural criticism in the early twentieth century. Their programme calls for the understanding and judgment of culture according to its success as a critical – that is to say, self-consciously rational – enterprise. In practice, the humanists judge other cultures by this standard, and implicitly they advanced their own critical practices as contributions to a model for the rational investigation of achieved aesthetic effects. In practice, then, we can find moments of both criticism and critique in these writers, as if the importance of tradition and transmission they highly valued over the terrible learning of critique still called for its counterpart in the cultural crisis that all stripes of modernism felt to be the condition of our world. For this reason, while many of the critical precepts of these critics – vortex, ideogram, paradox, and so forth – are now of limited critical significance, their progress towards the historically based and highly contextualized models of cultural criticism and critique we will examine in the following chapters has been of great importance indeed.

CHAPTER THREE
The Psychoanalytic Critique of the Subject

> Psycho-analysis is neither a *Weltanschauung*, nor a philosophy that claims
> to provide the key to the universe. It is governed by a particular aim,
> which is historically defined by the elaboration of the notion of the
> subject. It poses this notion in a new way, by leading the subject back to
> his signifying dependence.
>
> Jacques Lacan
> *The Four Fundamental Concepts of Psycho-Analysis*

THE PSYCHOANALYTIC SUBJECT

In a letter to Wilhelm Fliess written in June 1900, Freud mentions
visiting a house where he had once dreamed about his young female
patient 'Irma'. His subsequent analysis of that dream in *The Interpretation of Dreams* was his inaugural demonstration of how dreams could
be understood analytically. This early prototype of dream analysis led
Freud to the formulation of 'dream work', which then served as a
model for thinking about the many operations of the unconscious
that produce the irrational and yet revealing events of everyday life.
Freud summarizes the results of his breakthrough, saying that '*When
the work of interpretation has been completed, we perceive that a dream is the
fulfilment of [an unconscious] wish*' (1900: 121). At once grasping the
drama in this announcement of his displacing the conscious, knowing
'subject' as the key for interpreting experiences in favour of an
unconscious subject with its own desires and even its own agenda for
satisfying them, he writes to Fliess, 'Do you suppose that some day a
marble tablet will be placed on the house, inscribed with these words?

84

– In This House, on July 24th, 1895 the Secret of Dreams was Revealed to Dr. Sigm. Freud' (1900: 121).

Freud's discovery entails his description of the mechanism for producing dreams and other irrational events of experience, and all of this functions as a critique of the Western subject as a rational consciousness previously thought to be fully aware of its own intentions and motives. His critique amounts to a near-total theoretical reversal and a journey, as far as the subject goes, from the dark to the light of understanding, a metaphor that he manipulates to echo *The Republic*'s concluding men-in-a-cave sequence. Freud writes that his formulation of dream work was an event like 'passing [from a dark recess and] through a narrow defile' and emerging 'upon a piece of high ground . . . in the full daylight of a sudden discovery' (1900: 122). The 'discovery' destroys the barrier previously thought to divide the rational daytime personality from the far less rational and more erratic night-time personality who dreams about disparate and fantastical events. In place of the strictly rational and irrational sides of the subject, Freud postulates a less humanized and more mechanistic set of operations called unconscious processes that ultimately provide the staging for and even motivate all behaviour. He posits that irrational dreams 'can be inserted into' – and, in fact, are irrevocably a part of – 'the chain of intelligible waking mental acts' (1900: 122).

Freud then interprets dreams by emphasizing the application of impersonal laws concerning narrative sequencing and linguistic patterning. In the Irma dream, for example, he divides its narrative into minimal signifying units which he then explores for their potential as a system of meaning – as a *semiotic* system. Those units either connect metonymically with other units and clusters of units, or they serve as metaphorical compressions, that is, strategic substitutions, for previous connections, perhaps in other dreams or in waking experience. In the case of the Irma dream, his analysis uncovers a variety of 'other themes [that] played a part in the dream'. He discovers these themes not through natural or predetermined associations but through an analysis of the dream work mechanism that functions as a kind of organizing matrix for the dream. The themes uncovered through analysis 'were not so obviously connected with my exculpation from Irma's illness: my daughter's illness and that of my patient who bore the same name, the injurious effect of cocaine, the disorder of my patient who was travelling in Egypt, my concern about my wife's health and about that of my brother and of Dr. M., my own physical ailments, anxiety about my absent friend who suffered from suppurative rhinitis', and so on (1900: 120). These themes arise, rather, through analysis of the dream's narrative units and can be shown to comprise an order not directly expressive of Freud as a rational, knowing subject with conscious intentions towards Irma and her case.

In this way, what Freud advances in *The Interpretation of Dreams* is neither the transpersonal subject of the New Humanism nor the impersonal subject of the New Criticism, neither of which enacts a critique of the nineteenth-century conception of Romantic subjectivity that unquestioningly encompasses personal identity and personal responsibility. Psychoanalysis, whether Jungian revisions of Freud or classical Freudian theory, aimed – within the larger movement of modernism – to enact such a critique of subjectivity within Euro-American culture, the very culture that through colonization and cultural dominance had nurtured and promoted that Western notion of the subject from the late seventeenth century to the end of the nineteenth century. In this critique, psychoanalysis is an exemplary development of modernism in culture and literary studies for at least two reasons. The first is the tendency, inherent to psychological criticism, of interpreting disconnected or syncopated structures, the reading of disparate narrative details for example, as part of an interpretive pattern – such as a 'Great Mother' archetype, or an 'Oedipus complex' – not seemingly mandated explicitly by the narrative itself. The second is that psychoanalysis can show a text to have meanings of various kinds on several levels simultaneously. There could be, for instance, elements of Oedipus in *Hamlet*'s overall dramatic structure, as Ernest Jones, Jacques Lacan and many others have discussed, not confined to realistic character or personal psychology. This emphasis on the possibilities of interpreting fragments and on the potential for multiplicity of meaning in texts strongly connects depth psychology and the larger project of modernism in the first half of the twentieth century.

A more fundamental connection with the study of modern culture is the dialectical nature of psychological criticism – its attempt to bring a sophisticated critique to cultural study by relating a theory of mind to literary aesthetics, particularly in narrative structure, to a general system of cultural signification, and to the social and cultural context of texts. This potential for connection with various dimensions of culture is responsible – more than anything else – for the strong continuing interest in the psychoanalytic understanding of texts throughout this century. In the work of the French Freudians and others on the Continent and in the United States, the extension of psychoanalysis into the discourse on language, female sexuality and political power has positioned Freudian thought in the late twentieth century both as a part of modernist culture in the early twentieth century and also as an energetic force for psychological and cultural critique in contemporary discourse.

Freudian theory is at base, we are suggesting, a critique of the classical model of the subject – the 'subject' understood in the sense of the agency of knowing, feeling, interacting or inter-relating, the Cartesian articulation of an interior and isolated being that served as the official paradigm of subjectivity from the Renaissance through to the end of the nineteenth century. (Different, 'unofficial' paradigms can be seen in women's novels in eighteenth and nineteenth-century England; see Armstrong 1987.) It is this conception of the subject, analogous to Kant's transcendental sense of the term, that the New Humanism implicitly rejects, without endeavouring to analyse it, and the New Criticism simply avoids recognizing. The notion of the psychoanalytic subject, in other words, is a critique of this transcendental notion precisely because it localizes experience from a particular viewpoint that is historically marked, happening to someone at a particular moment within particular cultural institutions – the institutions of agency, language, ideals and social relations we are examining in this book. In this way, the 'subject' encompasses not only conceptions of personal psychology and communal membership but brings with it, as a construct produced by the culture, connections with the ideological dimensions of that culture itself.

The history of this critique begins with attempts by Freudians early in the twentieth century to apply psychoanalytic insights to cultural practices as if treating patients on a couch – particularly in the assumption of 'art' as the evidence of artistic neurosis – to more recent attempts by contemporary cultural theorists to reposition Freudian thought in relation to literary texts, language, female sexuality and political power. The Freudian critique has always tended to situate the 'subject' – and this is perhaps Freud's greatest 'discovery' and the innovation of psychoanalysis that Jacques Lacan emphasizes – as a dynamic and even problematic agency, as a cultural construction that is inherently 'undecidable' in the sense that it is continually being reformulated by unconscious operations. The Freudian subject, in other words, exists only in relation to ongoing and changing experience, as Freud makes clear in his case studies, in the essays that focus on metapsychology, in *The Psychopathology of Everyday Life* (1901), and in *Jokes and Their Relation to the Unconscious* (1905).

As a first step in mapping the ongoing Freudian critique of the subject that has taken place in psychoanalytic theory over the last century, we need to remember that a huge split has divided Freudian theory nearly from its inception – a difference profound enough to suggest two different Freuds. This is precisely the split that has divided 'criticism' and 'critique' in cultural theory and divided 'pedagogy' (criticism) and 'critique' in literary studies. The more influential of the two Freuds, for American practice certainly, is the later Freud, that of 'ego' psychology particularly prominent in American practice after 1920. This is the Freud of *The Ego and the Id* (1923), *New Introductory Lectures* (1933) and *An Outline of Psycho-Analysis* (1940). Known as the 'second topography', this version of Freud focuses on the relationship of ego, id and superego and the fixed structures of an ego-centred personality. This emphasis locates the source of libidinal energy, the foundation of any conception of the subject, in the id, which is then the primordial 'origin' in the psyche on which all other psychic structures are dependent. Inherently in conflict with the id is the repository of ethical and moral values in the superego, which embodies those standards put in place by parental and social prohibition. These two agencies, representing the potential for satisfaction and constraint, are antithetical.

The mediation of these agencies is the function of the ego. In this 'second' scenario the ego is the conflict negotiator of desire in its struggle with constraint, as well as the representative of the interests of (the essence of, the 'truth' of) the whole person. The ego can draw from the id's energy as it operates as a system's manager within the person; in doing so, it serves as the site of most immediate expression for 'narcissistic libido', or energy moving directly from the id. As the ego faces outwards to the world, it encounters the prohibitions of the superego, which restrains the ego's operation by instituting ethical aims and remorse, or guilt, when those aims are not met.

In this topography Freud positions ego, or 'self', as the practical extension of the id, always at odds with the disapproving superego, on the one hand, and in 'contact' with intractable 'reality', subject to the constraints of the superego, on the other. The ego, as the agent negotiating between internal and external forces, is an imperial if somewhat beleaguered self which is committed to protect the interests of the whole person – and thus its own sovereignty – from dangerous encroachments on two sides. The ego struggles against the world, against the reality principle (that is, against 'objects' of cognition and experience) as it tries to wrest a measure of freedom from necessity. In this struggle to survive, the ego also attempts to discover an authentic 'truth' in its negotiated versions of experience. This version of the subject *as ego* suggests the agency of self as a substantial *thing*, the actual 'self' of the person, as if an actual bodily organ. In short, this is the Freud of the centrally positioned and 'substantial' ego, the model of mind with the 'natural' and permanent ego locked directly in combat with external 'reality'. This is the Freud of Kantian Romantic subjectivity, the subject not as the transcendental subject of knowledge (as in Kant) but as the transcendental subject of the 'whole' person.

A second, 'other' Freud, distinct from the 'ego' version, is the precursor of the semiotic or 'French Freud' elaborated by Lacan. This is the Freud of 'Project for a Scientific Project' (1895), Chapter VII of *The Interpretation of Dreams*, the letters to Freud's friend Fliess, *Jokes and Their Relation to the Unconscious*, and the metapsychology pieces before 1920. This version of Freud focuses on three separate but at the same time 'bound' – that is to say, functionally connected – systems: (1) the unconscious, (2) preconscious, and (3) conscious systems. The unconscious covers the total apparatus of psychic discourse, the totality of human software as a kind of operating system, including the mechanism that creates the construction and effects of personal and communal experience. In this model, the unconscious is not so much the whole 'person' as the totality of forces that interact and come into play to construct a subject. The preconscious is that dimension of the unconscious, actual connections and associations, capable of becoming conscious 'ideas' or psychic investments, objects of cathexes. Consciousness is then the mere site of exposition where representations of ideas and psychic investments are monitored and, to an extent, played out in relation to each other. Consciousness, in this way, is a 'text' in which the unconscious system, operating according to 'distortion', 'repression' and 'deferral', inscribes traces to indicate the functioning of the total unconscious system.

Since the late 1930s, Jacques Lacan has urged a return to this earlier and more semiotically oriented foundation of Freud's approach to the subject. Lacan has reconceived – or at least foregrounded Freud's own critique of – notions about a fixed 'ego' of identity and personality as a shifting 'subject' of speech, as in the various positions occupied by pronoun references such as 'I', 'you', 'he', 'she', and so on. This non-'substantial' conception of the subject has had the deepest effect upon the connections among psychoanalysis, personal agency and culture, particularly the ideological dimension that always works through, some would even say 'underwrites', cultural formation. In fact, the whole project of psychoanalysis from 1900 and the publication of

Freud's *Interpretation of Dreams* through to the early 1920s can be understood as a sustained attempt at various levels to elaborate a semiotic theory of the human 'subject', what we know and how we know it, as opposed to the Cartesian assertion of the self-evidence of subjectivity. The attempt to do this – as modern intellectual history gives evidence – has had a pervasive and deep influence on the twentieth-century project of critique.

Beginning in the 1930s Lacan began specifically highlighting the complex relationship of the speaking subject – comparable in various limited ways to the ego as the agency which consciously thinks and speaks – to the unconscious processes which govern it. More to the point, in this model the centre of functioning, the agency of intention and action, is clearly not the ego in the prior sense of a governing system's manager for fixed personal identity, but the unconscious as an everchanging economy with a dialectical operation of external and internal forces. For Lacan, the projection of 'I' (or ego) in conscious experience is a limited inscription, not the executive agency, of unconscious functioning. The ego is not a substantial form but one position within a discourse (defined by the larger system of discourse) for the staging of an utterance, like the position of the 'I' in a long and otherwise complex utterance. One may conceive of Lacan's 'unconscious' much as one thinks of fluent speakers of a language as 'unconscious' of grammar – not consciously 'intending' grammar – while in the act of articulating it. In this conception, grammar structures the speaker's messages and creates horizons of possibilities for those messages which determine rather than express the speaker's intentions. Analogously the unconscious is composed of a set of structured and distinct but simultaneously 'bound' systems, rules and applications of rules, like language itself. The 'I', or ego, cannot be as in the other model, the ego-as-homunculus struggling directly with superego and reality. The 'I' is a site of positioning and strategic marking in discourse. This paradigm is characterized by 'positions' of speech and orders of discourse and, finally, suggests a 'semiotic' Freud because the subject is not a reservoir of meaning and identity. 'Subject' and unconscious 'discourse', rather, are *relational* concepts defined dynamically in their difference from other concepts and activities, 'subject' and 'discourse' being key constituent elements in Lacanian and post-structuralist thought. Lacan's debt to structuralism in these formulations will become clearer in the context of the next chapter.

THE FIXED SUBJECT: PSYCHOANALYSIS AS PERSONAL TRANSACTION

In a later section of this chapter we will more fully describe the context for understanding the 'undecidable' nature of the Freudian subject – in effect, we will present the case Lacan makes for a theory of the subject not defined so much by the ego's function or even by 'cognitive' development but rather by an inherently dynamic relation between the subject (as a construct) and knowledge. Here, however, we will examine the 'substantial' (later) Freud, where the ego is in direct contact with reality. This version of psychoanalysis tends to promote 'knowing' as information transmittal in a linear and highly rational sense, the pedagogy we described in the preceding chapter. In this view, 'experience' is a kind of unmediated cognitive processing of that which is unfamiliar or previously unknown. A patient or a student 'learns' about the world and acquires strategies for strengthening the ego and manipulating external dimensions of reality. A student, in this view, is one who learns strategies to extend the mastery of and defend an already-constituted and stable ego. A teacher is then a repository of knowledge about 'reality' and an agent for conveying it to students as accurately and efficiently as possible. The business of education, it follows, is for teachers to effect the transmission of information and for students to facilitate its reception with as little interference or distortion as possible.

In this rationalized 'scene of instruction', the deciphering of literary texts in psychological terms, as Henry Lowenfeld says, has historically assumed 'the coincidence of artistic talent and neurotic disposition' (1983: 59). From this perspective, all art is essentially derivative and a prosthetic extension of a normative version of experience, making art a deviation from the accurate and unbiased apprehension of reality. In this conception, art is an artificial limb or a 'psychic bandage' needed when there is a neurotic blockage to direct apprehension so that literary production relates to the writer's psyche as a kind of shell to the kernel of real, personal experience to the degree that personal experience belongs to the official domain of the 'ego'. In this model, a literary text is presumed to be, as William Barrett says, 'the product of the personal being of its author' in response to external reality (1983: 95).

Norman Holland is an example of an accomplished literary critic who works within the strict bounds of psychoanalysis conceived in the parameters of 'ego psychology' we are discussing. In his career he has consistently foregrounded the aim in criticism 'to understand the combination of text and personal association' in the act of reading (1980: 364). 'Instead of taking the text as a fixed entity,' he writes, 'let us think of it as a process involving a text and a person. Let us open up the text by assuming the person brings to it something extrinsic. It could be information from literary history, biography, or an archaic ritual like the flyting between primitive bards. It could even be some quite personal fact like my reading ["The Purloined Letter"] in Pocketbook No. 39 or my finding it at a time in my life when I had something sexual [masturbation] to hide' (1980: 363–4).

Working from these assumptions about the transactions between person and text, Holland proceeds to 're-cover' a story from the overly 'abstract, intellectual reading' characteristic of those who critique the notion of the subject. To do this, he strategically consults his own 'personal' responses to a text and finds a 'private' order of meaning and unity, what he calls a personality theme. By importing this degree of 'personal' association into interpretation, Holland is attempting to push aside intellectual barriers in order to attain a direct grasp of the reading transaction itself, a move calculated to take psychological criticism supposedly to the heart of a story.

Yet on closer examination, Holland's 'transactive criticism' is caught in a contradiction about textuality – precisely the contradiction inherent to the activity of critique that we have been discussing. In his essay on Poe's 'The Purloined Letter', Holland says, 'Instead of taking the text as a fixed entity, let us think of it as a process involving a text and a person.' In the first half of his sentence the text-as-fixed-object is rejected because it is not an objective thing 'out there' in any clear sense. In the second half of the sentence, the text-as-fixed-object is hastily retrieved in relation to a person's changing response, as a distinctly separate partner in an interpretive relationship.

In other words, in the transactive formulation Holland seems to reinstitute an absolute separation of text and interpretation, a separation central to his theory of textuality. 'According to Holland,' as Steven Mailloux notes, 'the reader makes sense of the text by creating a meaningful unity out of its elements. Unity is not in the text but in the mind of a reader' (1977: 417). But if the subject of reading is not positioned in the text, and the text is devoid of meaning, what has happened to subjectivity? Holland's answer, as Mailloux shows, is based on an assumption that the text does have an objective status (1977: 419). In *Five Readers Reading* Holland himself says that 'the reader is surely responding to *something*. The literary text may be only so many marks on a page – at most a matrix of psychological possibilities for its readers' (1975: 12). His answer says that the 'text'

– an empty 'matrix' of 'marks on a page' – is indeed objective but minimally significant in the reading transaction. The economy of textual order has actually vanished from the text in order to be relocated in the 'mind of the reader'. The reader, the individual ego and person, contains any meaning that can be attributed to the text and thus *brings* meaning to the supposedly empty text, just as Holland *brings* his own meaning to Poe's story. The text's structure and its own 'truth' are in this way made fully masterable by the individual ego. This minimalist text, in the process, has become a mere reflection of the reader's identity theme, or ego.

The subject of reading defined by Holland contrasts to the subject of critique as we have been discussing it in this book. Holland's fixed subject of a prescribed critical activity ultimately dictates substantial 'forms' of meaning in a text, which are conceived of as accurate reflections of the fixed subject rather than of processes. Such a fixed subject is a prerequisite of the reigning movements of formalism at mid-century in American and European criticism. We are speaking of the New Criticism in America, as we discussed in the last chapter, and *explication du texte* in France (which goes beyond our interest in this book). These movements drew upon the notion of the fixed ego, a notion implicit in the aesthetic ideology of Kantian metaphysics. Each approach prescribed a method of close reading, loosely suggesting the model of empirical investigation, and attempted to account for varieties of textual information, including imagery and image patterns, rhythm, sound, tone and overall structure. Each method presented itself as potentially exhaustive, able to discover and catalogue all pertinent textual details in a manner approximating empirical observation in thoroughness and supposed objectivity. Seen in this context, Holland's transactional ego psychoanalysis is a version of New Criticism (in which Holland was trained), which substitutes the fixed subject for the autonomous text of New Criticism while retaining in important ways its pedagogical imperative focused now, not on tradition and humanism, but on the 'personality theme' of the fixed subject of reading.

THE ARCHETYPAL ELABORATION OF THE SUBJECT

In the Anglo-American academy, however, the active development of the New Criticism came to an end in the late 1950s with the rise of archetypal criticism associated with the psychologist Carl Jung, which produced a critique of the New Criticism in practical influence and prestige. The archetypal elaboration of the subject succeeded in exploiting certain aspects of the New Criticism, mainly the deployment of 'paradox' and 'irony' as interpretive instruments, and then moved directly into areas that the New Criticism refused or failed to develop, particularly the relationship between literature and objects of study that exist 'outside' the narrowly formalist conception of literature. These included areas such as 'mind', or personal psychology, history, culture, and even relations simultaneously 'within' but transcending particular texts – what Northrop Frye in *Anatomy of Criticism* specifically called the 'conceptual framework' (1957: 7) of literature conceived within the 'systematic comprehension' (1957: 2) of an intellectual discipline, the whole 'system' of literature, that is, taken as more than a huge assemblage of literary documents and creative efforts (1957: 12). On this issue, New Critics such as Cleanth Brooks, Wimsatt and Beardsley, John Crowe Ransom, Mark Schorer and Joseph Frank were judged to have taken literary criticism outside of history – just as Kant situates the subject of knowledge outside history and Holland situates the fixed subject of experience outside history – in that they advocated critical practice as an ideal activity and a 'delicate learning' (1957: 72) which by its nature could not account for change in culture.

Approaches to archetypal criticism are varied, but the central paradigm for archetypal interpretation is Jungian, even though Jung was Freud's student up until the 1920s, and even though psychoanalysis already contained its own theory of archetypes as evidenced in Freud's *Totem and Taboo*. Jung's primary focus, and the point on which he sought to divide from Freud, was his approach to the 'collective unconscious', a realm of transpersonal imagery preserved and repeated throughout human experience. Like the transpersonal subjectivity Babbitt describes, the collective unconscious belongs to the human race and to individual people at levels 'below' consciousness, in the form of 'archetypes', or fundamental patterns and forms of human experience, such as 'mother', 'rebirth', 'spirit' and 'trickster'. At any one moment, while apprehensible only as fragments, or incomplete representations, the archetypes could, as it were, flicker on the walls of conscious awareness and constitute fragmented patterns that, while informative, are never quite unambiguous or completely unified, even though archetypes are the actual content of 'experience' as opposed to the more abstract mental processes in Freud such as repression, deferral, transference, and so on.

In literary interpretation, an archetype is 'a typical or recurring image' (Frye 1957: 99) that may include but also cut across developments in character, plot and setting. Apparently unrelated and seemingly discrete textual elements as well as realistic, representational details form patterns suggestive of one or more of the archetypes. The supposed presence of these patterns establishes an archetypal orientation in the work insofar as they reflect what lies 'beneath' the work's narrative and imagistic surface. In this way, archetypal interpretation organizes each literary text into a narrative surface composed of images and a textual 'depth' where the connection with archetypes takes place. The goal of a full archetypal interpretation is to make explicit what is only implicit in the text's fragmented evocation of archetypes. An archetypal understanding of a text, in short, necessitates seeing how the appearance of suggestive details in a minimal sequence signifies, in reality, a disguised and fully informative archetypal pattern, 'which connects one poem with another and thereby helps to unify and integrate our literary experience' (1957: 99). Such integration, Frye suggests, transforms literary experience into cultural experience.

The possibility of charting narrative progression in archetypal criticism is crucial for understanding archetypalism's critique of the New Criticism. After all, the New Critical emphasis on imagery as the object of analysis depended mostly on evidence drawn from poetry, particularly modernism's highly figurative, non-narrative poetry. As is often noted, the New Critics foundered precisely on the difficulty of applying imagery and paradox/irony (essentially static and even pictorial in their avoidance of temporal change) to fiction and its profoundly temporal dimension. Only late in the movement's development, during the late 1940s and 1950s, did Joseph Frank and Mark Schorer seek to recast an understanding of the poetic image as 'spatial form' and suggest technique as a form of discovery in prose fiction.

By contrast, archetypalism from its start attempted to define itself precisely in relation to a temporal order of narrative as embodied in the 'monomyth' or 'quest'. As Erich Neumann and others have shown, the coherence of the archetypes rests precisely on their placement within a narrative development that moves from total narcissism towards the hero's individuation and relative autonomy, each stage in the quest being a further step towards independence from the Great Mother (1955). This pattern is *mono*mythic by virtue of encompassing all possible human change and growth within a single story. The quest-narrative unites the repeatable form of each archetype with the principle of change dictated by the ongoing temporal development of a particular story. The potential circularity of merely locating self-defining archetypes in literature – in which discoveries are dictated by foreknown image and narrative patterns – is at least mitigated by the necessity of accounting for the dynamic operation of narrative ('mythic') progression in particular works.

The definitive archetypal approach to literature, without question, is Frye's *Anatomy of Criticism*, the text we have been following. Frye is the most formidable of archetypal critics, and he was the one to announce a decisive break, as he said, with the 'ironic provincialism' and 'delicate learning' of the New Criticism (1957: 62, 72). Uncharacteristically disdainful in his appraisal of New Criticism's formalism, Frye rejected what he considered its limited focus on the 'poem itself' and its weak articulation of cultural relationships. Also, the implicit religious and 'typological' perspective of Frye's criticism conflicts with the scepticism about the religious dimension of the cultural order implicit in the work – though contrary to many personal beliefs – of the New Critics. Frye's most direct slap at the New Criticism is the choice of a title for the *Anatomy*'s first essay, 'Historical Criticism: Theory of Modes', in which, with polemical bravado, he attempted to situate the archetypal project – his critique of literary study – on the very historical terrain of criticism the New Critics were popularly thought to have abandoned. Frye proclaims, in effect, that archetypal criticism's success would be grounded precisely where the prior movement was thought to have failed.

He then went on in 'four essays' to erect the monomyth's structure over the whole of culture in a 'proto-structuralist' reading of Western literature's archetypal development grounded on 'the assumption of total coherence' (1957: 16) – an arrangement beginning with prehistoric and sacred 'myth' and ending with present-day 'irony'. In a remarkably rich elaboration of literary archetypes, Frye presented a comprehensive catalogue of literary forms (genre, sound, rhythm, tone, and so on) as part of a projection of a complete archetypal paradigm. Explicit in his discussion is, in fact, a sense of the 'development' of Western literature: in his 'Historical Criticism', Frye simultaneously suggested both an archetypal 'conceptual framework' for criticism and an examination of the 'history' of literature as a crucial dimension of culture in a global sense.

Throughout the 1960s, Frye's version of archetypalism influenced much theory and practical criticism, especially in Medieval–Renaissance studies, an emphasis that continues on into the late twentieth century in the classroom, although much less in scholarship.

Frye

Gradually, however, Frye's approach came under attack from historical critics, structuralists and feminists. Historicists such as A.S.P. Woodhouse, Roy Harvey Pearce and Lionel Trilling began to point out the failure of both the New Criticism and archetypalism to deal with history except within extremely narrow bounds. It can be argued, for example, that archetypalism develops a historical theory of dominant literary modes in Western culture – from myth through romance, high mimetic, low mimetic, and finally to contemporary irony – in order only to turn Western literature itself into a huge, static image or structure, one unified and all-inclusive version of what Pound and others described in the local structures of imagism, so that history virtually becomes an 'image' and, consequently, a closed aesthetic system. Historical criticism reasonably should be able to analyse change and account for the as yet unmet and unthought, and it is not clear that the archetypal progression of images adequately does this, or does anything more than impose a static grid over literary history as a substitute for the difficulty of accounting for change, for developments that cannot be predicted in the progression of Frye's 'modes', and for historical eventualities that Frye's aestheticism simply has not begun to imagine.

From the vantage of linguistics, the structuralists of the 1960s and 1970s critiqued Frye's complicated but, in their view, often naive and overly rationalized schema of archetypal progressions. In the first chapter of *The Fantastic*, as we mentioned in Chapter 1, Tzvetan Todorov criticized Frye's tendency to analyse literature for 'content', actual images (like 'forest' and 'sea') in literature, when his professed aim was to examine literary structure as positioned beyond concrete examples (1970: 18). Todorov also notes both the rigidity of much of Frye's schema and the logical lapses in that schema (1970: 13). By contrast, in *The Fantastic* Todorov consistently derives genre distinctions from logical rules that can be applied in particular instances of texts, for example when he defines the genre of the 'fantastic' as lasting 'only as long as a certain hesitation: a hesitation common to reader and character, who must decide whether or not what they perceive derives from "reality" as it exists in the common opinion' (1970: 40).

Perhaps most devastating, though, is the feminist critique of Frye, which undermines the Jungian paradigm and Jung and Frye's notion of the monomyth. The archetypal hero is at base a male figure attempting to bring about reconciliation with an 'original' female (the Great Mother) and with a potential 'anima' figure who is both the hero's ideal mate and his reward for successful completion of the

97

quest. This exclusively male paradigm assumes a male subject, and nowhere in Jung's thought or Frye's is there a sustained attempt to reconceive a woman's experience outside of her subservient role. As Catherine Belsey comments in *Critical Practice*, 'underlying Frye's formalism, therefore, is a concept of human nature and of culture which sees literature as imitating not the world but rather "the total dream of *man*"' (1980: 23, emphasis added). These are major areas of historical and gender blindness in the *Anatomy*, which suggests that Frye's work does not situate itself historically and culturally any better than did the New Criticism, and these limitations seriously undermine archetypalism's efficacy as cultural theory.

While some teachers and practical critics still employ archetypalism for specific ends, especially to create contexts for genre distinctions, the work of Frye – the archetypalist par excellence – enacts, as our narrative has suggested, the transformation of critique back into criticism, a practice based on unexamined axioms and an inability to conceive of a framework of understanding that could make its axioms apprehensible. Certainly at the level of local readings and the making of intertextual connections among texts, 'supported', as Belsey says, by Frye's wide range of reading, his fluency and his wit, 'the *Anatomy* succeeds dazzlingly' (1980: 21). Yet even with such success, the *Anatomy* is a notable but failed attempt to configure cultural theory within a complex intellectual framework. If Frye is convincing in his local readings, the intellectual framework of the *Anatomy* is a closed system of largely unexamined assumptions about the nature of cultural order, class and gender.

PSYCHOANALYSIS AND PEDAGOGY: RESISTANCE AND CRITIQUE

While psychoanalysis is the intellectual parent of archetypalism, psychoanalytic criticism precedes both archetypalism in the first generation of Freudians beginning in the 1920s and 1930s (who based their work, paradoxically, on the later Freud of ego psychology) and the more recent movement of the semiotic 'return to Freud' associated with Jacques Lacan. Archetypal criticism, for all its virtues and power, and despite its critique of the New Criticism, finally participates in a version – a transpersonal version – of the assumptions of the fixed subject that govern the New Humanism, American formalism, and the criticism of Freudian ego psychologists (including Holland's later 'transactional' psychoanalysis). By contrast, the great strength of contemporary psychoanalytic criticism is that it goes beyond many positivist assumptions (even those of its origin) to use Freud's work to critique those assumptions and develop discursive and self-consciously rhetorical modes of reading.

In other words, throughout this century psychoanalysis has continued to influence cultural theory in specific and important ways. In writing this book, for example, we characteristically encounter psychoanalytic resistances, not only the resistances of theoretical blockages and blindnesses, but the more subtle 'resistance' Freud describes in 'Analysis Terminable and Interminable' to the very 'uncovering of resistances' (1937: 239). That is, the work of criticism and writing is a working through, as Freud would say, of the 'resistances' of a cultural text. At one level this is the difficulty of getting started on the page, the unexpected need for revision, the refocusing and recasting, the need for additional revision, the late rethinking, and so on. But on a more subtle level it is the 'resistance' which manifests itself in seeing clearly and getting things 'right': the unmarked resistance of self-evident truths (which are the objects of critique). In other words, we do not mean by 'resistance' solely the simple sense of putting off of a task, the simple resistance of meeting an opposing force – like that, as Freud says, 'of having worked in clay' to remove something unneeded. We are describing, further, the complex resistance inherent to the subject and evident in writing that Freud describes as producing the impression 'of having written on water' (1937: 241). Where language is concerned, that is, a writer necessarily encounters a kind of 'resistance' that cannot be located anywhere fixable and permanently addressable and cannot be directly overcome precisely because *it resists* analysis and critique in its own enabling assumptions. Freud's image of water writing (reminiscent of the epitaph on Keats's gravestone, 'Here lies One Whose Name was writ in Water') of course suggests erasure simultaneous with inscription that makes the constant repetition – what Geertz calls the 'intrinsically incomplete' nature (1973: 29) – of cultural critique so difficult.

Shoshana Felman elaborates the importance of *resistance* in this sense in 'Psychoanalysis and Education' in her description of psychoanalysis as functioning largely as pedagogy. An analyst inevitably treats a patient who suffers 'from a sort of ignorance'. When the analyst 'removes this ignorance by giving him [needed] information', Freud writes, '(about the causal connection of his illness with his life, about his experiences in childhood, and so on) he is bound to recover' (1910:

225). The ignorance that causes such neurotic suffering is not an innocent oversight or misapprehension, merely something unnoticed or a mere lapse of memory; as Freud says, it is 'not his ignorance in itself'. It is, rather, 'the *inner resistances*' (225), as these *resistances* – not accidents either, chance misalignments of intentions and method – are motivated by what Felman calls 'a *desire to ignore*'. This desire does not come from 'a simple lack of information but the incapacity', Felman goes on, 'to acknowledge one's *own implication* in the information' (1987: 79). Ignorance, as it happens, conceals an active resistance to the acquisition, or recognition, of knowledge and creates the inevitability that the uncovering of knowledge, as in the phases of writing a book such as this, will and must be performed in relation to, working through, that resistance.

Felman describes here a 'performative' conception of psychoanalysis as pedagogical practice. She tries to merge pedagogy into psychoanalysis, which Lacan conceived to be fundamentally and *already* a teaching anyway, and to show that, after the lesson of Lacan, a pedagogue should teach in relation to the student's '*unmeant knowledge*' (1987: 77), the unconscious as it is inscribed but at the same time hidden in teaching as a kind of text. In the conception of psychoanalysis as pedagogy – in this critique of received ideas about pedagogy – the 'unmeant' must be of paramount importance because 'teaching, like analysis', as Felman explains, 'has to deal not so much with lack of knowledge as with resistances to knowledge' (1987: 79). In this analysis, unmeant knowledge is significant because its lapses and breaks are unconsciously motivated and display a culturally marked disposition to what knowledge represents – the very idea of culture as a way of life or a horizon of experience that Raymond Williams describes. For the student, that is, that which is 'unmeant', or even 'not remembered', does not exist in 'a passive state' but in 'an active dynamic of negation, an active refusal of information' – an unconscious and active resistance to knowledge (1987: 79).

The resistance to knowledge, therefore, entails a working through that resistance by means of what Felman calls a 'new condition of knowledge' (1987: 80), which means *enacting*, or re-enacting, a transferential relation to knowledge much as a psychoanalytic patient must enact, or re-enact, an archaic parental relationship with the analyst for psychoanalytic therapy to be effective. In taking this critique of pedagogy, with its reversal of time-honoured educational priorities, Lacan virtually promotes 'ignorance' and decentres 'learning' as the primary preoccupation of teaching. Lacan the teacher then asks how he can interpret out of the dynamic ignorance he analytically encounters, both in others and in himself, <u>how he can turn ignorance into an instrument of teaching.</u>

Felman's rendition of Freud and Lacan on pedagogy is a plea for adoption of a complex and subtle response to pedagogical discourse – respect for the 'other' conceived as the unconscious within language. This respect is given through the performative enactment of reading and writing the unconscious text, by actively recognizing (for their signifying power) resistances and absences and 'unmeant' knowledge. Accordingly, Felman argues in her discussions of literature, criticism and education that students must read and interpret psychoanalytically so as to respond to the otherness of the unconscious, the text that cannot be read with complete and final success.

In the discontents of writing, writers encounter the 'resistance' Felman speaks as an 'other' desire internal to writing itself, surely the same 'resistance' students report when they cannot write. Teachers may on occasion be embarrassed at extremely poor student writing, but the resistance to language is also a paradox for teachers who, like Socrates – as Barbara Johnson says – come to teaching 'through a kind of compulsion to speak' (1982: v), teachers being those who 'must speak' and yet must also face the resistance of doing so in their students and in themselves. The deeper paradox, as Lacan insists, is that a common line of 'resistance' runs through and disorients the subject. Moreover, the problematics of psychoanalytic therapy – defined by 'resistance', 'transference' and 'repression' – are the same as the <u>problematics of the subject who writes.</u>

THE CRITIQUE OF THE SUBJECT

This broad concept of resistance in psychoanalysis covers virtually anything that 'interrupts the progress of analytic work' (Freud 1900: 555), that which blocks the overcoming of defences or the bringing to consciousness of unconscious desires – anything that 'finally brings [analytic] work to a halt' (1897: 266). Closely linked to repression and effected by the 'systems of the mind which originally carried out repression' (1920: 19), the concept of resistance comes up frequently for Freud as a <u>'rewriting'</u>, like the resistance in dreams that leads him 'to compare [dreams] with a system of writing' (1913: 177). In the 'Note on the Mystic Writing Pad' he describes this whole system of resistance in the model of a child's toy. The 'mystic writing pad' has 'a slab of dark brown resin or wax with a paper edging; over the slab is laid a thin transparent sheet . . . [and] one writes upon the celluloid portion of the covering-sheet which rests upon the wax slab'. He then says that one writes with a 'stylus' by pressing 'the lower surface of the waxed paper on to the wax slab, and the grooves are visible as dark writing upon the otherwise smooth whitish-grey surface of the celluloid'. To erase what has been written, he goes on, 'all that is necessary is to raise the double covering-sheet from the wax slab by a light pull' (1925: 228–9).

In this conceit Freud identifies two different kinds of 'resistance' at work, one passive and one active. Each undercuts the stable positioning of the subject since each represents a desire that does not emanate from the subject. The passive kind is seen in the 'traces' always etched directly on the wax board and showing through the sheet above it, the persistent record of past inscriptions. The active kind is the actual erasure and rewriting of a new text, the suppression of a message by another message as the moments pass. In foregrounding resistance as 'rewriting', Freud highlights the intrusion of desire *not belonging* to the subject that is none the less part of the process of situating the subject. The more common assumption about the subject is of the supposed 'ease' of contemplation and learning, the sense in which words are 'cheap' (and 'teaching' or analysis is just fifty minutes' worth of words) and in which the 'journey' of learning and specu-lation, as Henry James describes of the young Isabel Archer, is a pleasant stroll ending predictably with the bounty of a 'lapful of roses' (1881: 54).

In the semiotic Freud of the early phase we have been discussing, however, we must abandon the essential model of the subject and 'experience' for a science of 'positioning', that is, for an understanding of a particular relation to discourse. Discourse, in this conception, is understood as a *cultural* phenomenon, which, like the grammar we described earlier, is unconscious: it delimits possibilities of experience and apprehension, even when they feel 'immediate' and the sole possession of the self. When the subject-as-student projects the teacher as someone with mastery over knowledge, what Freud calls 'transfer-ence' takes place. This means that the student attributes to the teacher, like the analysand to the analyst, precisely what the student identifies unconsciously as a lack of access to the power and prestige of the entire semiotic system. Lacan explains that the object of transference 'is supposed to know that from which no one can escape, as soon as he formulates it – quite simply, signification' (1973: 253).

The teacher or analyst who elicits this transference can teach or effect analysis through an imaginary projection, which consists in the

Semiotic construction of a subject

student's or analysand's belief that the other person knows and can convey 'all' knowledge. The promise of knowing 'everything' – of possessing not only knowledge but a fully realized 'self' – lures the student/analysand into a new relation to knowledge. The student/ analysand then occupies a new place from which to produce (rather than merely repeat) language and gradually takes up some of the powers at first projected on to the masterful subject who is supposed to know something. The student/analysand in this model, more than anything else, is the embodiment of the ongoing possibility of speech – initially a suppressed articulation in someone else's language (who is 'supposed' to know) but eventually a new relation to language production.

Closely related to the critique of the subject inherent in the Freudian conception of resistance is the critique inherent in Freud's narrative account of the semiotic construction of a subject. This is very much in the tradition of the Hegelian critique we discussed in Chapter 1, and it is described in an essay from the period of Freud's first topography, 'Instincts and Their Vicissitudes'. In this metapsychology piece Freud details how 'visual' or 'scopic' experience is composed structurally of 'positions' for looking so that a person gazes at another person, for example, by taking up an initial voyeuristic and fixed location. Once that position is occupied, the subject has a relation to its object and has acquired a 'partial-object' identification in that it possesses to a degree the object through gazing at it. The subject now functions in relation to itself as a subject engaged in the act of looking but also in relation to the object of its regard. For an instant the subject position, as a relation, is constituted by both the position of looking *and* of the object seen. In the next moment the subject seems to *become* what it first focused on as an object. Freud's idea is that the 'single' act of looking in this way has created three positions in subject, subject/object, and object for the scopic drive, and in the visual 'text' at any one moment some of these positions are 'repressed' or cancelled to foreground and privilege the singularity of the remaining position.

Seeing, then, is not just a single act of a unified subject but a manifold construct that includes a lost object of vision within a series of functions. As Freud's account cycles through these positions, the reiteration of this loss in 'seeing' entails the continual reintroduction of a new and yet another new position, each of which entails a new subject who occupies the position left vacant by the previous subject 'to whom', as Freud says, 'one display[ed] one self in order to be looked at by him' when the new position is taken up (1915: 129). In this way, Freud's essay theatricalizes a mechanism of positioning in a text – of how a subject, as a condition of being a subject, continually gets repositioned in relation to other positions. The 'subject' is actually a set of relations, a function and not a thing, virtually the activity of shifting from position to position. Any hierarchy for the different positions of the subject will be necessarily unstable. That is to say, a fixed, or 'natural', hierarchy is not required for the constitution of a subject. A common literary dramatization of the subject as an activity of cycling through subject positions can be seen in the doubling of characters in Mary Shelley's *Frankenstein*, Poe's 'William Wilson' and Joseph Conrad's 'Secret Sharer', among others. These are narratives that emphasize the alternation of identical characters as at one moment subjects and at another as objects in either the story's point of view or in the main character's apprehension of another character. As such, the subject is embedded and constituted in relationships – in a *cultural* manifold.

The major challenge to this view of the semiotic, dynamic subject comes from Jacques Derrida. Derrida is particularly critical of the claims for constancy and stability that still remain in the Freudian model of the subject. The general Freudian view, as Geoffrey Hartman and others have noted, is that a prototype for the signifying capability comes out of Freud's paternal conception of how the signifying activity comes to be. For example, the Freudian 'foundation' for representing 'otherness' lies in what Lacan calls the *nom-du-père* and in the 'differential yet substitutive (compensatory) mechanisms' of this representation – in this *semiotic* function – 'acceptance of . . . the (absent) father, or, basically, of the mediacy of words, allows a genuine recognition of difference' (Hartman 1978: 92). This 'recognition' – based on the notion of language as a iterable operation of identical functions – implies or postulates a 'subject' who does the 'recognizing' as well as a site of difference and recognition. The *nom-du-père*, the 'paternal' or functional origin of language as a mechanical function, in this view actually structures and gives stability to the Freudian subject. The reliability of the linguistic function, in a sense, allows for the signifying process and guarantees that language will be significant and recoverable. In short, while not in any way a substantial 'thing', the *nom-du-père* as a function nevertheless facilitates and guarantees meaning *as if* meaning emanated from a substantial origin and as if the subject were a substantial category.

Derrida objects to this critical psychoanalytic analysis of the subject as an illusion, arguing instead that in reality the subject conceived as a function cannot be established as a reliable reference for experience and a standard for 'truth' in any sense. No signifier can be so uniformly meaningful, as if *to function* like a thing, and there is no such symbolic agency that can intervene in signification to forestall the dissemination of signifying activities that 'construct' a subject. There is no 'paternal' authority in language to underwrite the subject. Derrida does recognize 'undecidability' as a trope, and he also posits 'signification' and its *traces* in discourse. But signification, dependent as it is on an absolutely unknowable 'difference' in texts, cannot be limited as a concept or principle. For Derrida, *trace* itself is another name for dissemination and, by definition, is non-fixable as a point of stability in signification. (In Chapter 5 we will examine the repeated 'namings' in Derrida's work.) Derrida argues that there is no ground behind the 'other', no stability behind the apparent instabilities of signification. At issue in this dispute over the nature of meaning and significance is Derrida's claim that psychoanalysis (even Lacan's deconstructive version of it) reifies and substantializes as concepts possibilities and lines of force which cannot be fully encompassed within stable concepts or equated with substances. Such 'reification', in fact, precisely transforms the critique of subjectivity back into criticism based upon an idea of that reified subjectivity.

On the question of the subject, we believe, it is not exactly the point that Lacan is right and Derrida wrong. At issue is the fact that Derrida insists on a cognitive (informational) interpretation of what psychoanalysis *says* rather than a performative reading of it as an activity, as Felman and others interpret Lacan's Freudianism. Rather than the cognitive validity of psychoanalysis's 'truth value' or even its 'true' value, the problem is that the choice of the cognitive grasp over the performative event, the dimension of knowing over doing, mind over body, that is undecidable. Because the psychoanalytic 'subject' is the whole operation of the 'text' (as in the text of the 'scopic' drive) with the accompanying semiotic complexities entailed by the term 'text', 'the unconscious, in Lacan's eyes', as Felman explains, 'is not simply the object of psychoanalytical investigation, but its subject' (1987: 21). For Lacan the subject, one can say finally, is structured like an unstable but yet identifiable text.

A major theme of the discourse of Lacanian psychoanalysis, therefore, is that resistance to discourse constitutes the very activity of carrying on discourse. That is, the concept of 'resistance' as inherent to the system of language rather than to an ego directs attention to the performance, the activity, of discourse, as opposed merely to the noting (or positing) of the results of that discourse. In such resistance – and here the political as well as psychological force of the term is

105

active – we can see the negativity of transformative critique we examined in Chapter 1. For Lacan, then, one ignores the 'resistance' to discourse (the activity) only by ignoring the values being conveyed in the doing of this activity. The 'doing' does not happen all by itself, because discourse is always situated at a particular moment, place, and according to the particular and yet contingent constitution of the subject. The subject is situated, as Emile Benveniste says, at an 'instance' of enunciation (1966: 217).

The 'subject' throughout this discussion, we reiterate, does not mean 'I' in the sense of the person speaking at any one moment, nor does it mean the 'self' cast in the totalized identity of a 'real' person. And, as we said before, it also does not mean 'ego' even in the specifically Freudian (and sometimes Cartesian) sense of that term. The Lacanian 'subject' critically reframes notions such as 'experience' and 'selfhood' within a context of 'language' rules – that is, knowledge and information conceived as instituted constructions rather than as naturally occurring events and activities. From Lacan's perspective, in the broadest sense the 'subject' takes in the entire semiotic system of functioning, what Derrida, at a Freudian moment, calls 'the subject of writing . . . a *system* of relations between strata: the Mystic [Writing] Pad, the psyche, society, the world' (1967a: 227). This recasting of the subject enacts critique as a self-consuming activity distinct from criticism precisely because it is without fixed references to the truth.

For this reason, concepts such as 'inscription' and unconscious 'discourse' and their systematic elaboration have been the characteristic concerns of the psychoanalytic critique of the subject. The schema of a semiotic Freud can even be used to describe and frame the phenomenon of ego-psychology (such as we described in Holland) in its supposed direct relationship of language and world – ego and reality. Lacan understands this relationship – in which the ego appears to confront the world directly, without the mediation of semiotic representation – as a narcissistic illusion and a phase of discourse called the 'imaginary'. Supposedly the ego in this view, like Kant's subject of knowledge, is generated independently and without connection to the world. In ego psychology, Lacan asserts, the ego certainly appears to be a totally integrated inner person who in his or her autonomous constitution exists independently of and separate from the world, able, as in Holland, to engage in 'transactions' with the world.

In the semiotic model of psychoanalysis the literary text is no longer the exclusive 'object', the substance, of interpretation, it is read in conjunction with the Freudian text, not through it. Literature and psychoanalytic criticism, in this model, inform each other in textual interactions that are both psychoanalytic readings of literature and literary readings of psychoanalysis, a cycling through the positions of subject and object that enacts a dynamic series of reversals. Peter Brooks' reading of *Beyond the Pleasure Principle*, for example, attempts to understand Freud's discussion of the 'death instinct' in terms of a literary structure, what Brooks calls a 'masterplot' that describes 'a total scheme of how life proceeds from beginning to end' (1977: 285). For Brooks, the literary and psychoanalytic texts inform each other creatively outside of the 'therapeutic' application of psychoanalysis to literature.

In this sense, as Lacan argues, textuality proceeds and creates the matrix of signification and meaning, and not vice versa. 'We teach,' as Lacan says, 'that the unconscious means that man is inhabited by [constituted by] the signifier.' To be thus inhabited by the signifier, in Barbara Johnson's words, is to be 'knotted' up, entangled in semiotic relations. 'The letter as a signifier,' as Johnson goes on, 'is thus not a thing or the absence of a thing . . . but a *knot* in a structure where words, things and organs can neither be definably separated nor compatibly combined' (1980: 141). Signifiers create 'texts', and 'knot' captures the etymological sense of the figural weaving that constitutes them. Lacan's vision of a text based on his contention that the unconscious is structured like a language shows the problematic view of the text in psychoanalysis semiotically conceived.

The language of contemporary psychoanalysis, especially as influenced by Lacan, may be the most difficult of all contemporary attempts at critique in that it attempts as much to perform effects of 'power' in itself – effects 'on' and 'within' the reader – as it attempts to describe meaning. Just as the relations of patient and therapist are not simply interaction or transactions but the psychoanalytic drama of transference and projection, so the psychoanalytic use of language is also a working through unconscious resistance as well as a designation of meaning. Psychoanalytic critique offers a language whose force is as 'performative' as it is 'constative', as much a theatricalization as a statement of truth. With this difficulty in mind, we have been trying to situate psychoanalysis among contemporary attempts at critique at the same time as trying to situate psychoanalytic criticism generally within the recent history of literary studies.

PSYCHOANALYSIS AFTER LACAN: THE FEMINIST CRITIQUE

To this point we have been discussing how psychoanalytic theorists since the late 1930s have challenged a number of conclusions about the nature of the subject. Principal among these conclusions is the ego-centred theory of how psychoanalysis achieved its 'cures' and, in a closely related way, how psychoanalytic criticism accomplishes its interpretations of texts. This critique, particularly as advanced by Lacan, focuses on the theory of the 'ego' as key to the psychoanalytic critique of the subject. In the 1970s and 1980s, a new wave of French theorists and critics trained or influenced by Lacan began to extend and to revise psychoanalysis even further to address more directly institutional and ideological issues in relation to the critique of the subject. They argued that Lacan did not go far enough in probing precisely the areas that characterized his discourse – the psychoanalytic dimensions of the 'subject', psychoanalysis as both a clinical practice *and* a cultural institution, and psychoanalysis as ideologically committed and engaged.

These post-Lacanians include contributors to the French journal *Tel Quel*, feminists influenced by deconstruction, and Continental critics of the political left. They form no single school but in the ongoing attempt to revise Lacan's thinking instigate a discourse in three principal phases in the move beyond Freud. We will describe these phases and then return to discussions of each of them. In the first phase, in the late 1960s and 1970s, they tended to *combine* Lacan's insights with other perspectives in an attempt to enlarge both, but made no fundamental changes in Lacan's precepts, especially in regard to the subject. Hélène Cixous's criticism is representative of this phase in that she brought Lacanian strategies to feminism and deconstruction but did little to challenge psychoanalytic discourse about the subject. Cixous, for example, in the 1960s and 1970s, wanted to rethink the relations between gender identities but did little to reconceive the concept of the subject that informs gender. Next were those who made use of Lacan's discourse but proceeded to alter major Freudian and Lacanian concepts in response to the critiques instituted in other disciplines. Luce Irigaray and Michelle Montrelay, in exactly this manner, sought not to 'add' Lacan to feminist discourse so much as to place Lacan and feminist discourse in a strategic conflict that might create an occasion to rethink fundamental Freudian precepts in light of the concerns of post-modern culture. These theorists especially sought to alter the understanding of female sexuality, that is, female identity and feminine modes of cultural interaction and 'writing'.

There were also those who accepted certain of the semiotic and structuralist advances of Lacan's thought but worked to achieve a massive break with Freud and Lacan, their goal being to go 'beyond' Freud and Lacan altogether. This is the direction of the transformative psychoanalytic critiques of Nicholas Abraham, Maria Torok, Gilles Deleuze and Felix Guattari. Deleuze and Guattari, in particular, influenced those who wanted to go 'beyond' primary Freudian concepts and Lacanian innovations such as the critique of the subject, the postulation of the imaginary, the symbolic, the real, and so on. This twenty-year trajectory from Cixous to Deleuze and Guattari suggests a continuing psychoanalytic critique of the subject – first in the assimilation of Lacan's work and then in attempts to critique the subject in non–psychoanalytic but still nominally Freudian terms.

Cixous's work of the 1970s represents an early attempt to modify the Lacanian critique of the subject but within the bounds of a theoretical accommodation with Lacan. Cixous is generally known in America for 'The Laugh of the Medusa' and *The Newly-Born Woman*, works in which she is the visionary guide to reading and writing as a woman. The project of *écriture féminine* began in the middle 1970s when Cixous, Luce Irigaray, Julia Kristeva and Catherine Clement, among others, developed a body of thought about reading women's texts, both texts *by* women and texts characterized as *women's* texts. Their general strategy, at odds with biologically based readings of Freud, reflected a notion of femininity and feminine writing not based on biological conceptions of the sexes – a 'given' essence of male and female characteristics – but on culturally constructed conventions, such as that of 'openness' in feminine texts as a lack of repressive patterning and a tendency towards the indeterminant and random. They imagined 'feminine writing' not exclusively as composed by women but as a description of those texts marked by the requisite openness or divergence from patriarchal, rational decorum. This theorizing about gender, pursued in the atmosphere of post–May 1968 France and deconstruction, prompted questions about the relations of writing, politics and gender – what 'writing' is, how texts deploy power, how to read a feminine (non–patriarchal) text, and, with even greater urgency, what the 'feminine' is.

Cixous's aim was to engage Freud via Lacan in a dialogue with feminine sexuality, an engagement, however, that restrained feminist theory more than it revised psychoanalysis. Cixous, for example, argued for the primacy of the Freudian concept of 'castration', by which Lacan meant the linguistic function, or set of laws, through which discourse is organized and kept pure and orderly. 'Castration [in this sense]' as intrinsic to discourse, as Cixous says, 'is fundamental [to writing], unfortunately' (cited by Conley 1984: 156). 'Isn't it evident,' Cixous asks rhetorically, 'that the penis [the laws of discourse] gets around in my texts, that I give it a place and appeal?' (1975: 319). Referring to this symbolic function as determining what gets into discourse and what does not, she then asserts that it would be 'humanly impossible to have an absolute economy without a minimum of [masculine] mastery' as represented by castration (cited by Conley 1984: 139).

Perhaps more productive but also conservative in this phase of encounter with Lacan is Shoshana Felman, whom we discussed in relation to pedagogy. Authoritative, wide-ranging and always lucid, she is a major reader of Lacan, probably still the major interpreter of Lacan in America. She helped to shape Lacanian studies in America from the middle 1970s and, along with Anthony Wilden, Jane Gallop and Ellie Ragland-Sullivan, has been committed to exploring literary and cultural criticism in relation to the main registers of Lacan's thought – especially to what she frequently calls the force of his teaching, his 'revolutionary' pedagogy. Her work indicates, moreover, the movement of Lacanian studies in the 1980s towards an appreciation of Lacanian *practice* as actively engaged with post-modern modes of thought, particularly in pedagogical theory. In *Jacques Lacan and the Adventure of Insight* (1987), and elsewhere, as we mentioned earlier, Felman's rendition of Lacan is an implicit plea for adoption of a complex and subtle response to pedagogical discourse – respect for the 'other' conceived as the unconscious within language. Like Cixous, however, Felman basically accommodates other discourses to Lacan's thought and seeks few concessions of reformulation from Freud's discourse of patriarchalism.

Far more revisionary in her approach to psychoanalysis is Luce Irigaray. Psychoanalyst, linguist and philosopher, she goes beyond Cixous and Felman to analyse the ways in which Western discourse has effaced 'woman' by reducing her to the specular image of man. Conscious that 'every theory of the subject has always been appropriated by the "masculine"', as may well be the case with Cixous's discourse, Irigaray carefully eschews any formulation that is likely to approach the authority of what she calls the essentializing gestures of patriarchalism. She is extremely cautious, in other words, of routinizing her critique as criticism. Thus, *Speculum of the Other Woman* –

the book which caused her expulsion from Lacan's Freudian School and the loss of her teaching position at Vincennes – as she says, 'has no beginning or end. The architectonics of the text, or texts, confounds the linearity of an outline, the teleology of discourse, within which there is no possible place for the "feminine," except the traditional place of the repressed, the censured' (1977: 68).

Speculum takes its title from the curved mirror (or a mirror folded back on itself as if in a self-conscious critique) as opposed to the flat mirror which unselfconsciously privileges the relation of man to his fellow man and excludes the feminine. This book mimics the shape of the curved mirror by 'beginning' with a deconstruction of Freud's essay 'Femininity' and 'ending' with Plato, thus traversing history backwards and ending where one would expect it to begin. By 'beginning' with Freud, *Speculum* attempts to enact Irigaray's pre-occupation with the '*sexual indifference that underlies the truth of any science, the logic of every discourse*' (1977: 69). Conversely, Irigaray charges that by conceptualizing and standardizing female sexuality within masculine parameters, traditional psychoanalysis is unable to say anything about woman and her pleasure. In Freud's analysis of how a woman develops out of a child with a bisexual disposition, Irigaray detects the blindness that results from taking the penis as the only organ of recognized value. This, in turn, results in denying the specificity of female sexuality, as is clear from Freud's contention that the little girl is, therefore, a little man whose development is marked by envy for the possession of the penis and whose attachment to the mother must end in hate.

Irigaray, though, as we said, is careful not to construct another set of concepts to replace the ones that she aims to expose, and yet Irigaray does go back repeatedly to reiterate the blindness of psycho-analysis to the specifics of female sexuality. *Speculum of the Other Woman* presents all the difficulties of a text that uncompromisingly breaks with tradition while at the same time it attempts to enact some of the disruptions that it considers necessary to create the interstices in which a woman's voice can be heard. Because the main question of psychoanalysis lies in its failure to investigate its own historical determinants and the historical determinants of the sexual destiny assigned to woman, any attempt to raise the question of female sexuality cannot be content with inscribing itself within the accepted boundaries of Western discourse and reflecting it as a flat mirror, but must operate as a curved mirror and show its own *inside*, thereby involving a reinterpretation of Western discourse. This reinterpreta-tion concerns, of course, not only science and political economy but

111

also and particularly language. In this concern, the fields of critique we traverse in this book come together.

But given that the rules of language are laid out according to masculine parameters, how does one speak as 'woman'? The subject conceived as masculine has been able to maintain mastery over discourse because it has produced syntax – 'a syntax of discursive logic which is always a means of masculine self-affection, or masculine self-production, or self-generation or self-representation', 'whereas the "other" syntax, the one that would make feminine "self-affection" possible, is lacking, repressed, censured' (1977: 132). In a sense, *Speculum*, with its defiance of chronology and closure, and 'When Our Lips Speak Together', the last section in *This Sex Which is Not One* – with its emphasis on plurality, proximity and difference perceived as resemblance to another woman rather than to a masculine standard – are examples of a language which strives to make feminine self-affection possible.

On the one hand, Irigaray shows how psychoanalysis 'leaves completely aside whatever woman's "self-affection" might be' and, by valorizing the masculine sex alone, deprives woman of her 'self-affection' (1977: 133). On the other, in calling attention to psychoanalysis's effacement of the uterus, the vulva, the lips, the breasts, she capitalizes on the plurality of female genitals to construct her idea of woman's syntax. In doing so, she fashions her own version of Freud's notorious dictum 'anatomy is destiny' to indicate how, having '*sex organs more or less everywhere*', woman also enjoys a more diffuse, plural pleasure, and how as a result ' "she" is indefinitely other in herself' (1977: 28). Consequently, in a culture that numbers everything by units ('the *one* of form, of the individual, of the (male) sexual organ, of the proper name, of the proper meaning' [1977: 26]) she is an enigma, for '*She is neither one nor two*' (1977: 26), since she has no proper name and since her sexual organ, 'which is not *one* organ, is counted as *none*' (1977: 26).

But perhaps Irigaray's most critical analysis stems from her understanding of the unconscious and its relation to the feminine, as it appears in her intuition that the feminine may in part 'consist of what is operating in the name of the unconscious' and that 'a certain "specificity" of woman' may be 'repressed/censured under cover of what is designated as the unconscious' (1977: 123). If this is true, then the unconscious, in these terms the feminine element of history, still belongs to discursive logic, a logic which finds '*reserves* for itself in the unconscious as in any form of "otherness": savages, children, the insane, women' (1977: 126).

PSYCHOANALYSIS WITHOUT FREUD

The feminist critique of psychoanalysis – and Irigaray's critique is exemplary – has led to a further articulation by Gilles Deleuze and Felix Guattari (as well as Monique Wittig whom we discuss in Chapter 7). They have moved in their own work from avant-garde experiments and probings of contemporary discourse to radical discursive practices. As an academic philosopher, for example, Deleuze began his career with typically 'modern' critiques of the subject such as *Empirisisme et subjectivité* (1953), a book subtitled 'An Essay on Human Nature Since Hume', and *Kant's Critical Philosophy* (1963). Guattari began his work as a psychoanalyst trained in Lacan's school in Paris and also practised beginning in 1953 at La Borde clinic, an establishment providing anti-institutional versions of therapy. In different ways, in other words, both theorists enacted early 'institutional' (academic) critiques of the subject and other aspects of contemporary psychoanalytic discourse. When they began working together, they moved towards 'transformative' practices of the sort that Cixous and Irigaray call for. In this way, ranging from institutional to transformative critiques, their work summarizes several significant moments of contemporary discourse.

Deleuze and Guattari have sought to critique psychoanalysis in the most extreme sense in order to transform it altogether, ultimately to *destroy* it by unmasking its ideological foundation in the values of bourgeois culture. Accordingly, they focus their critique on psychoanalytic 'theory' and, just as intently, on psychoanalysis as an institutional representation of culture in its bourgeois and patriarchal dimensions. In this regard, *Anti-Oedipus: Capitalism and Schizophrenia* (1972) and *A Thousand Plateaus* (1980) try to dissect psychoanalysis so as to institute new understandings and discourses for contemporary culture on the ashes of the old. They advance a truly anti-Freudian critique along three lines: they try to expose the nature of repression and castration as fundamental to psychoanalytic machinery; they critique the psychoanalytic characterization of the unconscious as an ideal of static 'being' rather than active 'production'; and they try to expose the situating of discourse within the hegemonic constraints of the Oedipal narrative. These three arguments constitute their critique of the psychoanalytic subject.

In the classical version of psychoanalysis, 'repression' and 'castration' are related but distinctly different concepts. *Repression* belongs to what Freud calls the primary system and is a basic function of the mind's ability to operate, precisely the realization of 'difference,' which is the engendering basis in all binary and digital oppositions. Physiologically, it is the negation or closing of a neural pathway (or pathways) while another (or others) are left open for neural transmission. At the much higher level of actual experience, it reflects the elemental pairing of binary terms and the possibility of cancelling one of the terms – a switch that may be turned either on or off but cannot be both. As a function, however, repression cannot be positively contextualized as 'real' and must be inferred as a virtual activity creating a matrix of potential functions according to which, at the higher, cybernetic level, choices can be made. This is the level at which painful memories are 'lost' but pleasurable ones retained, and at which one experience is valued over others that are then 'out of mind' or forgotten, and so on. In this way a 'primary' operation of the 'primary' system, repression is fundamental to the very notion of 'mind'.

By contrast, *castration* is not an abstraction of the mind's function but a culturally encoded instance of repression – as in the specific application of a rule. If a father denies a child the pleasure of sleeping in the bed with his parents, the father's act is an act of repression that imposes a law to accomplish a particular cultural end – here the instituting of exogamy. Further, the father's shaping of the child's behaviour in this instance is done in the name, through the agency, of paternal authority. In this example the cultural 'rule' concerning desire and its blockage is implemented by a literal father, but in a patriarchal economy that authority *always* belongs to the position allotted to the (symbolic) father – the 'father' in this instance is analogous to the 'authority' of grammar operating impersonally within the cultural institution of language. In this usage, 'castration' is the culturally inscribed signal requiring denial or an act of substitution. As a concept, therefore, castration is actually a cultural effect, and the application of its rule turns the situation it is applied to into an instance of 'culture', too.

Deleuze and Guattari reject this notion of repression and castration as 'molar', by which they mean both overly general and false. The 'molar' is a cluster of suppressed assumptions united in an ideologically motivated pattern that is taken – mistakenly – to be 'scientific' and 'naturally' the way humans function. For example, the molar formulation of 'castration' conveys not only cultural restraint but a masculine 'presence'. The buried supposition behind the term castration, as Deleuze and Guattari show, is precisely 'that there is finally only one sex, the masculine, in relation to which the woman, the feminine, is defined as a lack, an absence' (1972: 294). Deleuze and Guattari challenge this hegemonic version of cultural regulation as promulgated to advance a 'molar' (and essentialist) conception of males. By contrast, the 'molecular', non-essentialist conception of the unconscious, like the repression that engenders it, 'knows nothing of castration' precisely because castration is an ideologically motivated construct, heavily weighted with much cultural baggage, and not attributable solely to the operation of repression (1972: 295). Deleuze and Guattari seek to explode the concept of castration and speak instead of the unconscious producing positive 'multiplicities' and 'flows' (1972: 295) – potentially not just 'two sexes, but *n* sexes', perhaps a 'hundred thousand' (1972: 296).

These distinctions lead, finally, to their critique of a key psychoanalytic concept, the unconscious. What allows the constitution of such 'molar' conceptions of castration to begin with is Freud's conception of the unconscious as a static *representation*. The fact of the unconscious as difference, as that which is not represented as such in a manifest text (including the 'text' of consciousness), is not objectionable in this critique of psychoanalysis, and to a great extent Deleuze and Guattari actually approve of Freud's conception of the unconscious as the site of the 'production of desire' and, without irony, call this conception the 'great discovery of psychoanalysis' (1972: 24). The problem comes, rather, in Freud's attempt to bury the unconscious as a productive function 'beneath a new brand of idealism' and to associate it with the *representation* (rather than 'production') of 'a classical theater' of 'myth, tragedy, [and] dreams' (1972: 24). In short, Freud, and Lacan after him, depict the unconscious in a passage through Greek myth inextricably bound up with the Western *family* and the ideological investments inherent to Western culture. For Freud and Lacan it follows that the unconscious is not a site of production, a machine capable of various modes of work, but is itself the 'essence of representation', and the 'essence of representation [is constructed in advance] to be a *familial* representation' (1972: 296, emphasis added). Jean-François Lyotard's essay we examined in Chapter 1, 'The Jewish Oedipus', is a good example of the logic of psychoanalytic 'representation'.

Deleuze and Guattari reject this absolute identification of the unconscious with the family and reposition the unconscious, instead, as a 'machinic arrangement' which *can* but need not produce the familial organization of narrative as one of its effects. In so doing, they resituate the 'order of desire' in the unconscious not as cultural representation, a static and permanent framing of familial (Oedipal) order, but as cultural '*production*' in all of its dizzying, polymorphous possibilities (1972: 296).

The final target of their attack on psychoanalysis and patriarchal culture in general is 'Oedipus'. In that the three areas of their attack are interrelated, certainly the attack on Oedipus recapitulates to a degree that on the 'familial' version of the unconscious-as-representation. But 'Oedipus' is an even broader concept and must be seen not merely as an ideological interpretation of psychological functions but in the most encompassing political sense, which, as Mark Seem asserts, is 'the [very] figurehead of imperialism [and] "colonization"' (Deleuze and Guattari 1972: xx). As Deleuze and Guattari argue, Oedipus is a construct 'more powerful . . . than psychoanalysis, than the family, than ideology, even [when all of these are] joined together' (1972: 122). Oedipus encompasses none other than the whole of the hegemonic regime that is 'Western culture', and it is 'Oedipus' at this encompassing level that Deleuze and Guattari oppose in their anti-Freudian fervour to be 'anti–Oedipal'. To oppose Freud at this stage is the same as opposing Western imperialism and derivatives of Western ideology that culminate in imperialism. It opposes the setting into position that is the constant danger for critique.

Deleuze and Guattari then posit the 'post-Oedipal' world as without the genital and Oedipal organization characteristic of Western culture – in other words, without the psychoanalytic subject as we have been discussing it. They argue that the loss of this version of the subject will yet produce, among many other things, a radically liberated human body, a 'body without organs' (1980: 285), a body of energy 'flows' and 'excesses' that is capable of 'becoming an animal' (1980: 259) in the specific sense that psychoanalysis, with its belief in castration and Oedipal commitments, 'doesn't understand becoming an animal' (1980: 259). In their terminology, 'becoming an animal' means dismantling the concept of Western humanism that understands *what it means to be human* (in Greco-ontotheological terms); it entails a particular configuration of the 'human' subject *other than* what psychoanalysis posits.

Their further aim is to provide a kind of cognitive bridge to the realm of 'becoming an animal', to the post-human, and so they advance the alinear logic and irrationality of what they term the economy of the 'rhizome'. By 'rhizome' they mean the economy of culture as composed of irrational eruptions and disruptions of the concept of the integrated subject, the possibility of unforeseen and erratic cultural connections and formations. Most notably in *A Thousand Plateaus*, it is clear that Deleuze and Guattari want to violate and suspend the model of the Western subject as they find it figured in the schemata of psychoanalysis. To this end, they advocate the pursuit of ratios and economies of thinking and experience *other than* those Freud could conceive in his own recapitulation of the values and commitments already evident in Western culture from the ancient Greeks forward. To the degree that Deleuze and Guattari evoke cultural possibilities 'other than' those defined by Western culture and its subject – that is, to the degree they critique the post–Lacanian subject – they evoke a rhizomic model of post–Freudian, post–Oedipal culture.

The violence and suspension of this project is, perhaps, the most thoroughgoing and extreme instance of critique we will encounter in this book. In the energy of their will to explode the focus of Freud and Lacan, Deleuze and Guattari seem to undermine important aspects of critique that we traced in Chapter 1 – its rationality, its questioning, its tireless circumspection. But in another way, by focusing on the individual as the unit of concern, their explosive critique, seeming to go beyond transformation to an apocalyptic starting over, remains conservative, a criticism and modification of Freud and Lacan for all its violence and suspension. That is, the aim of suspending rather than transforming the Western subject avoids examining collective cultural institutions; in their critical analysis of the subject Deleuze and Guattari leave out the collective institutional vectors of critique and its objects. In this chapter, we too have avoided such close examination of collective institutions by focusing on individual arguments and books and de-emphasizing, in the preceding section, the collective force of the feminist critique. Such collectivities are prominent in the field of critique we explore in the next chapter, the critique of language.

CHAPTER FOUR

Structuralism, Semiotics and the Critique of Language

It may be – it is a philosophic and not linguistic question – that the phenomenon of language as such is mysterious, but there are no mysteries in language.

A.J. Greimas
Structural Semantics

Throughout our discussion of the critique of the subject in the preceding chapter, we repeatedly described the economy of the subject we were discussing as analogous to linguistic structures. We even suggested that the work of Jacques Lacan introduced (or 'discovered') a 'semiotic' Freud, one in which the work of psychoanalysis, including literary criticism and the critique of culture it suggests, can be understood in the analogous terms of the structures of language and meaning. The very nature of that analogical relationship is of great importance to any discussion of critique precisely because the relationship between criticism and critique, as we described in Chapter 1, articulates the difference between conceiving of phenomena as 'examples' of pre-existing 'first principles' that exist *outside* of those examples and conceiving of phenomena as analogues to other frameworks of understanding, so that criticism can stand 'outside' itself and turn its own criticisms upon itself in the form of critique. In these terms, the central issue of the preceding chapter was whether, in describing the economy of the subject as 'structured like a language', we were presenting an analogy of two different things – using 'language' to help us to understand 'subjectivity' – or whether we were *situating* subjectivity upon the 'ground' of semiotics, making language, after all, *basic* to subjectivity. We will return to this seemingly undecidable dilemma in our concluding chapter.

We want to examine this dilemma in terms of the preceding chapter in order to provide an introduction to our discussion of the critique of language that has shaped literary and cultural criticism in our time. Throughout Chapter 3 we presented forms of psychological critiques of the subject – ego psychology, archetypalism, Lacanian psychoanalysis, the feminist critique of psychoanalysis – each of which, after enacting its own critique, became the subject of a subsequent critique. This sequence is one that we have followed in each of the chapters of this book, and it is one we will continue to follow. In other words, critique becomes the object of critique as it hardens into dogma of its own, as when Kantian critique becomes the aesthetic ideology of the New Humanism and New Criticism. This ongoing process of the particular critique of a pre-existing understanding is closely related to an aspect of language and semiotic systems more generally that A.J. Greimas calls 'substantification', that aspect of language that transforms dynamic relationships into seeming 'things' or 'substances'. It is the ability of language – its very genius – to create the 'effect' of reality so that whenever language articulates a relationship it seems to be *referring* to pre-existing entities. 'Whenever one opens one's mouth to speak of relationships,' Greimas writes, 'they transform themselves, as if by magic, into substantives, that is, into terms whose meaning we must negate by postulating new relationships, and so on and on. Any metalanguage that we can imagine to speak about meaning is not only a signifying language, it is also substantifying, freezing all intentional dynamism into a conceptual terminology' (cited in Schleifer 1987: 41).

Greimas is speaking specifically about the analysis of the 'double articulation' of language (see Schleifer 1987: esp. 89–93) in which the 'objects' of linguistic analysis are alternatively conceived of as *relationships* which create the effect of substances ('substance-effects') and *substances* which participate in relationships. In linguistics a phoneme – the smallest 'element' of language that distinguishes one meaning from another – is alternatively conceived of as a 'bundle' of relationships among aspects of sound production (for example the engagement or disengagement of the vocal cords, or the use or non-use of lips in sound production) and as phonemic entities which themselves combine to produce syllables and words(for example *t-r-e-e* [or more accurately /t/ + /r/ + /i:/]). All aspects of language, Greimas argues, participate in this dualism, this 'double articulation'. As Roland Barthes argues in *Elements of Semiology* – a book that was tutored in important ways through discussions with Greimas – it is precisely this double articulation that distinguishes language from other systems of meaning. 'In opposition to human language,' Barthes writes, 'in which the phonic substance is immediately significant, and only significant, most semiological systems probably involve a matter which has another function besides that of being significant (bread is used to nourish, garments used to protect)' (1964: 68).

In its double articulation – the articulation of *meaning* in language and the articulation of sounds ('phonic substance') into elements of signification ('phonemes', the elements which are 'immediately significant, and only significant') – language is structured, in Roman Jakobson's terms, as 'both *energeia* and *ergon* – in other words, language (or any other social value) as creation and as oeuvre' (1936: 179). Language is both the *process* of articulating meaning (signification) and its *product* (communication), and, as we shall see, these two functions of language are neither identical nor fully congruent. In any case, Jakobson's terms suggest that not only 'psychology' and the psychological critique of the subject we examined in the preceding chapter can be understood as a special case of the general phenomena of linguistic structures, but the very activity of critique and all critical understanding of literature and culture can themselves be seen as 'basically' – 'essentially' – reducible to the double nature of linguistic activity.

STRUCTURAL LINGUISTICS

Greimas and Jakobson and Louis Hjelmslev (whom we mentioned in Chapter 2) as well as the schools of linguistic and literary criticism – Russian Formalism, Prague Linguistics and French Structuralism – all base their understanding of language and signification on the studies of twentieth-century linguistics, and especially the work of Continental (as opposed to Anglo-American) linguistics. At the head of this tradition is the great Swiss linguist Ferdinand de Saussure. In the *Course in General Linguistics* (1916) – the transcription by his students of several courses in general linguistics he offered at the University of Geneva from 1907 to 1911 – he called for the 'scientific' study of language as opposed to the work in historical linguistics that had been done in the nineteenth century. In the course of that century the emerging science of linguistics developed intricate schemes of relationships among most of the European languages, what came to be called (because of this work) the 'Indo-European' languages. Taking particular words as the building blocks of language, historical, or 'diachronic', linguistics traced the origin and development of these languages from a putative common language source, first an 'Indo-European' language and then an earlier 'Proto-Indo-European' language.

It is precisely this study of the unique occurrences of words – with the concomitant assumption that the basic 'unit' of language is, in fact, the *positive* existence of these 'word-elements' – that Saussure's science of linguistics critiques. Diachronic linguistics assumed that an account of historical occurrences of words provided an accounting – an understanding – of the nature of language. Saussure's critique – his 'science' of linguistics – was an attempt to reduce the myriad facts about *signification*, studied so minutely by historical linguistics, to a manageable number of propositions about the functioning of the signifying process in human life by describing a rigorous conceptual framework. That is, Saussure saw that even the great achievement of historical linguistics in the nineteenth century – like the triumph of the 'individualism' of Romantic subjectivity – *assumes* the unity and self-identity of its object of study (self-identical 'words' in language, self-identical 'subjects' in psychology) rather than subjecting that object to the same rigorous analysis to which it subjected phenomena surrounding that object. The 'comparative school' of nineteenth-century philology, Saussure says in the *Course*, 'which had the indisputable merit of opening up a new and fruitful field, did not succeed in setting up the true science of linguistics. It failed to seek out the nature of its object of study' (1916: 3).

That nature, he argues, is not simply to be found in the 'elemental' words that comprise a language – the seeming 'positive' facts (or 'substances') of language – but in the *formal* relationships which give rise to those 'substances'. In other words, 'the linguistic phenomenon always has two related sides, each deriving value from the other' (1916: 8). This is the great initiating insight of Saussurean linguistics: the relational – 'double articulation' – of linguistic and, later, 'semiotic' phenomena. In this critique of historical linguistics we can see, again, the transformation Northrop Frye describes from naive induction to systematic understanding. Instead of taking words as the building blocks of language, Saussure tried to describe the conditions – what Frye calls the 'conceptual framework' (1949: 250) – that give rise to these seeming basic units of language.

Saussure's systematic re-examination of language is based upon three assumptions. First is the assumption that the scientific study of language needs to develop and study the *system* rather than the history of linguistic phenomena. 'If we fix our attention on only one side of each problem,' he notes, 'we run the risk of failing to perceive the dualities pointed out above; on the other hand, if we study speech from several viewpoints simultaneously, the object of linguistics appears to us as a confused mass of heterogeneous and unrelated things' (1916: 9). For this reason he distinguishes between the particular occurrences of language – its particular 'speech-events', which he designates as *parole* – and the proper object of linguistics, the system (or 'code') governing those events, which he designates as *langue*. Moreover, such an object, he argues, calls for the 'synchronic' study of the relationship among the elements of language at a particular instant rather than the 'diachronic' study of the development of language through history.

This assumption gave rise to what Jakobson came to designate as 'structuralism' in 1929:

> Were we to comprise the leading idea of present-day science in its most various manifestations, we could hardly find a more appropriate designation than *structuralism*. Any set of phenomena examined by contemporary science is treated not as a mechanical agglomeration but as a structural whole, and the basic task is to reveal the inner . . . laws of this system. What appears to be the focus of scientific preoccupations is no longer the outer stimulus, but the internal premises of the development: now the mechanical conception of processes yields to the question of their function. (p. 711)

In this dense passage Jakobson articulates the scientific aim of linguistics as opposed to simple, 'mechanical' accounting. Along with this, moreover, he is also describing the second foundational assumption in Saussurean – we can now call it 'structural' – linguistics: that the basic elements of language can be studied only in relation to their *function* rather than their *cause*. Instead of studying particular and unique events and entities (for example the history of particular Indo-European 'words'), those 'events' and 'entities' have to be *situated* within a systemic framework in which they are related to other so-called events and entities. This is a radical reorientation in conceiving of the world, one whose importance the philosopher Ernst Cassirer has compared 'to the new science of Galileo which in the seventeenth century changed our whole concept of the physical world' (cited in Culler 1981: 24), or, more appositely, to the 'Copernican revolution' that Kant claims his philosophical critique effected in the eighteenth century.

Saussure specifically redefines the 'word', now conceived as the linguistic sign, in functionalist terms. The sign, he argues, is the union of 'a concept and a sound image' which he called '*signified* [*signifié*] and *signifier* [*signifiant*]' (1916: 66–7), and the nature of their combination is functional in that neither the signified nor the signifier is the cause of the other. Rather, they exist within the linguistic sign in what Greimas calls a relationship of 'reciprocal presupposition'. The signifier presupposes the signified which, after all, it signifies. But at the same time the signified presupposes the signifier, otherwise it couldn't be 'signified [by something]'. In this way Saussure defines the basic element of language, the sign, *relationally*. (It is important to note that by 'sound image' Saussure does not mean physical sound. Rather, he is describing the *phoneme* of language, the basic *formal* articulation of physical sound (which Barthes calls the 'phonic substance'), the second of language's 'double articulation'.) In defining language relationally, he makes the basic assumption of historical linguistics, namely the *identity* of the basic units of language and signification (i.e. words), subject to rigorous analysis. The reason we can recognize different occurrences of the word *tree* as the same word (whether those occurrences take place at different times historically or in the different pronunciations of two speakers in a conversation) is that the word is not defined by inherent qualities. It is not a 'mechanical agglomeration' of such qualities but is defined, rather, as an element in a system (the 'structural whole') of language.

This relational definition of an entity (it is also called a 'diacritical' definition) governs the conception of all the elements of language in structural linguistics. It is most evident in the development of the concepts of the 'phonemes' and 'distinctive features' of language. Phonemes, the smallest articulated and signifying units of a language, are opposed to 'phones' or phonic substance, which are the actual sounds that a language utilizes. In other words, phonemes are not the sounds which occur in language but the sounds which are apprehended by speakers – phenomenally apprehended – as conveying meaning. Such apprehension, as we suggested at the end of the preceding chapter, is essentially collective. As Prague semiotician Jan Mukařovský noted in 1937, 'structure . . . is a phenomenological and not an empirical reality; it is not the work itself, but a set of functional relationships which are located in the consciousness of a collective (generation, milieu, etc.)' (cited in Galan 1985: 35). For this reason, phonemes, the smallest perceptible elements of language, are not *positive* objects but a 'phenomenological reality'.

In English for instance, the /t/ phoneme can be pronounced with an aspiration (a slight 'h' sound seemingly added to it) as in an emphatic pronunciation of the word *take* [t']; or it can be pronounced unaspirated as in *steak*. In both cases an English speaker will recognize these pronunciations as variations (or 'allophones') of a /t/ phoneme so that someone speaking with an accent that aspirates all /t/s could still be understood. The difference between languages is such that phonemic variations in one language can constitute distinct phonemes in another. Thus English distinguishes between /l/ and /r/ whereas in many oriental languages these articulations are considered variations of the same phoneme, just as [t] and [t'] are variations of /t/ in English. For this reason native Chinese speakers have great trouble with the distinction between these English phonemes precisely because in their native language they are simply variations of the 'same' sound. In the same way, native English speakers have great trouble with languages in which /t/ and /t'/ are distinctive phonemes. In every natural language, the vast number of possible words is a combination of a small number of phonemes. English, for instance, possesses less than forty phonemes that combine to form over a million different words and the vast number of *different* pronunciations to which these words are susceptible.

The phonemes of language, as we noted earlier, are themselves systematically organized as 'bundles' of features. In the 1920s and 1930s, following the lead of Saussure, Jakobson and the Russian phonologist N.S. Trubetzkoy isolated the 'distinctive features' of phonemes. These features are based upon the physiological structure of the speech organs – tongue, teeth, vocal cords, and so forth – and they combine in 'bundles' to form phonemes. No distinctive feature can exist outside of combination with others within a phonemic articulation (one cannot engage the vocal cords without doing other things to produce a sound), but, more importantly, combinations organize and *define* themselves through a logic of binary opposition in terms of their presence and absence. In English the difference between /t/ and /d/ is the presence or absence of 'voice' (the engagement of the vocal chords), and on the level of voicing these phonemes reciprocally define one another. The difference between /p/ and /t/ is that the former possesses the feature of 'labiality' (it is produced by the lips), while the latter is 'dental', and again they are defined in relation to one another. In this way, phonology is a specific example of a general rule of language Saussure (1916) describes.

> . . . in language there are only differences. Even more important: a
> difference generally implies positive terms between which the difference
> is set up; but in language there are only differences *without positive terms*.
> Whether we take the signified or the signifier, language has neither ideas
> nor sounds that existed before the linguistic system, but only conceptual
> and phonic differences that have issued from the system. The idea or

phonic substance that a sign contains is of less importance than the other signs that surround it.   (p. 120)

In this framework, 'positive' identities – what constitutes 'sameness' and, finally, meaning itself – are determined not by inherent qualities but by systemic ('structural') relationships.

This conception of the elements of signification being diacritically determined through a system suggests a third assumption governing Saussurean linguistics and semiotics, what Saussure calls 'the arbitrary nature of the sign'. By this he means that the relationship between the signifier and signified in language is never necessary (or 'motivated'). One could just as easily use the sound signifier *arbre* as the signifier *tree* to unite with the concept of 'tree'. But more than this, the *signified* is arbitrary as well. One could as easily define the concept 'tree' by its woody quality (which would exclude palm trees) as by its size (which excludes the 'low woody plants' we call *shrubs*). This relationship is not necessary because it is not based upon *inherent* qualities of signifier or signified. The nature of the sign – and of signifiers and signifieds – is governed by systematic diacritical relationships. Moreover, the numbering of assumptions we have been making is not an order of priority. Each assumption – the systemic nature of signification (best apprehended by studying language 'synchronically'), the relational or 'diacritical' nature of the elements of signification, the arbitrary nature of signs – is in relationships of reciprocal presupposition with the others.

Within this analysis we can see that the science of linguistics, like the 'science' of psychoanalysis, or that of chemistry, is governed by a conceptual framework that understands the phenomena it studies in overarching relationships of *contrast* and *combination* – the *energeia* and *ergon* with which we began. The elements of language are defined on any particular 'level' of understanding in terms of the ways in which they contrast with other elements on that level, just as the periodic table offers the chemical elements in a *systematic* framework of contrasts. Elements combine with elements from their own level to create the elements of the next linguistic level, just as chemical elements combine in a systematic fashion determined by their contrasting qualities. Thus, distinctive features combine to form phonemes, and phonemes combine to form morphemes (the smallest units of meaning such as prefixes, suffixes, etc.), and morphemes combine to form words, and words combine to form sentences. (A linguistic phenomenon such as the word 'I' in English is alternatively a phoneme, a morpheme and a lexeme [word] depending on the question brought to that phenomenon.) In each instance, the 'whole' of an element is greater than the sum of its parts, just as water, H_2O, in Saussure's example (1916: 103), is more than the mechanical agglomeration of hydrogen and oxygen.

The great difference between a 'human' science such as linguistics (or psychoanalysis, for that matter) and a natural science such as chemistry is Saussure's third assumption, the arbitrary nature of the sign. In chemistry the elements of the framework of understanding – particles, chemical elements, molecules – are not 'arbitrary' but rather inherent and necessary within the object of study. In studying meaning, on the other hand, the elements *are* arbitrary. Signification can use *any* phenomena to signify, just as in studying psychology, as Freud suggests, the subject can direct its desire at *anything*. It is for this reason that Barthes mentions the signifying nature of bread and clothes in the Eucharist and in fashion, even though they are not necessarily signifiers ('bread is used to nourish, garments used to protect' [1964: 68]). The arbitrary nature of the sign is clearest in those instances in which language uses the *absence* of some feature as part of its signifying system, when, as Saussure says, 'a material sign is not necessary for the expression of an idea; language is satisfied with the opposition between something and nothing' (1916: 86). In chemistry material is always necessary, and the absence of oxygen, say, is simply its absence. But in language – in signification – the absence of 'voicing' is more than the simple absence of the sound produced by air rushing across vocal cords. It also produces a signification that, in English, can be perceived in the difference between *site* and *side*, *dew* and *two*. Absence here is not simple. As Jacques Derrida says in another context, it, like signification in general, is 'irreducibly nonsimple' (1972: 13). Such non-simplicity is what Saussure meant when he asserted that 'the linguistic phenomenon always has two related sides, each deriving value from the other' (1916: 8).

Such an understanding of the arbitrary nature of the sign leads to the assumption that there is a great difference between the natural sciences and the human sciences: the assumption of the absolute opposition between nature and culture which, we will see, is subject to its own critique at the hands of 'post-structuralists'. The linguist Emile Benveniste (1966) has argued that:

> one should draw a fundamental distinction between two orders of phenomena: on the one side the physiological and biological data, which present a 'simple' nature (no matter what their complexity may be) because they hold entirely within the field in which they appear . . . on

the other side, the phenomena belonging to the interhuman milieu, which
have the characteristic that they can never be taken as simple data or
defined in the order of their own nature but must always be understood
as double from the fact that they are connected to something else,
whatever their 'referent' may be. A fact of culture is such only insofar as
it refers to something else.   (pp. 38–9)

The overriding 'fact' of culture is signification, the fact that phenomena – whatever we can 'perceive' – always mean something, always
signify. Linguistics studies such signification in language.

The three assumptions of the *Course in General Linguistics* lead
Saussure to call for a new science of the twentieth century that would
go beyond the double articulation of language to study 'the life of
signs within society'. Saussure names this science *semiology* (from
Greek *semeion*, 'sign'). 'Semiology,' he predicts, 'would show what
constitutes signs, what laws govern them. Since the science does not
exist, no one cay say what it would be; but it has a right to existence,
a place staked out in advance. Linguistics is only a part of the general
science of semiology' (1916: 16). Almost simultaneously with Saussure's *Course*, in the first decade of the twentieth century the American
philosopher and logician Charles Sanders Peirce attempted to describe
the general science of the functioning of signs in various sciences in
the study of 'semeiotic' [*sic*] – what Jonathan Culler calls the 'science
of sciences' (1981: 23). Peirce saw semiotics in relation to logic, and
developed elaborate taxonomies of types of signs. The coincidental
articulation of the 'same' neologism to describe a science which did
not exist but which, as Saussure said, had 'a right to exist', is a key in
the history of ideas, comparable to the coincidental development of
calculus by Isaac Newton and G.W. Leibniz at the turn of the
eighteenth century.

Most important, the 'science' of semiotics widens the study of
language and linguistic structures to the realm of cultural artifacts
constituted (or articulated) by those structures. As semiotics came to
be practised in Eastern Europe in the 1920s and 1930s and in Paris in
the 1950s and 1960s, it examined *meaningful*, cultural phenomena
from the viewpoint of the conditions that make such meaningful
phenomena possible, including the structures that give rise to that
meaning. That is, semiotics takes its methods from the structural
linguistics Saussure initiated (and, sometimes, from the *pragmatics*
Peirce initiated) in order to understand the conditions governing
meaning in human culture. It does this whether that meaning is the
particular 'effects' of literature produced by the 'elements' of literature
and narrative Russian Formalism studied in the 1920s, or the phenom-

enon of temporality in literature and film that Prague semiotics studied in the 1930s, or the myths of 'primitive' societies that structural anthropology studied in the 1950s. Semiotics also focuses on general cultural concepts such as that of the Virgin Mary, as Julia Kristeva has shown, or particular cultural phenomena, ranging from wrestling to advertising, that French structuralists studied in the 1960s and 1970s. In each case, the widening purview of the structural study of language creates models and procedures for the structural study of literature and culture itself.

RUSSIAN FORMALISM

The first use of the tenets of Saussurean structuralist linguistics for the study of literature occurred in Russia at the beginning of the twentieth century. This movement has come to be known as Russian Formalism. The connection of literary study and linguistics was effected, in part, by the presence of Roman Jakobson, a central figure in the Moscow Linguistic Circle, in the work of the Russian Formalists. Jakobson was also instrumental in organizing the Prague Linguistic Circle. Russian Formalism took modernist aesthetics and epistemology to heart and attempted to analyse literature not by its identifiable or 'natural' (or 'representational') content but consistently by its form – how it is constructed and how it functions so as to have meaning in the first place. In 1929 in an essay entitled 'The Literary Fact', Yuri Tynjanov wrote that 'it is self-evident that "material" is not at all the opposite of "form"; it is also "formal" because there is no material which would be external to a construction. . . . Material is that element of the form that is subordinated for the benefit of the foregrounded constructive elements' (cited in Steiner 1984: 115). In this description of literary fact, Tynjanov is using an argument parallel to Saussure's description of phonemes (language's 'sound image'). The so-called 'material' of language and literature is itself 'formal'; as Saussure notes in the *Course*, each element of linguistic science is '*a form, not a substance*' (1916: 113).

The focus on form in the literary study of Russian Formalism entailed a re-examination – that is, a critique – of traditional ways of understanding literature. Peter Steiner notes:

> Traditional critics had not treated literary texts in terms of psychology, sociohistory, or philosophy just to be perversely 'unscientific,' but

because they saw these works as expressions of the authors' mental lives, documents of their time, or philosophical meditations. The Formalist view was quite different. For them literature was an autonomous reality governed by its own regularity and more or less independent of contiguous spheres of culture. From this perspective the vital issue for literary science was no longer the investigation of other realities that literary texts might reflect, but the description of what it was that made them a *literary* reality.   (p. 245)

Russian Formalism enacted its critique of literary study – it produced a 'science' of literature in the same way Kant attempted to produce a 'science' of philosophy – by relentlessly focusing on the formal 'devices' that created *literary* effects.

The emphasis on form in literary criticism has two general applications: an understanding of a text's interior patterning, or how it works, and the recognition that form marks a work as belonging to a particular genre – a novel, lyric, drama, and so on. Thus, formalism in the broadest sense views literature as a complex system of forms that may be analysed in relation to one another at different levels of generality – from the specifics of a poetic image or line through that poem's genre. Formalism, in short, attempts to view literature not as constituted by its intrinsic ('natural') meaning, as an imitation of reality, but by relational patterns that are meaningful in and to a particular work and genre.

Russian Formalism was the work of two groups of critics, the Moscow Linguistic Circle, begun in 1915, and Opojaz (Society for the Study of Poetic Language), set up in 1916. Both groups were disbanded in 1930 in response to official Soviet condemnation of their willingness to depart from the ideological standards of socialist realism. Their influence continued strongly in the work of the Prague Linguistic Circle (founded in 1926) and in a few key works such as Vladimir Propp's *Morphology of the Folktale* (1928). It is an oddity of the modern history of ideas, however, that after 1930 the Russian Formalists (and, to a lesser extent, Prague structuralism) had almost no impact on Western criticism and theory but resurfaced thirty years later with the advent of literary structuralism in France in the 1960s. The importance of Formalism to Prague semiotics is, as we shall see, almost inestimable, but the politics of Czechoslovakia, as in the Soviet Union, helped to erase the intellectual legacy of Russian formalism and Prague Semiotics from the 1940s through to the 1980s. With the exception of Claude Lévi-Strauss's important critique of the work of Vladimir Propp, 'Structure and Form: Reflection on a work by Vladimir Propp' (not translated into English until 1976), much early

French Structuralism, very important to American criticism in the 1960s and 1970s, was unaware of the work in Moscow and Prague.

Like Eliot and the modernists in general, the Russian Formalists sought to move away from nineteenth-century Romantic attitudes in criticism and to avoid all Romantic notions about poetic inspiration, genius and aesthetic organicism. Instead, the formalists adopted a deliberately mechanistic view of poetry and other literary art as the products of *craft*. As Viktor Shklovsky, the self-proclaimed 'founder of the Russian school of Formal method', says, 'in its essence the Formal method is simple – a return to craftsmanship' (cited in Steiner 1984: 44–5). Considered as craft, literature may be investigated according to immediately analysable literary functions. While the formalists believed that no particular deployment of words, images or other language effects is intrinsically literary (there being no such thing as literary language), they saw that literature, like other usages of language, could have a particular *function*, could 'work' to accomplish particular ends, an assumption articulated in Jakobson's description of 'structuralism'. Such functionalism is also important to the historical criticism of Mikhail Bakhtin or the later 'sociological' criticism (as he called his work) of Kenneth Burke (1937: 303–4). But the Russian Formalists grounded their study in linguistics. They wanted to see language deployed as *language* and highlight its linguistic functioning as the object of criticism. The linguistic properties of a poem's meaning and effect then become the primary concern, instead of 'inspiration' or 'poetic genius' of the psychological subject, or the socio-historical context of literature, or even the philosophical nature of things. The formalists attempted to maintain and to extend this view at every step of analysis by identifying formal properties as *effective* properties through detailed analyses of poetic (and narrative) technique.

This impulse in theory towards a literary formalism can be seen most clearly in Shklovsky's definition of literary 'devices' as aimed at effecting some end (a concept analogous to Saussure's 'functional' definition of linguistic entities). Central to formalism, for example, is Shklovsky's argument in 'Art as Technique' against the aesthetic notion of 'art as thinking in images' (1917: 7) and his promotion, instead, of the importance of literary and non-imagistic devices. A concentration on images, Shklovsky maintained, leads one to view a poem as having actual 'content', and this assumption inhibits any truly formal or relational analysis. What may appear as 'content' needs to be considered as 'device', or any operation in language that promotes 'defamiliarization'. That is, because language is a medium of communication before it is used in art (just as, in Barthes' example, bread is food before it signifies in church services), its expressions and conventions inevitably will be overly familiar to the reader and too feeble to have a fresh or significant impact in a poem. Perception, Shklovsky writes, 'becomes habitual, it becomes automatic'; the habit of ordinary speech 'devours works, clothes, furniture, one's wife, and the fear of war' (1917: 12). For this reason, he goes on, 'art exists that one may recover the sensation of life; it exists to make one feel things, to make the stone *stony*' (1917: 12). To be made new and poetically useful, language must be 'defamiliarized' (1917: 13) and 'made strange' through linguistic displacement, which means deploying language in an unusual context or effecting its presentation in a novel way. Rhyme schemes (or lack of rhyme), chiasmus (rhetorical balance and reversal), catachresis (the straining of a word or figure beyond its usual meaning), conceits, mixed metaphors, and so on – all these devices for producing particular effects in literature can be used to defamiliarize language and to awaken readers to the intricacy and texture of verbal structure.

Defamiliarization is, therefore, the manner in which poetry functions to rejuvenate and to revivify language. In fact, defamiliarization shares much with the aim of critique in its impulse to subject self-evident truths to critical scrutiny. Russian Formalist accounts of *how* literature works closely position literature and its critical study as forms of critique of the *cultural* institution of language. This accounting is quite different from Romantic criticism's view of poetry as the expressive channel for transcendent (or divine) feelings or poetic (or personal) genius. It is also quite different from the seemingly related phenomenon of New Critical formalism insofar as New Criticism does not examine the formal nature of the 'devices' it utilizes, such as 'irony' or 'paradox' or even its originary gesture of assuming the self-enclosed nature of the literary work. New Criticism hardly conceived of these aspects of poetry as 'devices' or historically determined elements of discourse at all – and neither did it subject the assumption of the *value* of its work to critique.

Russian Formalism departs from New Criticism on the key issue of the *function* of forms. (There are moments in New Criticism – as when Cleanth Brooks asserts in 'The Language of Paradox' that Donne's effect 'is to cleanse and revivify metaphor' [1947: 17] – that are close to Shklovsky's definition of 'defamiliarization'.) Rather than conceiving the formal properties of literature as a means of achieving particular effects, the New Critics conceived literature to be a self-sustaining 'artifact', a 'spatial form' in Joseph Frank's term (1945), and form as a self-contained 'autonomous' entity, what Brooks meant by a 'well-wrought urn'. Perhaps most telling about the New Criticism was its reliance on 'imagery' as a concept with which to define form. While the Russian Formalists sought to avoid any focus on literary content, the New Critics posited paradox and irony (particular *effects* of literature) as controlling figures and, in effect, turned them into content. As Brooks asserts in his reading of Donne's 'The Canonization', paradox and irony actually reflect the structure of the imagination itself (1947: 21). His reasoning, based on Kantian aesthetics, is that since poetry is produced by the imagination, it must reflect the imagination's own structure. That structure, or 'form', is opposition, as seen rhetorically in the figures of paradox and irony. These figures, it follows, although they are intended to be poetry's form, virtually become its *content* in that they are the ultimate referents for all the indications (largely imagistic) of meaning. From this New Critical standpoint, all poems are about, or 'contain', these patterns.

In this dispute over imagery is the largest difference between the 'substantial' formalism of the New Criticism and the 'functional' formalism of Russian Formalism. As Jurij Striedter notes, 'for New Criticism the aesthetic norm is paramount, for Formalism the devia-tion from the norm' is paramount (1989: 70). Whereas the Russian Formalists attempted merely to lay bare the operation of local devices, rejecting any authoritative and final interpretation of a work, the New Critics believed that a work can be read objectively and accurately in light of its actual structure or form. A work can, thus, have a single, or 'correct', interpretation. W.K. Wimsatt and Monroe C. Beardsley in 'The Intentional Fallacy' even stipulate the manner of reading a work the 'right' way: 'judging a poem', they say, 'is like judging a pudding or a machine. One demands that it work' (1946: 4). They explain the interference and inaccuracies possible when authorial intentions become a consideration in close reading – the 'wrong' way. In 'The Affective Fallacy', further, they show how at the other extreme a reader's undisciplined 'affective' responses to a text may distort the correct apprehension and interpretation of images. Whereas the Russian Formalists concentrated on form as a plurality of literary devices and on interpretation as an activity, the New Critics retrieved from Romanticism the concept of aesthetic wholeness and unity as well as a unified or definitive interpretation of a work. They argued that a work, properly read, will always be unified by a set of tensions expressed in paradox and irony. In short, the New Critics assumed total coherence in a work; the Russian Formalists did not.

PRAGUE SEMIOTICS

Still, Russian Formalism grounded its study of literature on an unexamined assumption too. That assumption, implicit in Shklovsky's essay 'Art as Technique', was that 'literature' could be legitimately – that is, 'scientifically' – isolated from other cultural phenomena for the purposes of study. It is this assumption of Russian Formalism that Prague Structuralism critiqued – and, in fact, it is precisely this opposition that led Jakobson and Mukařovský to oppose 'structure' to 'form' as the central concept of understanding. The opposition implicit in formalism between 'form' and 'content' does not allow for the examination of historical change in literature (even in a 'school' as loosely formed as 'Russian Formalism'). In order to counter this tendency in formalism, Jan Mukařovský emphasizes the *dynamic* nature of structure. Before describing structure as 'a phenomenological and not an empirical reality' in the passage we quoted earlier, he asserts that the relation between the parts of any structure 'is felt to be not static, as if given beforehand, but unique and unrepeatable . . . structure is not a stable but a fragile equilibrium' (1937; cited by Galan 1985: 35).

Such a critique of formalism can be directed towards Saussurean linguistics as well as Russian Formalism. On the level of the sign, Sergej Karcevskij offers such a critique in 'The Asymmetric Dualism of the Linguistic Sign' (1929). In this essay Karcevskij tries to *account for* linguistic change rather than assuming, as Saussure himself does, that 'no characteristic [of language] has a right to permanent existence; it persists only through sheer luck' (1916: 229). 'Mere phonetic modifications,' Saussure adds, '. . . are due to blind evolution' (1916: 231). Here and elsewhere in Saussure, the implication is that historical change, like the sheer multiplicity of *parole*, is not the proper object of scientific inquiry but simply a realm of chance and accident. Karcevskij (1929) argues, on the other hand, that the historical movement of language can be understood in terms of the very structure of the sign.

> The signifier (sound) and the signified (function) slide continually on the 'slope of reality.' Each 'overflows' the boundaries assigned to it by the other: the signifier tries to have functions other than its own; the signified tries to be expressed by means other than its sign. They are asymmetrical; coupled, they exist in a state of unstable equilibrium. It is because of this asymmetric dualism in the structure of its signs that a linguistic system can evolve: the 'adequate' position of the sign is continually displaced as a result of its adaptations to the exigencies of the concrete situation. (p. 54)

133

In this way, the relational structure of the sign calls for transformation in that the signifier 'seeks functions other than its proper one' and the signified 'seeks to express itself by means other than its sign' precisely *because* language is relationally structured. That is, the 'parts' of elements of the sign are *always* related to something other than themselves.

This radically relational definition replaces, as Mukařovský says, 'form' with 'structure' in which what is structured is not simply 'content' but rather phenomena *already structured* on a different 'level' of apprehension. In this way, phonemes are the 'content' structured into morphemes, but the phonemes themselves, understood in another context – as 'bundles' of distinctive features – are already 'structured'. The same relational definition replaces the object of study of Russian Formalism with a new way of thinking of that object of study. This can be seen, as F.W. Galan has argued, in contrasting Roman Jakobson's 1921 description of the object of study in terms of scientific formalism to his later description of it when he was a member of the Prague Linguistic Circle.

In 1921 Jakobson claimed that literary study should examine not literature but 'literariness', those elements that make an utterance characteristically 'literary'. As Galan (1985) describes it:

> . . . for Jakobson poetry is simply 'language in its aesthetic function,' that is, utterance produced solely 'for the purpose of expression,' one in which the communicative function, consequently, 'has only minimal importance.' The formalist critic thus investigates the procedures that help render standard language literary, focusing attention on the laying bare of devices and the realization of verbal structures, but stays away at all cost from anything extraliterary – from biography, psychology, politics or philosophy – for fear of behaving, in Jakobson's provocative simile, like a policeman who arrests the culprit and all the innocent passersby into the bargain. (p. 107)

In 1933 in Prague, Jakobson presented a subtle but important modification of this position in a famous essay entitled 'What is Poetry?'. In it he argued that the poetic function, 'poeticity', should be viewed as only one constituent part of the complex structure of poetry. 'According to Jakobson's structural view, in contrast to his formalist stance,' Galan writes, 'the difference between art and nonart, or between literary and nonliterary language, is one not of kind but of degree. Unlike "literariness," "poeticity" is not equated with the poetic work as a whole; it is identified merely as a part of that whole: the dominant part' (1985: 107–8). In other words, 'poeticity' (unlike 'literariness') is a *relational* rather than an absolute element of a poetic work: that work is 'poetic' precisely because the poetic and aesthetic functions relationally dominate the other functions.

At the time of 'What is Poetry?' Jakobson conceived of language consisting of a bundle of four functions (see Galan 1985: 72), but later he defined six functions of linguistic activity in relation to six factors which are 'inalienably involved in verbal communication' (1960: 66). The following chart (1960: 66, 71) describes the functions of language with the 'factors' of the actual situation of verbal communication in brackets.

Referential function [context]
Poetic function [message]
Emotive function [addresser] —— Conative function [addressee]
Phatic function [contact]
Metalingual function [code]

These functions are arranged in relations of binary opposition in which, in Saussure's terms, 'each deriv[es] value from the other' (1916: 8): the emotive function versus the conative function, the poetic function versus the phatic function, and the referential function versus the metalinguistic function. All six functions are always present in linguistic activity, but any function can dominate a particular instance of linguistic activity in such a way that it is 'the focusing component of a work of art. It rules, determines, and transforms the remaining' functions of language (Jakobson 1935: 41).

In this way, the relationships among functions are not fixed immutably but are interactive. In the terms we have been pursuing, the *focus* on the emotive function of any work leads to a species of psychological analysis. A focus on the conative function suggests 'reader-response' analyses of discourse or versions of the ego-psychology we examined in the preceding chapter. It can also suggest sociological aspects of the persuasiveness of rhetoric (as found in Bakhtin and Burke) when the whole relationship between the addresser and addressee is taken into account. Focus on the referential function leads to historical analysis. Focus on the metalinguistic function leads to linguistic analysis and some versions of philosophical linguistics (which underscores the *tendency* towards ahistoricism in structuralism and semiotics). Focus on the poetic function leads to the aestheticization of language, to both Russian and New Critical Formalism, but it also suggests kinds of philosophical (or ontological) analysis. Focus on the phatic function leads to the study of the materiality of language – the phonetics (as opposed to phonemics) from which Saussure departed. It is precisely this sense of 'focus', a *phenomenological* sense of attention and 'feeling', that allows for the various 'extraliterary' examinations of 'literature' and also allows so-called 'nonliterary' texts to find their way into the literary canon. When the poetic function is dominant, Jakobson argued in 'What is Poetry?', 'the word is *felt* as a word and not a mere representation of the object being named or an outburst of emotion, when words and their composition, their meaning, their external and internal form, acquire a weight and value of their own instead of referring to reality' (1934: 387, emphasis added).

In other words, Jakobson, and Prague Semiotics more generally, emphasizes the global *cultural* (or 'collective') existence of literary discourse in emphasizing the existence of 'literature' within configurations of the cultural *activity* of language. It is for this reason that Mukařovský defines art in particularly anti-formalist terms. Thus, he asserts in 'Aesthetic Function, Norm and Value,' that 'the work of art emerges, in the final analysis, as a genuine ensemble of extra-aesthetic values and as nothing else than exactly such an ensemble . . . [because] aesthetic value dissolves into the particular extra-aesthetic values and is but a global designation for the dynamic integration of their reciprocal relationships' (cited in Galan 1985: 198). For this reason, in Jakobson's terms, 'although poetry is a totality set apart by a series of specific signs and determined as a totality by its own dominant – namely, poeticity – it is at the same time a part of the higher totalities of culture and of the overall system of social values' (cited in Galan 1985: 133).

Such a relational conception of art led Prague Semiotics to examine structure on levels besides that of the poetic function. For instance, Prague Structuralism focuses upon the conative function of discourse much earlier than recent articulations of reader-response criticism, and it did so by and large by focusing on *social* rather than individual responsiveness – unlike ego psychology and versions of speech-act theory. In 'Intentionality and Unintentionality in Art' (1943–45), Mukařovský addresses the question of the reader. 'Only unintentionality,' he writes, 'with its resistance to semantic unification, is able to incite the perceiver's active attention; and only unintentionality . . . through the contact between perceiver and work, set in motion the whole of the perceiver's life experience' (cited in Galan 1985: 183). In this way, Prague Structuralism focuses on the relation between the conative and emotive functions of language to describe aesthetic experience relationally rather than formally.

In a similar way, Felix Vodička emphasizes the social role of the literary critic. The critic, for Vodička, is an individual who from the start experiences works of art with 'the consciousness of a collective (generation, milieu, etc.)' that Mukařovský describes (Galan 1985: 35). As such, the critic is 'the mediator, not only between individual aesthetic experience and the literary public, but also between the individual work and the momentary state of literary and social evolution' (Striedter 1989: 127). Vodička, Galan suggests, 'avoids the twin traps of aesthetic dogmatism, which holds that there is an ideal model that all art must approximate' – this is the 'trap' of the Kantian aesthetic ideology that plagued the New Criticism – 'and aesthetic subjectivism, which claims that all aesthetic judgments are ultimately personal and lacking general validity'. This last is an extreme of Freudian ego-psychology in a critic like Norman Holland. 'Vodička,' Galan continues, 'falls into a third snare of historical relativism, which perceives the process of change as chaotic and uncontrollable' (1985: 160). In this, he repeats Saussure's gesture of seeing history as simply the realm of accident and chance.

Prague Semiotics fell into this 'snare' precisely to the degree to which it focused on the *linguistic* structures of literary art. That is, if Prague 'structuralism' performs a critique of Russian Formalism in terms of the cultural and individual contexts in which literature is experienced, it itself is subject to the critique to which Mikhail Bakhtin and his circle subjected Formalism in the 1920s, especially in the critique of Saussurean linguistics in V.N. Vološinov's *Marxism and the Philosophy of Language* (1929). In that book (which was probably written by Bakhtin; see Clark and Holquist 1984) Vološinov critiques Saussure for focusing on *langue* as the constituent element of meaning rather than the social *functioning* of discourse best understood in terms of ideology. Much later in his career in 'The Problem of the Text in Linguistics, Philology, and the Human Sciences', Bakhtin notes that 'every utterance makes a claim to justice, sincerity, beauty, and truthfulness. . . . And these values of utterances are defined not by their relation to language (as a purely linguistic system), but by various forms of relation to reality. . . . Linguistics deals with the text, but not with the work. What it says about the work is smuggled in, and does not follow from purely linguistic analysis' (1976: 123). In Chapter 6 we will more closely examine Bakhtin's critique of semiotics from a socio–political standpoint, but it is appropriate to mention it here because it was precisely socio–political forces of German occupation in World War II and subsequent Soviet hegemony over Czechoslovakia that led to the dissolution of Prague Semiotics and the rise of French Structuralism which found its origin not in the remarkable work in literary and cultural studies in Moscow and

Prague, but in a fateful meeting between the young anthropologist Claude Lévi-Strauss and Roman Jakobson in New York. Both were in exile from the European war, and Lévi-Strauss discovered a method, in Jakobson's linguistics, for understanding the nature of human culture.

FRENCH STRUCTURALISM

The 'method' of the semiotic or structural study of myth and culture has been the life-work of Lévi-Strauss, who has studied a wide range of myths, mostly Amerindian, and has attempted to discover the structure – or what might be called the grammar – of mythological narrative. He has attempted to apply the methods of structural linguistics to narrative so that, in just the way linguistics analyses sentences, structural anthropology analyses anonymous cultural narrative discourses. A particularly influential example of his achievement is his early essay 'The Structural Study of Myth' (1955; reprinted in *Structural Anthropology* [1958]), which heavily influenced subsequent literary studies. In this essay Lévi-Strauss presents a structural analysis of narrative in which the syntagmatic dimension (the story line) is eclipsed in favour of a paradigmatic 'reading' of 'mythemes' (recurrent narrative structures) in several versions of the Oedipus story from cultures with little or no contact with one another. He isolates and codifies the structures of semantic meanings underlying the particular differing cultural contents that informed various 'versions' of the myth by conceiving of 'the true constituent units of a myth' not as 'isolated relations but *bundles of such relations*' and by conceiving that 'it is only as bundles that these relations can be put to use and combined so as to produce meaning' (1955: 211). In this analysis he abandons the possibility of a 'true version' of the myth (1955: 218) – analogous to the 'true' meanings of words etymology discovers – and instead attempts to articulate the 'combinatory variants' of mythic narratives and then 'formulate the law' of those combinations (1955: 223, 228).

His method, as he described it more fully in 'Structure and Form' (1960), follows that of linguistics so that the 'elements' of cultural narration are *structured* phenomena. As he notes in 'Structure and Form', 'we define a "universe of the tale", analyzable in pairs of oppositions interlocked within each character who – far from constituting a single entity – forms a bundle of distinctive features like the phoneme in Roman Jakobson's theory' (1960: 182). In the procedure of 'The Structural Study of Myth' – a procedure, as he says, based on relationships like those of linguistics that focus on 'the combination of sounds, not the sounds in themselves' (1955: 208) – Lévi-Strauss is *performing* his critique of humanistic readings of myth as unique expressions of the 'human spirit'. He calls these expressions 'plati-tudes' describing 'feeling common to the whole of mankind' (1955: 207). But equally important, as he came to see later, he is critiquing formalism. 'For formalism,' he writes in 'Structure and Form' (1960), 'form' and 'arbitrary content'

> must be absolutely separate, as form alone is intelligible, and content is only a residual deprived of any significant value. For structuralism, this opposition does not exist; structuralism does not treat one as abstract and the other as concrete. Form and content are of the same nature, amenable to the same type of analysis. Content receives its reality from its structure, and what is called form is a way of organizing the local structures that make up this content.   (p. 179)

In contending that form and content both have 'the same nature' and yet are distinguishable Lévi-Strauss is elaborating his assertion in 'The Structural Study of Myth' that linguistics can help cultural anthropol-ogy because 'language itself can be analyzed into things which are at the same time similar and different' (1955: 209). Moreover, the 'local structures' Lévi-Strauss mentions are *cultural* structures, and it is precisely the effacing of culture that Lévi-Strauss sees as the 'error' of formalism.

At the same time, this effacement is the focus of a recurring critique of Lévi-Strauss's structural anthropology. As Edmund Leach argues, a powerful abstract rationalism informs Lévi-Strauss's work that can be seen in both his faith in science and in the 'intelligibility' of phenomena. His rationalism takes the form of what Leach calls Lévi-Strauss's search for 'mind' as an objective 'attribute of human brains' (1970: 40). The basis for this rationalism, as we mentioned in Chapter 1, is precisely the opposition between 'nature' and 'culture', an opposition of elements which, in Lévi-Strauss's work, must be 'absolutely separate' (just as Lévi-Strauss critiques formalism for its 'absolute separation' of form and content). Later in this chapter we will examine the critique of structuralism that emphasizes this oppo-sition. Here we want to emphasize that Lévi-Strauss's rationalism, as we noted in Chapter 1, articulates the highest ambition of structural-ism and semiotics by attempting 'to transcend the contrast between the tangible and the intelligible by operating from the outset at the sign level. The function of signs is, precisely, to express the one by means of the other' (1964: 14). In this way, semiotics and structuralism as they developed in France in the 1950s and 1960s attempt, as does Prague Structuralism, to isolate and define the conditions of meaning in culture. More so than the Prague Structuralists, however, Lévi-Strauss emphasizes the *formalism* inherent in Saussure's linguistic project in his attempt to articulate the relationship between the tangible entities of nature and the intelligible meanings of culture.

This 'formal' aspect of French Structuralism – beginning with Lévi-Strauss's analyses of narrative discourse in the early 1950s in France – explains its impact on literary studies in England, America and France. (See Lentriccia 1980 for a version of this argument.) In fact, structuralism is closely related to literary formalism, as represented by both American New Criticism and Russian Formalism. The principal aim of these movements, as we have seen, was to displace 'content' in literary analysis and to focus instead on literary 'form' in a detailed manner analogous to the methods of empirical research. In this aim critique is institutional rather than transformative, Kantianism without the transcendental subject. Both movements also sought to organize the generic structures of literature into a system consistent with the inner ordering of works that close reading revealed. In each case, literature is viewed as a complex system of 'forms' analysable with considerable objectivity at different levels of generality – from the specific components of a poetic image or line through the poem's genre to that genre's place in the system of literature. New Criticism and Russian Formalism, in short, promoted the view of literature as a system and a general scientific approach to literary analysis. (Northrop Frye, as we noted in Chapter 2, called for an analogous systematization of literary studies in 'The Function of Criticism'.) This systematizing and 'scientific' impulse, especially as formulated in the linguistically oriented theories of Russian Formalism, is a major link between early modern formalism and French Structuralism of the 1960s.

The rise of structuralism was at first greeted with considerable hostility by critics in the United States and Europe. It was generally acknowledged that this movement was attempting an ambitious 'scientific' examination of literature in all its dimensions. To some, however, the supposed detachment of such an investigation appeared to be offensively anti-humanistic and unrelated to the values of a Western liberal education. Anthropologist Alfred Kroeber argued that 'structure' is a redundant concept that needs no articulation, and many literary critics judged this new movement to be an ephemeral fad. Not only was structuralism considered anti-humanistic; to the

Anglo–American world it was further suspect as a French import, merely an exotic dalliance for a few intellectuals who were arrogantly and blindly worshipping a foreignism. In 1975, however, the Modern Language Association awarded Jonathan Culler's *Structuralist Poetics* the annual James Russell Lowell prize for a literary study, and the Anglo–American academy (if not critics and readers generally) began to acknowledge that, for good or ill, structuralism was in place as a functioning critical system.

In fact, French Structuralism has proved to be a watershed in modern criticism, causing a major reorientation in literary studies. This reorientation can be seen in the functioning of cultural critique within the field of literary studies. Prior to structuralism, literary studies often seemed insular and isolated even by the standards of the humanities. After it, literary criticism seemed more actively engaged in the discourse of the human sciences, a vital participant and in some areas a guide. By basing its methods on those of linguistics, structuralism helped to condition the transformation we described in Chapter 2 of the traditional 'humanities' into what have come to be called the 'human sciences'. Moreover, in retrospect, the influence of French Structuralism on literary studies vividly dramatizes the extent to which modern criticism, in its impulse towards critique, has become an interdisciplinary phenomenon. 'Semiotics' has even come to constitute a field in itself, which takes meaning and the varying conditions of meaning as its 'objects' of study in a way that cuts through, without being confined to, traditional humanities and social sciences such as literary studies, philosophy, history, linguistics, psychology and anthropology – all the fields of cultural critique.

For this reason, the transformation of structural anthropology to structuralist literary criticism was without great difficulty and, in retrospect, almost inevitable. As a school of literary criticism, French Structuralism was dedicated to explaining literature as a system of signs and codes and the conditions which allow that system to function, including relevant cultural frames. With its intense rationalism and sophisticated models, structuralism at its inception seemed without bounds in what it could 'understand'. Like the linguistic methodology it assumed, structuralism, most importantly, has conceived of itself as a *scientific* project, assuming, as Lévi-Strauss says, the essential *intelligibility* of the phenomena it studies. This is clear in the work of A.J. Greimas, perhaps the most rigorous follower of Lévi-Strauss's structuralism. In *Structural Semantics* (1966) he attempted to widen Lévi-Strauss's structural anthropology to include *all* cultural signification, writing that 'it may be – it is a philosophic and not linguistic question – that the phenomenon of language as such is mysterious, but there are no mysteries in language' (1966: 65). For French literary structuralism (as well as structuralist linguistics and anthropology), the same assumption held. Its aim was to 'account' for literature as fully and objectively as possible, without recourse to such mysterious and unanalysable concepts as 'genius' or 'mind' (the language of Romantic subjectivity and Freudian psychology) or 'the spirit of the time' (the language of sociology) or even Steiner's 'ontological' difficulty we mentioned in Chapter 1 (the language of philosophy). If structuralism derives from, as Greimas says, the 'mysterious' *phenomenon* of language – its 'givenness' as the ground of critique – it quickly looks away from the mystery of that phenomenon to focus on language through rational, scientific analysis. Not since the Russian Formalists had literary theory aimed at such lofty theoretical goals and expected so much of itself as practical criticism. As the most ambitious movement in recent literary studies, French Structuralism in the 1960s seemed poised to explain literature in every respect and to create, as Greimas says, 'an efficient science of man' that could construct 'functional models capable of bending individuals and collectivities toward new axiological structures' of interpretation and meaningful behaviour (1966: 160).

Structuralism's strength as an analytical technique, however, was connected to what many conceive to be its major weakness. The power of structuralism derived, as Roland Barthes said, from its being 'essentially an *activity*' that could 'reconstruct an "object" in such a way as to manifest thereby the rules of functioning' (1963: 214). These rules are manifest as the 'generally intelligible' *imitation* of a literary object. By this, Barthes meant that structuralism focused on the *synchronic* dimension of a text (*langue* as opposed to *parole*), the specific ways in which a text is like other texts. The structural comparison of texts is based on similarities of function (character development, plot, theme, ideology, and so on), relationships of 'the same nature' (Lévi-Strauss 1960: 179) that Lévi-Strauss called *homologies*. The predominantly synchronic analysis of homologies recreates the text as a paradigm, a timeless system of structural possibilities. Following these precepts, Todorov, to take this one example again, attempts to *position* the fantastic as a genre within a configuration of other literary genres.

A more rigorous example of literary structuralism is Greimas's *Maupassant: The Semiotics of Text*, a book-length analysis of Maupassant's six-page story 'Two Friends'. Especially useful as an example, this book is governed by the achievement of Prague Structuralism as well as Lévi-Strauss's work. In his important essay entitled 'Poetry of Grammar and Grammar of Poetry' (1968) Roman Jakobson argues that the very grammar of poetry is inhabited by what he calls the 'intense dramatization' of poetic art.

> Any unbiased, attentive, exhaustive, total description of the selection, distribution and interrelation of the diverse morphological classes and syntactic constructions in a given poem surprises the examiner himself by unexpected, striking symmetries and antisymmetries, balanced structures, efficient accumulations of equivalent forms and salient contrasts . . . [which] permit us to follow the masterly interplay of the actualized constituents. (p. 127).

It is precisely such a structuralist, semiotic analysis – attentive, exhaustive and striking – that Greimas pursues in *Maupassant*. As Paul Perron notes in the Introduction to Greimas's book, its subtitle, 'A Demonstration,' announces Greimas's aim of presenting an analysis of a literary text analogous to a 'scientific demonstration' (Greimas 1976: xv). *Maupassant* is indeed a tour de force of the highest order in its reading of Maupassant's short story, parallel to Jakobson's readings of the many poems he analysed – for instance Jakobson's structuralist analyses of Baudelaire's 'Les Chats', written with Lévi-Strauss, a Shakespeare sonnet, Yeats's 'Sorrow of Love', Pushkin's poems, and Blake (Jakobson 1987). Jakobson demonstrates what Greimas calls 'a certain way of approaching texts, with procedures of segmentation, with the identification of certain regularities and especially with models of predictability of narrative organization, models which can be applied, in principle, to all types of texts' (1976: xxiii).

By 'all types of texts' Greimas means prose as well as poetry, and early in *Maupassant* he describes the difference between 'poetic' discourse and 'logical' discourse to shed light on structuralist readings of literary texts. Jakobson defines poetry and the 'poetic function' as the projection of 'the principle of equivalence from the axis of selection into the axis of combination' (1960: 71), and Greimas argues that this definition remains 'vague' and attempts to replace it with 'precise grammatical definitions' (1976: 11). He writes:

> The existence of discourse, and not of a series of independent sentences, can be reaffirmed only if we can postulate a common isotopy, recognizable through the recurrence of a category or of a network of linguistic categories as it unfolds, for the totality of sentences constituting it. We are therefore inclined to think that 'logical' discourse must be supported by an anaphoric network which, by referring back to each sentence, guarantees its topical permanence. On the contrary, poetic discourse – especially if it consciously attempts to 'abolish syntax' – because of the omission of marks of recurrence, manifests a certain

143

grammatical incoherence at the surface level. Between these two extremes we can find all sorts of discourses that can be said to be imperfect in relation to the ideality of the grammatical forms we postulate for them.   (p. 9)

Greimas situates his analysis of 'Two Friends' between these extremes in his attempt to join together the more *formal* 'grammatical' studies of poetry pursued by Jakobson and the 'syntactical' study of folktales developed by Lévi-Strauss and himself. In other words, in *Maupassant* Greimas brings together formalism and structuralism in a 'demonstration' of the semiotic functioning of texts.

That demonstration is impressive especially in addressing the difficulty of semiotic analyses of discourse. That difficulty, Greimas has noted, is to find ways of equating in importance discursive elements of uneven length – ways of discovering what Lévi-Strauss calls 'things which are at the same time similar and different' (1955: 209). The 'system we have introduced over the last fifteen years to indicate subdivisions and sub-articulations of semiotic or linguistic texts', he writes in *Maupassant*, 'serves no other purpose' (1976: 230). Such a 'system' began with the assertion in *Structural Semantics* that 'discourse, conceived as a hierarchy of units of communication fitting into one another, contains in itself the negation of that hierarchy by the fact that the units of communication with different dimensions can be at the same time recognized as equivalent' (1966: 82). Jakobson's definition of the poetic function – the projection of *equivalence* onto syntax – avoids this problem by making the poetic function the principle of poeticity altogether.

In treating 'Two Friends', however, Greimas is forced to demonstrate this projection in his very method of analysis. He does so by superimposing similarity and difference in reading a literary text. The 'similarity' within a text – the sense that it is 'whole' and that, whatever its length, it finally conveys a *unified* impression on the reader – Greimas calls the isotopy of discourse. The difference within a text is the felt sense that, no matter how 'unified' its experience, it also conveys a sense of distinguishable parts. In *Maupassant* he accomplishes this complex superimposition by developing procedures of 'engagement' and 'disengagement' along with the conception of 'isotopy' (first developed in *Structural Semantics*). Disengagement detaches an utterance from the situation of enunciation, 'the subject, the place, and the time of the enunciation' (Greimas and Courtés 1979: 88). Engagement creates the conditions that can make 'an effect of identification between the subject of the utterance and the subject of the enunciation' (1979: 100).

In focusing as it does on both the differences of discourse and its isotopy, *Maupassant* offers an unbiased, attentive, exhaustive, total description of Maupassant's story and, at the same time, an unbiased, attentive, exhaustive (if not quite 'total') description of the methodology of a 'semiotics of text' that includes but goes beyond the 'grammar' of poetry to the 'semantics' of discursive meaning. As in Jakobson's analyses, Greimas (and his readers) are 'agreeably surprised' (1976: 241) by the thoroughness of the 'striking' discoveries of meaning and systems of meaning 'everywhere' in 'Two Friends', from the smallest details of colour and narrative glances to the largest 'cosmological' orders of signification (1976: 242). Like the alternative contrasts and combinations of structural linguistics, *Maupassant* offers the rigorous analyses of contrasting disengagement and engagement of the narrative and, in doing so, describes the global combinations of its isotopic significance.

Greimas's *Maupassant*, in its pretensions to scientific rigour, its revelation of single (isotopic) principles governing disparate phenomena, and its thoroughness – the principles of 'economy of explanation; unity of solution; and ability to reconstruct the whole from a fragment' that Lévi-Strauss describes as governing 'any kind of structural analysis' (1955: 211) – stands as an elaborate example of literary structuralism. (Roland Barthes' *S/Z*, published several years before *Maupassant*, works as a parody of this 'scientific' enterprise; see Schleifer 1987: 150–1 for a discussion of this parody.) *Maupassant* also demonstrates structuralism's undeniable achievement in practical criticism, as does Roland Barthes' work in charting a course through the early and late stages of structuralism, semiotic theory, the system of fashion, narrative structure, textuality, and many other topics (even if, as we have suggested, in a later 'post-structuralist' phase he goes 'beyond' structuralism in using the methods and procedures of structuralism to very different ends). Tzvetan Todorov, as we have seen, has also contributed to the understanding of narrative structure, genre theory, and the theory of symbolism. Further, in semiotic approaches to semantic theory, closely allied to structuralism, there is significant work by Michael Riffaterre, Umberto Eco, Gerard Genette, Jonathan Culler and others that constitutes important achievements in modern criticism.

THE CRITIQUE OF STRUCTURALISM

Structuralism's self-imposed limitations, especially its focus on general systems rather than on individual cases and, in its French and

American manifestations, its lack of concern with diachronic change – all of which marks its Kantian tendency to veer away from transformative critique – became increasingly evident in the late 1960s. The French philosopher Jacques Derrida offered a particularly decisive critique, a central example of which is 'Structure, Sign, and Play in the Discourse of the Human Sciences' (1966), and *Of Grammatology* (1967) which focuses on the structural anthropology of Lévi-Strauss. In 'Structure, Sign, and Play' Derrida connects structuralism to a traditional Western blindness to the 'structurality' of structure (1966: 248), an unwillingness to examine the theoretical and ideological implications of 'structure' as a concept. Derrida points out that the attempt to investigate structure implies the ability to stand outside and apart from it – as if one could move outside of cultural understanding in order to take a detached view of culture. In specific terms, Derrida's critique of Lévi-Strauss is a critique of the privileging of the opposition between 'nature' and 'culture' – what Lévi-Strauss calls in a different context the tangible and the intelligible. Derrida claims that Lévi-Strauss sets up this opposition as the very *enabling* opposition for his whole scientific project, yet 'in the very first pages of the *Elementary Structures* [*of Kinship*], Lévi-Strauss . . . encounters something which no longer tolerates the nature/culture opposition he has accepted' and rather seems at once both 'natural' and 'cultural' – namely, the incest-prohibition fundamental to the *Elementary Structures* (1966: 253).

In the next chapter we will closely examine Derrida's philosophic deconstruction of conceptual frameworks such as Lévi-Strauss's, so here we will merely note that Derrida's critique of Lévi-Strauss specifically and structuralism more generally is a critique of an apparent absolutism in the conception of binary oppositions – what Derrida describes as the apprehension of difference as opposition. In 'Structure, Sign, and Play' Derrida critiques the unexamined premise of Lévi-Strauss's scientific objectivity. Because one never transcends culture, Derrida argues, a scientifically objective examination of culture and meaning can never take place from the outside; there is no 'outside' or standing free of structure (and 'culture' and 'meaning'), no so-called 'natural' state free of the structural interplay that, in the structuralist analysis, constitutes meaning – in short, no objective examination of structure. Therefore, as Derrida shows, the attempt to 'read' and to 'interpret' cultural structures cannot be adequately translated into exacting scientific models. And if 'structure' cannot be isolated and examined, then structuralism is seriously undermined as a method.

Nevertheless, structuralism and semiotics have learned from the critique of the structuralist enterprise concerning the enabling assumption of the opposition between the tangible and the intelligible, nature and culture. The development of structuralism can be seen in Derrida's work as well as in Roland Barthes's career spanning structuralism and post-structuralism (from the rigorous linguistic analyses of *Mythologies* [1957] and *Elements of Semiology* [1964] to the post-structuralist playfulness of *S/Z* [1970] and *Roland Barthes by Roland Barthes* [1975]). However, the work of Julia Kristeva shows most clearly the labour of transformative critique within structuralism. 'What semiotics has discovered in studying "ideologies" (myths, rituals, moral codes, arts, etc.) as sign systems,' she writes, 'is that the *law* governing, or, if one prefers, the *major constraint* affecting any social practice lies in the fact that signifies' (1973: 25). Kristeva argues that semiotics has produced a form of cultural critique and has reached the 'crucial point . . . of its possible deployment as a critique of its own presuppositions' (1973: 27). Semiotics itself, as she argued earlier, not only 'models' phenomena in the same way the sciences do but also produces 'the theory of its own model-making'. That is, 'semiotics cannot harden into *a* science let alone into *the* science, for it is an open form of research, a constant critique that turns back on itself and offers its own auto-critique' (1969: 77).

Kristeva enacts this critique in writings that transgress the opposition between literature and non-literature as that opposition has often seemed to govern our own exposition in this book. In 'Stabat Mater' (from *Tales of Love*), for instance, Kristeva (1976) presents an analysis of the cultural concept of the Virgin Mary and, more generally, 'motherhood' itself in what Mikhail Bakhtin could call a 'double-voiced' discourse (Bakhtin 1935: 341; see also Toril Moi [1986] for the importance of Bakhtin to Kristeva's use and critique of structuralism). In this essay Kristeva presents two discourses in separate columns on the page that seemingly do and do not intersect, versions of Lévi-Strauss's 'culture' and 'nature'. The first is a 'scholarly' examination of the Virgin Mary's history in Western culture, and the second is a largely autobiographical 'experience' of motherhood that is not quite private but rather the 'collective' species 'experience'. Our language here, with all these quotation marks, is particularly tortured because in 'Stabat Mater' (as elsewhere) Kristeva is attempting to present a third-person account of 'culture' and a first-person articulation of something that transgresses ordinary linguistic usages based, as they seem to be, on some form of the distinction between culture and nature.

Clifford Geertz comes close to analytically describing the element in Kristeva of *collective* experience that does not oppose itself to individual experience in describing the *difficulty* of cultural analysis. 'What the ethnographer is in fact faced with,' Geertz writes, '. . . is a multiplicity of complex conceptual structures, any of them superimposed upon or knotted into one another, which are at once strange, irregular, and inexplicit, and which he must contrive somehow first to grasp and then to render' (1973: 10). In 'Stabat Mater' Kristeva is attempting to 'grasp' both 'mother' as cultural concept and the biology of 'primary narcissism' (1976: 235) – the cultural semiotics of the Virgin Mother and a discursive articulation of the 'experience' of motherhood that is almost pre-linguistic. The 'natural' discourse here is that of the 'tangible' rather than the 'intelligible', for motherhood is described as the birth of 'pain', as 'rhythmic' and essentially bodily (1976: 241). 'A woman,' she writes, 'is neither nomadic nor a male body that considers itself earthly only in erotic passion' (1976: 254). Instead, motherhood emphasizes the material, corporeal nature of human life, the (natural) 'otherness' to intelligibility itself.

Against this 'natural' reading of motherhood, Kristeva describes its most 'cultural' manifestations in the Catholic Church. Parallel to the 'natural' articulation, Mary's 'motherhood' is analysed as a semiotic phenomenon. That is, Kristeva describes the 'position' of the Virgin like that of the fantastic in Todorov's analysis or Greimas's positioning of the actors of 'Two Friends' as subjects and anti-subjects of cosmological wars between life and death. In Kristeva's argument, the Virgin Mother is in a position of structural 'homology' with the positions of the Father and the Son of the Trinity (1976: 245). As well as positioning the Virgin semiotically, she also examines the social function of the Virgin in different historical contexts, and the tradition itself in relation to a mistranslation from the Semitic term that means a young unmarried woman into the Greek term for 'the physiological and psychological condition of virginity' – an example of the arbitrary nature of the sign with a vengeance (1976: 236–7). Finally, even the opposition between nature and culture is explored as a *determining condition* of the semiotic concepts of 'mother' and 'virgin mother' in that 'a woman as mother . . . changes culture into nature, the speaking [mind] into biology' (1976: 259).

Yet within this semiotic analysis the opposition between nature and culture becomes problematic in these two discourses in just the way Derrida suggests it does for structuralism generally. At the heart of the semiotics of motherhood – its analysis as a cultural phenomenon susceptible to rigorous structuration – Kristeva discusses the tears and milk of the mother. 'They are,' she writes, 'the metaphors of nonspeech, of a "semiotics" that linguistic communication does not account for' (1976: 249). This 'natural', 'material' aspect of mother-hood is 'repressed', she claims, in the semiotic analysis, which she relocates in the bodily experience of separation from the mother – a pre-Oedipal splitting without the benefit of a transcendent signifier. For this reason, it is something we can apprehend only retroactively within language (hence all our quotation marks); it is that aspect of the *power* of language – what Herman Rapaport has called the 'spell' of discourse (1985) – that structural linguistics cannot account for. Although, as Kristeva claims, this is repressed in the semiotic analysis, it returns both in the analytical dimension of this text and in the autobiographical discourse 'outside' (or alongside) it. Similarly, 'semiotics' finds its way into the 'natural' bold-faced discourse of motherhood when it creates a way of examining 'the bipolar structure of belief' (1976: 252), the opposition between the passionate 'intelligibility' of the Word and the proverbial 'tangibility' and immediacy of mother-love. Such proverbiality is the element of the self-evident that critique attempts to question, but which, as here, finds multiple ways of returning to understanding and discourse.

In other words, Kristeva offers a structural/semiotic analysis which is informed by both structuralism and that tendency within structuralism that leads to post-structuralism – that is, by both the scientific method of semiotics, its existence as an institutional critique, and the deconstructive extension of that method. Her essay *grounds* itself in the semiotic 'discovery' that discourse and language are the basis for social formations and institutions – even 'formations' as philosophically general as religious ontology and as private and personal as birth giving. In Kristeva's work the opposition between social and personal, public and private, is *transformed* in the suggestion that the 'private' is also 'collective' – experience that is not representable, yet because it is situated in the field of representation it makes the 'semiotic' a crucial place of cultural production antedating ego-formation, desire and language.

In the transformation of its own grounding oppositions, 'Stabat Mater' presents 'a transgression of systematicity' (1973: 29) which articulates 'its own auto-critique' (1969: 77). Such a transformative critique is immanent in the institutional 'scientific' critique of structuralism. That is, by situating critique on the level of collective cultural institutions – language, meaning, even the phenomenality of feeling – semiotics creates the possibility of imagining institutions, including the institutions of self-evident 'truths' and ideas we will examine in the next chapter, different from themselves. Such difference transforms language, meaning and the phenomenality of feeling – those things at the heart of literary studies – in a way that changes literary criticism and the history of philosophy into genealogies of transformative critique. In this, structuralism and semiotics demonstrate their importance to contemporary cultural and literary studies even if, like Kantian critique, they possess a strong element of seeming disinterestedness that often functions to sever literary and cultural studies. It is precisely a critique of such disinterested objectivity and the separation between aesthetic and interested experience that poststructural critical philosophy pursues.

CHAPTER FIVE

Deconstruction, Post-structuralism and the Critique of Philosophy

Philosophy has an essential relation to time: it is always against its time, critique of the present world. The philosopher creates concepts that are neither eternal nor historical but untimely and not of the present.

Gilles Deleuze,
Nietzsche and Philosophy

The preceding chapter ended with a discussion of Jacques Derrida's 'deconstructive' critique of structuralism in relation to 'Structure, Sign, and Play in the Discourse of the Human Sciences'. We also discussed how Julia Kristeva used and transformed that critique in her semiotic analysis of motherhood in the West, pointing out an important difference between structuralism and post-structuralism. Structuralism and semiotics, unlike the critical philosophy of Derrida with its orgins in Nietzsche and Heidegger and its analogies with Wittgenstein and at least certain strains of literary criticism, are firmly embedded in the Kantian tradition of Western thought and science. Their aim, exemplary of Western thought, is to find ways of 'understanding' phenomena through models of explanation that offer coherent pictures of the order of things, a picture which embodies what Michel Foucault calls a 'principle of . . . unity' (1969: 111). As Jonathan Culler comments on the relation between Derrida and the English philosopher J.L. Austin, the aim of understanding is to master the context of whatever is to be understood. 'Meaning,' Culler writes, 'is context-bound' (1982: 123). Kristeva treads close to the limits of this project in her attempt to describe the materiality of motherhood – the creaturely pre-representational (as opposed to intellectual or spiritual) nature of mothering – which she identifies as a dimension of 'otherness'. In her essay she multiplies contexts *almost* to the point

151

of incoherence. Even there, however, can be seen the great project of structuralism and semiotics, to 'account for' cultural practices and their 'conditions' of existence.

The aim of Derrida's philosophical critique is different from this project. Instead of attempting to account for how things are, their order, Derrida aims to describe the limits of understanding. In 'The Search for Grounds in Literary Study', J. Hillis Miller writes that 'the fundamental sense of [a deconstructive] "critique" [is] discriminating testing out' (1985: 30). A deconstructive critique examines and tests the assumptions supporting intellectual insight in order to interrogate the 'self-evident' truths on which they are based. It tests the legitimacy of the contextual 'bounds' that understanding both presents and requires. Rather than seeking a way of understanding, a way of incorporating new phenomena into coherent existing or modified models, deconstructive critique seeks to uncover the unexamined axioms that give rise to those models and their boundaries.

NIETZSCHEAN CRITIQUE

Such a critique differs significantly from the institutional critique of language we examined in Chapter 4, even while sharing a good deal with that critique. Those similarities and differences can be seen in the work of Friedrich Nietzsche, and especially in the method of *genealogy* that we introduced in Chapter 1 – a concept, as we noted in relation to Raymond Williams, that is closely related to linguistic etymology. Trained as a philologist, and studying the place of discourse in thought and culture, Nietzsche often undertakes the philological examinations of particular words and concepts. In *The Genealogy of Morals* (1887), a short volume consisting of three essays exploring the genealogy of moral conceptions such as 'good', 'evil', 'guilt', the phenomenon of 'bad conscience' and the meaning of 'ascetic ideals', he investigates the relation between words and concepts and the connection between philosophical genealogy and linguistic analysis. '*What light,*' Nietzsche explicitly asks in the *Genealogy*, '*does linguistics, and especially the study of etymology, throw on the history of the evolution of moral concepts?*' (1887: 55). As a kind of response to this question he argues that 'it is of no small interest to ascertain that through those words and roots which designate "good" there frequently still shines the most important nuance by virtue of which the noble felt themselves to be men of higher rank' (1887: 27).

There is a striking difference between Nietzsche's philosophical critique and Saussure's linguistic critique – the difference between Nietzsche's attempt at a transvaluation of value and Saussure's attempt at a scientific accounting. Like Saussure, Nietzsche, in his critique of nineteenth-century philosophy, is most interested in the *conceptual* aspect of words that are governed not by the similarities between words – the 'sameness' of meaning – that diachronic linguistics focused upon, but by the *differences* that inhabit language. But rather than the systematic, 'scientific' critique that Saussure offers, Nietzsche's genealogical critique leads to a critique of what he calls in the *Genealogy* 'the will to truth'. 'The will to truth,' he writes, 'requires a critique – let us thus define our own task – the value of truth must be for once experimentally *called into question*' (1887: 153). In *Beyond Good and Evil* he asks, '*what* in us really wants "truth"? . . . Granted we want truth: *why not rather* untruth? and uncertainty? even ignorance?' (1886: 9). As part of this critique Nietzsche redefines the will to truth in *The Will to Power* as 'essentially an art of interpretation' (1901: 317). By making truth and reason the very object of critique, the concept or 'method' of genealogy in Nietzsche is directly a response to and a reworking of Kant's critical philosophy. It is a critique of Kant's attempt, as Rorty says, to establish philosophy as a *scientific* endeavour that is rigorous, generalizing, and grounded in reason (Rorty 1982: 141–46).

This critical project makes Nietzsche's purpose two-fold. In a critique of the will to truth he is 'rewriting', as Gilles Deleuze argues, Kant's *Critique of Pure Reason* (Deleuze 1962: 88). But at the same time he is also criticizing the positivism of nineteenth-century science and philosophy that takes *positive facts* (including the so-called factual nature of words that Saussure critiques) as the substance of the 'true'. In a way, then, the *Genealogy of Morals*, with its first essay exploring, philologically, the words 'good' and 'evil', its second examining the psychology of 'bad conscience', its third examining the phenomenon of religion, and its whole developing the concept/method of 'genealogy' throughout, recapitulates our own project of examining criticism and critique within the frameworks of language, psychology, philosophy and history. In this analogy the simultaneous critique of positivism is parallel to our discussion of humanism and pedagogy in Chapter 2 and, more generally, to Arnold's critique of positivism embodied in his critique of the terrible learning of Newman's Homer. In other words, Nietzsche's two-fold genealogical analysis directs its criticism at the 'truth' (and the 'will to truth') in Kant's critiques and at the 'real' world that nineteenth-century positive science attempted to describe and manipulate.

Unlike the logic and reason governing Kant's critiques and the relentless reference to existing 'facts' in positivism, genealogy above all seeks to trace the *conditions* governing concepts, behaviours and values. These 'conditions' are historical (rather than logical inferences), but at the same time they exist *in relation to* the concepts, behaviours, and values Nietzsche examines (rather than as positive, factual aspects of those things). 'A certain amount of historical and philological schooling,' Nietzsche writes, 'together with an inborn fastidiousness of taste in respect to psychological questions in general, soon transformed my problem [the problem of 'where' good and evil originate] into another one: under what conditions did man devise these value judgments good and evil? *and what value do they themselves possess?*' (1887: 17). To question the conditions governing the emergence of moral values and to question the value that seems to be, at first glance, self-evidently *part* of concepts – their very 'definition' – is both the method and conception of Nietzsche's genealogy. That is, genealogy brings together semiotics and history in precisely the way that Saussurean structuralism – or, for that matter, Kant's *scientific* philosophy – separates them. If science, as Rorty says, traces 'inferential chains between [general] principles and more particular . . . propositions' (1982: 141) – as Saussure does in applying the principle of binary oppositions in language to concrete linguistic phenomena or Kant does by applying the principles of impersonality and universality to the definition of 'truth' (as opposed to the particularity of the 'real') – then genealogy disrupts the causal hierarchy between principle and example.

It does so by describing concepts and principles – in a manner similar to Saussure's description of the 'elements' of language – as always susceptible to further *relational* analysis, always significant in relation to something outside themselves, the 'conditions' under which they arise. In this way, the 'inferential' relationship between principle and example, the relationship between general concept and historical fact, is confused. Discussing the concept 'punishment' (which, he says, 'possesses in fact not *one* meaning but a whole synthesis of "meanings"'), Nietzsche argues that 'today it is impossible to say for certain *why* people are really punished: all concepts in which an entire process is semiotically concentrated elude definition; only that which has no history is definable' (1887: 80). Earlier, in *The Wanderer and his Shadow*, he had described words as 'pockets into which now this and now that has been put, and now many things at once' (1880; cited in 1887: 180). In these linguistic examples, the *universality* of the truth and of facts is questioned.

Genealogy also questions the *impersonality* of the 'truth' of concepts and of the 'reality' of facts. Such questioning is ineluctably *historical*. As Nietzsche said a little earlier in the *Genealogy* (1887):

> . . . there is for historiography of any kind no more important proposition than the one . . . which really *ought to be* established now: the cause of the origin of a thing and its eventual utility, in actual employment and place in a system of purposes, lie worlds apart; whatever exists, having somehow come into being, is again and again reinterpreted to new ends, taken over, transformed, and redirected by some power superior to it; all events in the organic world are a subduing, a *becoming master*, and all subduing and becoming master involve a fresh interpretation, an adaptation through which any previous 'meaning' and 'purpose' are necessarily obscured or even obliterated. . . .   (p. 77)

This description, like those of structuralism and semiotics, presents phenomena (here intellectual phenomena) as best defined in terms of their function, in terms, that is, of a schema of *means and ends* rather than the positivist schema of *cause and effect*. The positivist schema necessarily hypostatizes causes by making them the subjects of sentences, the 'agents' of events. Nietzsche criticizes causality in the *Genealogy* as the assertion of a false ' "being" behind doing, effecting, becoming' (1887: 45).

Yet while he criticizes such understanding by describing phenomena functionally (as simply deeds, effects, and the 'becoming' of phenomena itself), unlike structuralists and semioticians, Nietzsche goes on in the next paragraph to situate this 'functional' analysis within a framework of struggles of powers and purposes – a framework of interests which cannot be 'impersonal'. In other words, if the functionalism of semiotics satisfies itself with a critique of linguistic positivism that 'understands' linguistic phenomena without asking the further question of the wider purposes to which linguistic phenomena are put – without examining the wider 'meaning' of linguistic phenomena *within* the 'interhuman milieu' Benveniste describes – then Nietzschean genealogical critique goes beyond precisely this satisfaction with 'understanding', this seeming 'will to truth'. Nietzsche goes on (1887):

> 'purposes and utilities,' are only *signs* that a will to power has become master of something less powerful and imposed upon it the character of a function; and the entire history of a 'thing,' an organ, a custom can in this way be a continuous sign-chain of ever new interpretations and adaptations whose causes do not even have to be related to one another but, on the contrary, in some cases succeed and alternate with one

> another in a purely chance fashion. The 'evolution' of a thing, a custom, an organ is thus by no means its *progressus* toward a goal, even less a logical *progressus* by the shortest route and with the smallest expenditure of force – but a succession of more or less profound, more or less mutually independent processes of subduing, plus the resistances they encounter, the attempts at transformation for the purpose of defense and reaction, and the results of successful counteractions. The form is fluid, but the 'meaning' is even more so.   (pp. 77–8)

Nietzsche situates the 'functionalism' of semiotics within the study of its history, its changing (as opposed to its *universal*) forms. But he does so not in order to examine, scientifically – which is to say, as he says here, 'progressively', 'logically', 'economically' ('with the smallest expenditure of force') – the 'conditions' governing the emergence and existence of meaning. This *impersonal* scientific aim is the project of structuralism and semiotics: the criteria Nietzsche articulates are the same as those we described governing 'science' in Chapter 1. (With the introduction of 'chance' in this description, even the empirical criterion of an 'exhaustive' accounting of phenomena is countered in Nietzsche.) Instead of presenting a scientific accounting, then, Nietzsche traces the *place* of meaning within the changing contours of cultural relationships and values – within the framework of forces, power and activity that is neither universal nor impersonal.

For this reason Nietzsche's conception of history does not comprise simply positive 'facts' and 'events'. 'The fact,' he writes in *On The Use and Abuse of History*, 'is always dull, at all times more like a calf than a god' (1873: 53). 'The virtuous man,' he adds, 'will always rise against the blind force of facts, the tyranny of the actual' (1873: 54). Later, in the *Genealogy*, he argues further that 'fact' is 'only an interpretation' (1887: 129) and that the will to truth (the *'faith in truth'* [1887: 150]) embodies 'that *desire* to halt before the factual, the *factum brutum* . . . that general renunciation of all interpretation (of forcing, adjusting, abbreviating, omitting, padding, inventing, falsifying, and whatever else is the *essence* of interpreting) – [a renunciation which] . . . expresses, broadly speaking, as much ascetic virtue as any denial of sensuality' (1887: 151). In other words, Nietzsche's genealogy attempts to explore not only 'under what conditions did man devise [conceptual] value judgments' (1887: 17) – *conditions* which are never universal – but also the very judgment attributing 'objectivity' and 'factuality' to phenomena – *judgment* that is never impersonal. Michel Foucault (1971) notes in his study of Nietzschean 'genealogy' that

> an event . . . is not a decision, a treaty, a reign, or a battle, but the reversal of a relationship of the forces, the usurpation of power, the

appropriation of a vocabulary turned against those who had once used it. . . . The world we know is not [an] ultimately simple configuration where events are reduced to accentuate their essential traits, their final meaning, or their initial and final value. On the contrary, it is a profusion of entangled events. . . . [T]he true historical sense confirms our existence among countless lost events, without a landmark or a point of reference.   (pp. 153–4).

NIETZSCHE AND ART

The double critique of Nietzsche's genealogy directed against impersonal positivism and universal (Kantian) philosophy is most clear in his treatment of art and aesthetic experience. In an important section of the *Genealogy of Morals* Nietzsche subjects the Kantian notion of the 'disinterestedness' of art we touched upon in Chapter 2 – what Paul de Man later came to understand as the 'aesthetic ideology' governing literary and philosophical studies in the twentieth century in his 'critique of the aesthetic' (1984: 136; and Norris 1988: Ch. 2). 'Kant,' Nietzsche writes, 'thought he was honoring art when among the predicates of beauty he emphasized and gave prominence to those which establish the honor of knowledge: impersonality and universality' (1887: 103). 'That is beautiful,' Nietzsche quotes Kant as saying, 'which gives us pleasure *without interest*' (1887: 104).

Nietzsche ridicules this definition of the disinterestedness of art as touched 'with the naiveté of a country parson'. In its place, he presents Stendhal's definition of beauty as the 'promise of happiness' (1887: 104). The 'promise' of this definition of beauty is always personal – it is always a promise of personal fulfilment – and the concept of 'happiness' in it always describes particular ends rather than a general and universal conceptual abstraction. The example Nietzsche gives to demonstrate this is Schopenhauer's *use* of Kant's conception of the disinteresedness of art for personal and particular ends. In Schopenhauer the 'disinterestedness' of art is reinterpreted 'to new ends, taken over, transformed, and redirected by some power superior to it' (1887: 77). Art, for Schopenhauer, serves the particular end of 'calming' his own '*sexual* "interestedness"' so that in Schopenhauer the very "disinterestedness" of beauty gave pleasure precisely 'from an "interested" viewpoint, even from the very strongest, most personal interest: that of a tortured man who gains release from his torture' (1887: 104, 105–6).

In arguing that even a conception of the 'disinterestedness' of art can be employed to serve personal and particular interests, Nietzsche is attempting to 'reinterpret' art 'from the point of view of the artist (creator)' (1887: 103). He does this not so much to glorify the artist as to take over and transform the problem of aesthetics from a framework of *passive* and objective behaviour, to one of forceful ('powerful') activity. As Deleuze says, 'Nietzsche demands an aesthetics of creation, the aesthetics of Pygmalion' (1962: 102). (As we will see, such an 'aesthetics' becomes, as Hillis Miller argues in *Versions of Pygmalion*, an 'ethics' of art precisely because it entails personal interests along with seeming impersonal experience.) Nietzsche's philosophy, Deleuze writes, has 'three fundamental points', and 'Nietzsche attaches so much importance to art because art realises the whole of this programme' (1962: 196). Deleuze articulates the points of this programme negatively to underline the *critical* (and, we might add, the *ethical*) nature of Nietzsche's genealogy: 'not the true nor the real but evaluation; not affirmation as acceptance but as creation; not man but the Overman as a new form of life' (1962: 185). The first of these points, in contrasting interpretive evaluation (and the manifestation of power in such evaluation) with the 'true' of Kantian philosophy and the 'real' of positivism, emphasizes the double critique in Nietzsche we have been describing. The second point emphasizes a Nietzschean conception and method of critique in contrast to the institutional critique of Kant. The third point, in focusing on the forms of life, emphasizes the ethical nature of critique in relation to philosophy and literary studies.

Kant, Deleuze argues, 'merely pushed a very old conception of critique to the limit, a conception which saw critique as a force which should be brought to bear on all claims to knowledge and truth, but not on knowledge and truth themselves; a force which should be brought to bear on all claims of morality, but not on morality itself' (1962: 89). This critique, Deleuze says, becomes a 'politics of compromise'. It ends up *accepting* the status quo instead of transforming it – 'transvaluing' it in Nietzsche's term – into 'a new form of life'. 'The point of critique', Deleuze says, 'is not justification but a different way of feeling: another sensibility' (1962: 94), 'another way of knowing, another concept of truth' (1962: 99). Such critique confuses aesthetics ('feeling'), espistemology ('knowing'), and ethics ('morality'). Thus Deleuze argues that Kant's is a 'false critique' (1962: 197) precisely because it separates these areas of concern. In terms of the two forms of critique we described in Chapter 1, we might better say that Kant's critique is institutional while that of Nietzsche is 'transformative'. And it is in this distinction that the Kantian impulse within the *scientific* project of structuralism and semiotics is most clear, and the critique of that project in 'post-structuralism' is also clear. For if structuralism attempts to describe the 'truth' of meaning, then post-structuralism – taking its impetus, as it often does, in Nietzsche's critique of the will to truth (in philosophy) and the impersonality and universality of Kantian aesthetic ideology (in literature) – attempts to transform ways of knowing and the conception of truth. It does so in conceptions of the true and the real which are neither impersonal nor universal but of the realm in which the personal and the universal come into conflict, the realm of ethics and culture.

DECONSTRUCTION

Such a conception of critique entails the striking – and, to many, the disturbing – abandonment of the opposition, implicit in Kant, between literature and philosophy. As Richard Rorty says, in the Nietzschean, post-structuralist project philosophy becomes 'a kind of writing' in which the very borders that govern scientific inquiry – in the linguistic terms Greimas uses in *Maupassant*, the very procedures of 'segmentation' that define the 'object' of investigation – break down. This breakdown is implicit in the doubling of critique in Nietzsche, the critique of Kantian idealism as well as positive materialism.

Deconstruction is a mode of critique in this broad sense. It was named in the 1960s by Jacques Derrida, who in 1967 began to describe certain events he saw taking place in the history of philosophy, that is, events in Western modes of conceiving and articulating knowledge. In sweeping analyses, Derrida notes that embodiments of 'legitimate' authority have traditionally been taken to be self-evident in their absolute 'rightness', as is the case with concepts such as 'goodness', 'purity', 'naturalness' and 'truth'. The same is true of more abstract versions of authority such as (in Derrida's examples) '*aletheia*, transcendentality, consciousness, or conscience, God, man, and so forth' (1966: 249) – all assumed in the West to be self-evident givens of understanding and 'correct'. He also argues that such concepts are necessarily defined in relation to their opposites. Further, Derrida explains in 'Structure, Sign and Play', that authority in the West is generally conceived as existing in a structure and thought to be the precise *centre* 'at which the substitution of contents, elements, or terms is no longer possible' (1966: 248). 'It has always been

159

thought,' Derrida writes, 'that [this] center, which is by definition unique, constituted that very thing within a structure which governs the structure, while escaping structurality' (1966: 248). Certain aspects of understanding, in other words, are themselves taken to be self-evidently 'true'. Thus, the concept of 'centre', or foundation of knowledge, is an epistemologically immovable point, on which structures and hierarchies of belief or understanding have been thought to be based or securely 'centred' or 'grounded'.

Most importantly, Derrida argues that this 'centre' – a conception which he says in a telling phrase is 'contradictorily coherent' (1966: 248) – has traditionally taken on two manifestations which correspond to the critiques of scientific functionalism and positive humanism we have seen in Nietzsche. In each case, as Derrida says, 'centre' was understood to be an 'origin' – 'a truth or an origin which is free from freeplay and forms the order of the sign' (1966: 250). In one case, the original is *structurally* conceived – that is, conceived as a function of structurality – and it corresponds to the grammatical structure (or what de Man calls the 'semiology' [1979: 6]) of meaning. In a second case, the original is *humanly* (or referentially) conceived – that is, conceived as an intention of a person. For this reason Derrida's critique of Western philosophy, like that of Nietzsche, has been two-fold. On the one hand he has subjected structuralism – especially the structuralism of Claude Lévi-Strauss (as in 'Structure, Sign, and Play') and that of Saussure as well – to his deconstructive critique. On the other hand he has also subjected Continental phenomenology and Anglo-American speech-act philosophy to his critique.

The word 'deconstruction' is Derrida's coinage in response to Martin Heidegger's idea of 'destructive' analysis, the attempt to introduce 'time' as a decisive element in the way we understand the world. (Nietzsche similarly makes time decisive in his genealogical work.) In the same way that time inevitably upsets and reshapes any human scheme of understanding – as Derrida shows – so meanings and values, by their very nature, are so mutually interdependent in systems of thought as to be continually destabilizing to each other and even to themselves. Deconstruction as a concept or practice which focuses on this instability of meaning rises out of Derrida's recognition that in modern conceptions of knowledge there is a temporal 'decentring' or a 'rupture' in the conventional order, a dramatic and decisive shift in traditional relations to authority, what might be termed a challenge to all authority. Understanding, Derrida says in *Of Grammatology*, 'is not to be thought at one go' (1967: 23). Herman Rapaport argues in his study *Heidegger and Derrida* (1989) that in deconstruction there is a radical break with 'Kantian teleology, which views time as linear, progressive, continuous'. He continues:

> from a post-Heideggerian prospective, time is anything but such a linear movement of the history of being or meaning; rather, time is a manifold of relations in which the difference between moments is itself undecidably given in a trace structure in whose indeterminacy the various modalities of time (arche, moment, lapse, eschaton, duration, present, past, future, suspension) are given not simultaneously but also not unsimultaneously. (p. 65)

The 'difference between moments' is, after all, our common-sense understanding of time. But Heidegger – and, after him, Derrida – argues that 'time is neither something nor nothing even if it is the condition without which it would be impossible to talk about that which is and is not' (Rapaport 1989: 93).

The articulation of 'neither . . . nor' – which is repeated throughout Derrida's work (see Schleifer 1987a) – is the articulation of the negativity of critique beyond criticism. This critique, as in Nietzsche, describes *neither positivism nor idealism* – or, as we are arguing in this chapter on the philosophical critique of literary studies, *neither philosophy nor literature*. Derrida himself, speaking of Nietzsche and the relationship 'between the "work" and the "life"', says he focuses on the dynamics of the 'borderline between the system and the subject of the system. This borderline,' he continues, 'is neither active nor passive, neither outside nor inside' (1985: 5). In such locutions, the investigation or 'interrogation' of deconstructive critique attempts to reveal that the underlying 'authority' is an arbitrary and, as in Nietzsche, an *interested* stopping-place in a regressive structure ('doing, effecting, becoming') of conceptual and temporal boundaries. (In 'Structure, Sign and Play' Derrida uses the term 'centre' for such authority; in 'The Search for Grounds in Literary Study' Hillis Miller uses the term 'ground'.)

Such questioning of authority can be seen in Derrida's critique of Lévi-Strauss's seemingly unconscious valorization of 'nature' over 'culture' within his attempt to demonstrate the relationship between the tangible and the intelligible. Moreover, this critique reveals, as de Man argues in 'Semiology and Rhetoric', no coherent reason for choosing one or another as a ground – it reveals the very 'undecidability' Rapaport describes. De Man describes 'two entirely coherent but entirely incompatible readings' of Yeats's 'Among School Children' which hinge upon one line ('How can we know the dancer from the dance?') which calls for both a 'grammatical' and a 'rhetorical' reading (1979: 11–12). In this regression of certainty and absolute

161

reference points, critique itself calls into question conventional cultural references and 'self-evident' concepts such as 'truth', 'objectivity', 'man', and so forth. This 'decentring', in other words, deeply undercuts all notions of self-evident and absolute grounds in knowledge. In short, as Nietzsche said, God, or any absolute reference point, really does 'die' (does become 'decentred') for the modern world. This declaration, as Deleuze writes, 'synthesizes the idea of God with time, becoming, history and man' (1962: 152). Accordingly, there is the recognition in modern thought of what Derrida calls the 'structurality of structure' (1966: 248) or Western culture's ironic ability to know and not to know something at the same time – in effect, to *know* that knowledge conceived as spatial structures, conceived as ideal 'form' beginning with Plato and Aristotle, is ultimately problematic and 'undecidable'. As Derrida says in *Spurs: Nietzsche's Style*, 'the decidable opposition of true and non-true' is suspended (1978: 107). 'Knowledge' is neither true nor not true.

As it bears on reading (including, of course, literary criticism, but not simply 'literature' precisely because the borderline between the literary and the non-literary comes into question), deconstruction is a strategy or 'tactics' of reading – what Derrida describes as 'a strategy without finality. We might call it blind tactics' (1967b: 135). Elsewhere Derrida describes deconstructive reading as starting from a philosophical hierarchy in which two opposed terms are presented as the 'superior' general case and the 'inferior' special case. These oppositions are Western culture's most important categories of thought as in truth/error, health/disease, male/female, nature/culture, philosophy/literature, speech/writing, seriousness/play (see Derrida 1972a: 41; 1972: 329–30). De Man adds to this list the opposition between the certainties of grammar and the uncertainties of rhetoric; and Derrida, in his critique of speech-act theory (1972; 1977), includes the opposition of language conceived as 'constative' (as essentially a system of true or false meanings) with language conceived as 'performative' (linguistic activity in its *situated* functioning between and among people). In all these cases, these oppositions present an implicit hierarchy. Another example is the generally accepted use of 'man' to mean 'human' and 'woman' to mean only the special case of a female human being. Such general acceptance is based (or 'grounded') on the linguistic 'fact' that 'man' is semantically unmarked, but the very 'naturalness' of these 'facts' also calls for critique, just as Lévi-Strauss's implicit elevation of 'nature' over 'culture' calls for Derrida's assertion that the seeming *prior* category of 'nature' is a special case of 'culture'.

Beginning with these generally accepted hierarchical oppositions, deconstruction in an initial 'phase' reverses such crucial hierarchies so as to elevate the 'inferior' over the 'superior' – making, as Culler says, 'the constative a special case of the performative' (1982: 113). The purpose of these reversals, however, is not merely to invert value systems. This 'reversal', Derrida says in *Spurs*, 'if it is not accompanied by a discrete parody, a strategy of writing . . . if there is no style, no grand style, this [reversal] is finally but the same thing, nothing more than a clamorous declaration of the antithesis' (1978: 95), a 'renewal of the hierarchy or the substance of values' (1978: 81). In a second 'phase' deconstruction attempts to 'explode' (in Derrida's metaphor, 1972a: 45) the original relationship of 'superior' and 'inferior' which gives rise to the semantic horizon – the possibility of any particular meaning – of a discourse. Deconstruction attempts, in Derrida's words, to confront one interpretation 'of interpretation, of structure, of sign, of freeplay' – one which seeks 'a truth or an origin which is free from freeplay and from the order of the sign' – with another interpretation of interpretation 'which is no longer turned toward the origin, [but] affirms freeplay and tries to pass beyond man and humanism' (1966: 264). In de Man's terms, this second interpretation refuses to distinguish between the specific meanings of grammar and the 'suspended' meanings of rhetoric – and, in a style and a procedure much more serious and single-minded than that of Derrida, de Man calls the discourse that articulates the inability to distinguish 'literature' (1979: 15).

The confrontations of deconstruction attempt to avoid their own constitution ('construction') into a new hierarchy. In fact, Derrida himself subjects this whole description of deconstruction (which he is at great pains to demonstrate is *not* a 'method') to the very critique being described (1982).

> I am not sure that 'phase two' marks a split with 'phase one,' a split whose form would be a cut along an indivisible line. The relationship between these two phases doubtless has another structure. I spoke of two distinct phases for the sake of clarity, but the relationship of one phase to another is marked less by conceptual determinations (that is, where a new concept follows an archaic one) than by a transformation or general deformation of logic; such transformations or deformations mark the 'logical' element or environment itself by moving, for example, beyond the 'positional' (difference determined as opposition, whether or not dialectically).   (p. 72)

Instead, the very procedure of deconstruction presents 'undecidability', an inability to choose, what de Man describes in the rhetorical term *aporia* – a use of discourse which presents mutually exclusive alternatives without any criteria for choosing between them – and Derrida describes as 'the Nietzschean *affirmation* – the joyous affirmation of the freeplay of the world and without truth, without origin, offered to an active interpretation' (1966: 264).

DECONSTRUCTION AND LITERARY CRITICISM

Derrida's deconstructive critique of founding assumptions in Western philosophy has led him to deconstruct many institutions of Western culture – that is, to extend critical analysis into areas of actual practice and thus to investigate at first hand the cultural institutions (like the *institution* of sexual difference examined in *Spurs*) he first described in general terms. He has done this explicitly with psychoanalysis, structural linguistics and literary criticism (especially theories of representation, or mimesis) as well as in the focus, as in his analysis of Nietzsche which we will examine in this chapter, on particular 'stylistic' and literary articulations of 'philosophy'. From his general theories and specific commentaries, there are three issues we have already touched upon that have a direct bearing on literary theory and criticism: textuality, undecidability and strategy. By textuality Derrida means largely what the structuralists mean by that term. Anything that can be known will be articulated *as a text* within a system of differences that exist, in Saussure's description, *without positive terms*. Because it is a system without positive terms (without a 'centre'), textuality is subject to a certain instability or undecidability. That is, texts of any sort (social or literary phenomena, for example) will produce meanings, but because the production of meaning cannot be arrested through a relationship with absolute referents (the positive terms of positivism) or absolutely closed contexts (the centres or grounds of idealism), textuality will always be in progress and unfinished – and thus undecidable. The notion of deconstructive textuality, as Paul de Man, Henry Louis Gates Jr, J. Hillis Miller, Barbara Johnson, Shoshana Felman and others have shown, is easily applicable in practical criticism, in which indeed the dimension of undecidability separates the structuralist from the deconstructionist version of the text.

Most decisive for deconstructive literary criticism, though, is the issue of deconstructive strategy we have described above, its two strategic 'phases'. A deconstructive analysis of literature involves reversing and reinscribing the terms of a hierarchy. This reversal and reinscription are of course playful, but of a playfulness intended to be disruptive as if to institute a kind of nonsense, something other than a 'will to truth'. But however innocuous such a strategy of 'nonsense' may seem, Derrida is playful in the 'serious' Nietzschean sense; that is, his play is intended to subvert the most fundamental strictures of seriousness and thus to displace and 'contaminate' the very basis of (Western) philosophic authority. It is play, in other words, aimed at producing, as in Nietzsche's transvaluation, a 'new way of feeling', 'a new way of thinking' (Deleuze 1962: 163). In fact, deconstructive play offers a virtual model of continual revolution (political and cultural) in its drive to overturn the status quo and then to institute a new order. In this way, as Derrida and other post-structuralists have become more playful, rhetorically and conceptually, they have also become more intent about instituting new practices in writing and thinking.

Such an analysis of literature can be seen in de Man's *Allegories of Reading*, particularly in his reading of Yeats and Proust in the first essay of that book, 'Semiology and Rhetoric'. More than most critics, de Man takes the disruptions of deconstruction seriously indeed. He is interested primarily in the manner in which a text *says* one thing and *does* another. To show this, following Charles S. Peirce, he opposes 'rhetoric' to 'grammar' and projects 'pure rhetoric' as an interpretive swerving or 'deflection' of meaning, a mode of error, whereas 'pure grammar . . . postulates the possibility of unproblematic, dyadic meaning' (1979: 9) De Man then deconstructs the opposition between rhetoric and grammar: first, a text has a 'meaning', or a given and somewhat static significance. Next, the text 'asserts' or 'performs' (as the reading continues) a quite different meaning, as if to constitute a different 'text' inconsistent with the first. This discrepancy between meaning and assertion in the same text – the text as *information* and as *activity* – de Man shows to be 'a constitutive part of their logic', of 'textual' logic (1979: 9).

The text, in this way, swerves from meaning to assertion, from 'insight' to 'blindness', from truth to falsehood, and the gap between terms (which allows the swerving) in each case de Man calls irony or 'error', not the 'mere error' of a factual mistake but a dynamic constituent of textuality. This irony, or error, is generated specifically because of a text's inability to *say* what it *does*, to unite saying and doing. Irony is generated by the fact, as Hillis Miller says, that 'a piece of language cannot logically be both performative and constative at the same time' (1990: 112). To one extent or another deconstructive readings of 'literary' texts confront the performances of authors/

165

narrators/texts with their 'constative' meanings in order to examine what is going on in literature.

Along with this confrontation, as Derrida himself suggests, deconstruction involves a reversal and reinscription of the usual patterns of interpretation – that is, it examines criticism as well as literature, and one hierarchical opposition that it has brought into question is the opposition between literature and criticism, 'primary' and 'secondary' texts. In this distinction, perhaps more than anywhere else, deconstructive criticism has encountered resistance. Many 'deconstructive' critics (such as those who taught and wrote at Yale University during the 1970s – Hillis Miller and Geoffrey Hartman along with de Man) attempted to challenge the 'superiority' of literature over criticism. De Man, in particular, claims a 'literary' status for critique itself: 'the key to this critique of metaphysics', he writes, '. . . is the rhetorical model of the trope or, if one prefers to call it that, literature' (1979: 15). He makes a claim for the essentially 'critical' nature of literature. Such 'criticism', focusing on the very hierarchy of 'literature' and 'criticism', does so performatively by submitting all kinds of texts – philosophy, science, ethics, and so forth: in other words, all kinds of cultural *practices* – to the critique of 'literary' criticism. A striking example is Derrida's figural reading of the word and the concept of 'woman' in Nietzsche's work that we will examine in the next section. But equally notable is Hartman's articulations (not always successful) of traditionally 'literary' uses of language to gloss and to examine texts.

The 'uncanniness' of the critique of the will to truth, as we noted in Chapter 1, sets deconstructive criticism apart in the Anglo-American academy. In a manner largely alien to the American tradition of philosophical pragmatism and temperamental optimism – against the native impulse to focus all of experience in the 'light of common day', within the bounds of empiricism (see Berman 1988) – deconstruction has tried to 'bring the plague' to American scholarship and teaching. The history of criticism, of course, is a history of such imports and exports, some more unsettling than others, but the importation of deconstruction has produced an 'uncanniness' calculated to decentre humanistic formalism (whether New Critical, archetypal or even linguistic) with an irony and undecidability foreign and almost completely 'other' to it. More than any other feature, it is this deliberate introduction of irony (of absolute loss, of death – not New Critical irony) that has alarmed many American academics and has prompted the charge that current theory 'turns literature against itself' (Graff 1979) – against, that is, the very concerns about the *function* of literature and criticism in human affairs, the very ethics that Derrida mentions in relation to his treatment of Nietzsche and 'woman' in *Spurs*.

In an important sense, this charge is entirely accurate. As Derrida and de Man show (indeed, as they *enact* in their analyses), language/literature is irrevocably divided against itself – is at each moment different from itself, turned against itself in the temporal folds of error and irony. To concede this 'fact' of discourse, however, misses the point of the self-division inherent in critique as well as deconstructive literary studies, even if the severity of the work of de Man seems to lead to such a concession. In fact, precisely because of what Christopher Norris calls the 'negative compulsion' in de Man, 'the entire effort of that singular intelligence . . . devoted to foreclosing, regretfully but firmly, whatever new dimensions of sense the adventurous reader might hope to find' in literature (1988: 115), de Man is not fully situated within 'critical literary studies'. (We are coining this term in relation to the use of deconstructive critique within the law under the designation 'critical legal studies'.) Neither is Hartman: if de Man emphasizes the *critical* in critical literary studies, then Hartman emphasizes the *literary*. Rather, Derrida's 'literary' reading of Nietzsche and Hillis Miller's recent attempts to describe what he calls the 'ethics' of reading should serve as instructive examples of deconstructive critique in more or less conventional literary criticism.

DERRIDA READING NIETZSCHE

Derrida's examination of Nietzsche's misogyny in *Spurs: Nietzsche's Style* is an example of the critique of the will to truth Nietzsche calls for in the *Genealogy*. Examining what he calls the 'scene' Nietzsche makes before women – the 'spectacle' of his misogyny 'which is overdetermined, divided, apparently contradictory' (1982: 69) – Derrida attempts to articulate an 'affirmative' deconstruction (1978: 37). Focusing on 'style' in Nietzsche, Derrida seems to reverse the opposition between philosophy and literature, truth and pleasure. Throughout his writing, Nietzsche articulates positions which are virulently anti-feminist. As Christopher Norris notes, Nietzsche 'repeats with hysterical insistence . . . that woman is the source of all folly and unreason, the siren figure who lures the male philosopher out of his appointed truth-seeking path. "Progress of the idea," Nietzsche writes: "it becomes more subtle, insidious, incomprehensible – *it becomes female*"' (1987: 202; Norris is quoting Derrida

167

quoting Nietzsche's *Twilight of the Idols* [Derrida 1978: 89; Nietzsche 1889: 485]). Yet insofar as Nietzsche himself is attempting a critique of reason, insofar as he finds, in Deleuze's words, that 'art realises the whole of [his critical] programme' (1962: 185), the very fact, as Derrida quotes Nietzsche saying (1886: 162) that 'from the very first nothing has been more alien, repugnant, inimical to woman than truth – her great art is the lie, her supreme concern is appearance (*Schein*) and beauty' – this very fact makes the power 'woman' playing 'at dissimulation, at ornamentation, deceit, artifice, at an artist's philosophy', as Derrida says, 'affirmative' (Derrida 1978: 67).

As we have seen, Derrida is not simply reversing philosophy and art; he is not, as Norris says, merely inverting 'the terms of this basic opposition and declar[ing] that metaphor is henceforth the "truth" of philosophy, or woman the name of some transcendent principle "beyond" the reductive strategies of male reason' (1987: 203). Instead, he is presenting 'undecidability' (Derrida 1978: 105): 'woman' which is neither the truth nor not the truth. Derrida writes (1978):

> Indeed, it is clear from the context [of Nietzsche's aphorism in *Twilight of the Idols*] that it is the idea that becomes woman. The becoming-female is a 'progress of the idea' (*Fortschritt der Idee*) and the idea a form of truth's self-presentation. Thus the truth has not always been woman nor is the woman always truth. They both have a history; together they both form a history. . . . [–]a history which philosophy alone, inasmuch as it is included therein, is unable to decode. (p. 87)

This 'history' is beyond 'philosophy' – indeed, it is a critique of philosophy – insofar as it describes Nietzsche's genealogical project. If the second 'phase' of deconstruction we have described – 'neither . . . nor' – transforms hierarchy into something 'outside' hierarchy – really, 'neither outside nor inside hierarchy' – it does so through the transformation of opposition into difference; as Derrida says in a note in *Spurs*, 'at the moment that the sexual difference is determined as an opposition, the image of each term is inverted into the other' (1978: 149). In precisely these terms Deleuze describes Nietzschean genealogy: 'opposition can be the law of the relation between abstract products, but difference is the only principle of genesis or production; a principle which itself produces opposition as mere appearance. Dialectic thrives on oppositions because it is unaware of far more subtle and subterranean differential mechanisms: [the] topological displacements, typological variations' of genealogy (1962: 157).

For Derrida, however, the project is 'grammatological' rather than (or along with) 'genealogical'. *Grammatology* is a term Derrida coined to describe the 'science' of writing (as opposed to speech) even as he raised questions about the opposition between writing and speech (and between science and whatever might be called non-science – rhetoric, art, style, play, or woman). 'Grammatology' makes clearer than 'genealogy' the element of interpretation that Nietzsche describes, the 'problem', as Derrida describes it, for reading (1978: 95). In reading Nietzsche, 'rather than examin[ing] the larger number of propositions which treat of the woman', Derrida instead formalizes 'their principle, which might be resumed in a finite number of typical and matrical propositions' (1978: 95). He then gathers together 'three fundamental propositions [which] represent three positions of value'.

> 1. Woman is censured, debased, despised as a figure or potentate of falsehood. In the name of truth and dogmatic metaphysics, she is accused here by the credulous [i.e. philosophical] man. . . .
> 2. Woman is censured, despised as a figure or potentate of truth. In the guise of the christian, philosophical being she either identifies with truth, or else she continues to play with it at a distance. . . . Up to this point, woman is twice castration: truth and non-truth.
> 3. Beyond this double negation, woman is recognized and affirmed as an affirmative power, a dissimulatress, an artist, a dionysiac. And no longer is it man who affirms her. She affirms herself, in and of herself. Castration, here, does not take place. And anti-feminism, which condemned woman only so long as she was, so long as she answered to man from the two reactive positions, is in its turn overthrown. (1978: 97; translation modified)

In this narrative the 'phases' of deconstructive practice are enunciated. Moreover, in the term 'reactive' Derrida underlines the fact that the 'split' between the 'phases' of deconstructive activity – here, 'reactive' opposition and affirmative difference – is less a 'conceptual determinination' than 'a transformation or general deformation of logic' (1982: 72). He does so by taking up a crucial term in Deleuze's analysis of Nietzsche. In *Nietzsche and Philosophy*, Deleuze defines genealogy as 'the art of difference or distinction, the art of nobility; but it sees itself upside down in the mirror of reactive forces' (1962: 56). Reactive forces, Deleuze argues, triumph over the active by separating active force 'from what it can do'. Reactive forces function by means of fiction, mystification, or falsification – the 'good' and 'evil', the 'bad conscience' and the ascetic ideals of the *Genealogy* (1962: 61, 57). In other words, 'active' and 'reactive' are not absolutely opposed, but the transformation and deformation of one another. Here, then, the very opposition between active and reactive – which, as Derrida points out in *Spurs*, governs the traditional opposition between male 'activity' and female 'passivity' (1978: 77–79) – is not absolute but finally 'undecidable'. 'What remains undecidable,'

Derrida says elsewhere, 'concerns not only but also the line of cleavage between the two sexes. As you recall, such a movement reverts neither to words nor to concepts' (1982: 75).

In this analysis, as we have suggested, Derrida is pursuing a grammatological critique. This can be seen in his tracing of the 'word' – the *mark* – 'woman' in *Spurs*. That is, as Gayatri Spivak has noted, 'woman' in *Spurs* takes its place among the other 'names' that Derrida has articulated throughout his career – 'names such as différance, trace, parergon and the like' (Spivak 1984: 24). We could add 'supplement', 'Sarl', 'hymen', 'life death', even 'deconstruction' itself, which Derrida describes as simply 'a word in a chain with many other words – such as trace or différance – as well as with a whole elaboration which is not limited only to a lexicon' (1985: 86). With such 'names' he is finding ways of 'naming', what Spivak calls 'citationality' (1984: 22), the fact that concepts have histories, and those histories can be traced genealogically, grammatologically through textual citations. Citations mark the very repeatability that makes language function. They are grammatological marks of 'itera-tiveness', as Derrida describes in 'Limited Inc.' (1977: 190), that is part and parcel of language and meaning.

The name 'woman' in Derrida, Spivak argues, is not a 'special case' but 'occupies the place of a general critique of the history of Western thought' (1984: 22). 'Woman' marks the general critique precisely because 'woman' *differs* from truth in Nietzsche, because, as Derrida says, 'the question of the woman suspends the decidable opposition of true and non-true and inaugurates the epochal regime of quotation marks' (1978: 107): because ' "woman" – the word made memorable (*époche*) – no more believes in castration's exact opposite, anti-castration, than she does in castration itself' (1978: 61; translation modified). The name 'woman', then, possesses a 'special quality' for a deconstructive critique. *Spurs* begins with the declaration that 'woman' will be Derrida's subject, and, Spivak (1984) argues,

> one must always remember that the word 'subject' can mean both subject matter (object) and the self. . . .
> Of all the names that Derrida has given to originary undecidability, women possess this special quality: she can occupy both positions in the subject-object oscillation, . . . something that différance, writing, parergon, the supplement, and the like – other names of undecidability – cannot do without special pleading. (p. 24)

In acts of self-citation – the 'strategies' of writing such as parody and the 'grand style' Derrida describes in Nietzsche's 'philosophy' – the speaking subject 'woman' can become an object of discourse. As

Nietzsche says in *The Gay Science*, women ' "give themselves," ' even when they – give themselves' (1882: 317; Derrida 1978: 69). 'Women,' Spivak says, ' "acting out" their pleasure in the orgasmic moment, can cite themselves in their very self-presence. It is as if the woman *is* quotation marks and vice versa. If men think they have or possess women in sexual mastery, they should be reminded that, by this logic women can destroy the proper roles of master and slave' (1984: 22). With such self-citation, as Derrida says, 'all the signs of a sexual opposition are changed. Man and woman change places' (1978: 111).

For this reason, Derrida repeatedly asserts that 'there is no such thing . . . [as] an essence of *the* woman or the sexual difference' (1978: 121); 'there is no truth in itself of the sexual difference in itself, of either man or woman in itself' (1978: 103). For this reason, Derrida argues, 'it is impossible to dissociate the questions of art, style and truth from the question of the woman. Nevertheless the simple formulation of this common problematic suspends the question "what is woman?" One can no longer seek the woman or woman's femininity or female sexuality. At least one cannot find these in any familiar modes of concept or knowledge, even if one cannot resist seeking them' (1978: 71; translation modified).

One can no longer seek these 'things' ('woman', 'femininity', 'female sexuality') because, Derrida argues, the very gesture of attributing properties, of making 'sense' (articulating 'truth' and 'knowledge') – what Derrida calls (in another 'word' to add to his list) 'propriation' – is somehow tied up with sexual difference. 'Not only is propriation a sexual operation,' he writes, 'but *before* it there was no sexuality' (1978: 111). This 'before', like the ambiguities of time in Heidegger – 'the condition without which it would be impossible to talk about that which is and is not' (Rapaport 1989: 93) – underlines an understanding of sexual difference as neither essential nor accidental. It is for this reason that Derrida pursues the name 'woman' in Nietzsche as an itinerary for a critique of the will to truth. 'There is no such thing as the truth of woman,' he writes in *Spurs*, 'but it is because of that abyssal divergence of the truth, because that untruth is "truth." Woman is but one name for that untruth of truth' (1978: 51).

Such a 'conclusion' to a deconstructive critique is haunted by questions of ethics in the very 'untruth of truth', in the very critique of the will to truth. 'The possibility of ethics could be saved,' Derrida notes, 'if one takes ethics to mean that relationship to the other as other which accounts for no other determination or sexual character-istic in particular. What kind of ethics would there be,' he asks, 'if

171

belonging to one sex or another became its law or privilege. What if the universality of moral laws were modelled on or limited according to the sexes?' (1982: 73). The universality of moral law, like the impersonality and universality of both knowledge itself and aesthetic experience that Kant asserts and Nietzsche denies, is a *crisis* as well as an object of critique for deconstruction, as it is a crisis for literary studies in the twentieth century – a crisis, as we have suggested here and as we will discuss in the conclusion, exemplified and generated in the gendered nature of the subject.

HILLIS MILLER, DECONSTRUCTION, AND THE 'ETHICS' OF READING

When Miller speaks of the 'ethics' of reading, he does not focus on the particularities of human relationships that Derrida suggests with the word 'woman'. But neither is he specifically speaking of the theme of ethics in works of literature. Instead, in a figurative use of parasite and host – an opposition he pursued in an essay in the 1970s entitled 'The Critic as Host' (1979) – he describes 'the "body" of literature . . . invaded by a necessity of being ethical, whether it wishes to or not, as a virus reprograms its host cell to its own pattern. This necessity is not thematic' (1987: 133). In fact, as we hope to show, this necessity is not even 'necessary' in the conventional opposition between necessity and accident that deconstruction attempts to critique. In describing the 'invasion' of literature by ethics Miller is glossing Derrida's assertion in *Signponge* that 'the ethical instance is at work in the body of literature' (1984: 53). In Miller's literary studies, the 'ethical instance' is at work in his understanding of the ethics of 'responsibility' in reading as taking the form of 'conduct' in which, in terms from Henry James that he cites in both *The Ethics of Reading* and *Versions of Pygmalion*, 'the whole conduct of life consists of things done, which do other things in their turn' (1987: 102; 1990: 14). This conduct takes place in 'the painful encounter with the otherness of other people in ordinary human relations' (1990: 11). This 'otherness', we will argue, is a constitutive element in the *sublimity* of Miller's reading, which explains literature's privileged place in his work. Still, such literary sublimity is also denuded, as it is here, of any sense of sexual difference operating in ethical reading.

Rather than taking second place, as ethics does in Kant's great critique (and, indeed, in any intellectual pursuit, such as the institutional critiques of psychoanalysis or semiotics, that is driven by the will to truth), intellectual activity conceived of as 'ethics' (as opposed to ontology or aesthetics) will *necessarily* take the form of genealogy or grammatology. Moreover, as Miller suggests in his repeated assertion that there can be no ethics without narrative (see, for instance, 1987: 23; 1990: 16), such 'activity', even when it seems, as it does in Kant, to be abstract philosophical inquiry, will take the form of literature. It is precisely 'in the commitment to the idea that ethics precedes ontology' that the Jewish theologian, Emmanuel Levinas (to whom Derrida has devoted several important studies) departs from Heidegger (Rapaport 1989: 216). Levinas (1986) noted in an interview:

> Man's ethical relation to the other is ultimately prior to his ontological relation to himself (egology) or to the totality of things that we call the world (cosmology). The relation with the other is *time*: it is an untotalizable diachrony in which one moment pursues another without ever being able to retrieve it, to catch up with, or coincide with it.   (p. 21)

Such priority makes philosophy *interested*, as Nietzsche says; and, equally important, it focuses its *interest* on the narratives of ongoing interpersonal conduct.

In this interest in the activities of time we can see another purpose in Derrida's strategy of multiplying 'words' for the double articulation of undeniability, for the unfolding of his grammatology. Miller's deconstructive criticism, as has often been noticed, repeats this strategy by closely focusing on particular words. In 'Ariadne's Thread' he describes his pursuit of etymologies as a means of indicating 'the lack of enclosure of a given word. Each word inheres in a labyrinth of branching interverbal relationships going back to a referential source but to something already, at the beginning, a figurative transfer' (1976: 70). In a later essay, 'Ariachne's Broken Woof', he goes even further by focusing on the confusion between *Ariadne* and *Arachne* in Shakespeare's use of 'Ariachne' in *Troilus and Cressida*. (In this focus he is following Derrida's coining of the term *différance* in French, spelt with an *a*, to gather together such meanings as 'difference', 'differ', 'deference'.) 'The word "Ariachne" leaps to the eye of the reader,' Miller (1977) argues. He continues:

> The principle of identity is the basic assumption of monological metaphysics. Only if A is undividably A, or, in this case, C equals C, does the whole structure hang together, in a chain that is described in Ulysses' famous speech on order. The order in question includes the religious, metaphysical, or cosmological links binding earth to heaven; the political or social order which is so largely in question in the play; the

ethical or intersubjective order of the vows of love between one person and another; the order of perception or of epistemology which sees and identifies things unequivocally, each as that one single thing which it is; the order of reason which makes a person or a mind one indivisible thing gathering various faculties under a unifying power or authority; the order, finally, of language, of rational discourse which posits unified entities and names them as what they are. The 'whole shebang' of Occidental metaphysics is, the reader can see, brought into question in Troilus's experience and in his speech.   (p. 47)

The focus on words and the elements of words, like Miller's repeated etymologies, is a *genealogy* of words that enacts, as in Derrida but more abstractly, a kind of ethical inquiry. Later, Miller describes such a moment in deconstructive criticism, in terms he cites from Nietzsche, as 'scrupulous slow reading', and he does so to situate his literary studies within the 'long and venerable tradition . . . of philology and of critical philosophy' (1985: 28, 34).

Such scrupulous reading takes on the force of an 'ethics' of reading that assumes, as Miller says in *Versions of Pygmalion*, that 'meaning does not go without saying' so that 'each phrase, however common-place and idiomatic, must be *read*' (1990: 60). 'By "the ethics of reading,"' Miller writes, 'I mean that aspect of the act of reading in which there is a response to the text that is both necessitated, in the sense that it is a response to an irresistible demand, and free, in the sense that I must take responsibility for my response and for the further effects, "interpersonal," institutional, social, political, or historical, of my act of reading' (1987: 43). In part, this turn to ethics, as Norris has argued, is a response to criticism of deconstruction 'as a species of last-ditch nihilism bent upon destroying the ethical and humanistic bases of literary study' (1988: 102). But more important, as we are arguing here, it is a working out of the 'logic' of deconstructive genealogy. That logic, as Miller's discussion of 'Ariachne' suggests, is haunted by fracture and dread, by what Miller calls elsewhere 'literature's death-dealing power that makes the notion that a work expresses a universal truth that is at the same time unique, cut off from historical, social, and political determining conditions, seem so scandalous to many' (1990: 75).

The scandal of ethics, after all, is, as Derrida suggests in his discussion of sexual difference, the very problem of the relation between the universal and the unique. It is 'something', Miller says, following Blanchot, 'that enters into the words or between the words' – 'something encountered in our relations to other people, especially relations involving love, betrayal, and that ultimate betrayal by the other or our love for him or her, the death of the other' (1985: 21).

For Miller – as it is for Derrida as well (see Schleifer 1990: Ch. 8) – this scandal is gathered up in the 'name' *Death* in part because, as Blanchot argues, dying is something, 'though unsharable, I have in common with all' (1980: 23). 'Death,' Miller writes, 'is perhaps the most radical name, though still only one figurative name among others, for the intermittences that break the continuity of human life all along the line. Of those blank places nothing can be known directly. They can only be named in trope' (1990: 125). This figuring of relations between people – and the equally scandalous relation between universal and particular – in terms of death explains Miller's interest, in *Versions of Pygmalion*, in the rhetorical figure of prosopo-poeia (the giving of voice and face to the dead). It is the 'attempt, necessarily destined to fail, to make up for the ultimate loss of death' (1990: 48).

The ethics of reading becomes in Miller a kind of deconstructive sublime – his attempt 'to notice', if not to 'account for', 'oddnesses, gaps, anacoluthons, non sequiturs, apparently irrelevant details, in short, all the marks of the inexplicable, all the marks of the unaccount-able, perhaps of the mad, in a text' (1985: 20). 'The essential claim of the sublime,' Thomas Weiskel has argued, 'is that man can, in feeling and in speech, transcend the human' (1986: 3). The nature of 'true acts of reading', Miller argues, is that 'something always fortuitous and unpredictable' happens so that 'a genuine act of reading . . . is always the disconfirmation or modification of presupposed literary theory. . . . You can never be sure what is going to happen' (1990: 20–1). In this fact lies the 'ethics' of responsive and responsible reading. But more is at stake here, what Miller calls a 'disruptive energy . . . [which] is properly religious, metaphysical, or ontologi-cal, though hardly in a traditional or conventional way' (1985: 21).

In *Versions of Pygmalion* Miller figures this almost inexplicable sense in the person of Bartleby from Melville's story – even while, as Miller himself suggests, the act of choosing an example re-enacts the *ethical* problem of the relation of the particular to the universal (1987: 42; see also 2, 11, 121). He writes (1990):

> What Bartleby brings is not a realm in the sense of place we might go. It is the otherness that all along haunts or inhabits life from the inside. This otherness can by no method . . . be accounted for, narrated, rationalized, or in any other way reassimilated into ordinary life, though it is a permanent part of that ordinary life . . . . Bartleby is the invasion of death into life, but not death as something from outside life. 'Death,' nevertheless, is not the proper name for this ghostly companion of life, as if it were an allegorical meaning identified at last. Nor is 'Death' its

175

generic or common name. 'Death' is a catachresis for what can never be named properly. (p. 172)

What can never be named properly is the *undecidability*, 'the impossibility of distinguishing clearly between a linguistic reading and an ontological one' (1987: 122). This dilemma is properly *ethical* because it entails the confusion between obligation and necessity in the word 'must' (1990: 240), a confusion of the universal and unique – 'the experience of an "I must" that is always the same but always different, unique, idiomatic' (1987: 127).

This experience is 'human' experience, and it founders on the confusion of grounding – the grounds of psychology, language, philosophy and social life we saw in Miller's analysis of the 'grounds' of literary study in Chapter 1. For Miller events 'just happen as they happen' (1990: 139) so that 'the unlawful law of human life may be that things happen by sheer unreasonable accidents' (1990: 117). In this understanding of events, Miller is following de Man's terrible assertion that 'nothing, whether deed, word, thought, or text, ever happens in relation, positive or negative, to anything that precedes, follows, or exists elsewhere, but only as a random event whose power, like the power of death, is due to the randomness of its occurrence' (de Man 1984a: 122; cited in Miller 1990: 94; see also Schleifer 1990: Ch. 4). The great danger of conceiving of events, as de Man does, as ultimately 'random' is precisely the danger of reducing ethics to particularities without any touchstones of universality, what we have called the collective institutional phenomena of culture. Such a reduction is a parody of genealogy or grammatology, genealogy without connection to ongoing affairs – transformative critique transformed to beginning over and over again, apocalyptically. In this context, Miller's concentration on prosopopoeia and his contention that 'prosopopoeia seems always liable at any moment to shatter into fragments that are a revelation not of a ubiquitous spiritual life but of the senseless, shapeless, and illegible matter of which both statues and human bodies are made' (1990: 225) seem a moment, and not the end, of critique. Yet even this articulation of a sense of life and language – the ('philosophical' or 'ethical' or even 'religious') *problem*, as we have argued, is precisely distinguishing the two – becomes a critique of language and the will to truth when understood, as Miller understands it, in relation to the universality of ethical imperatives.

In its opposition to the absolute universality 'truth' – in its understanding of this universality as a *problem* – Miller's critique takes on the form of the sublime – the 'encounter with the absolutely-other' that Derrida describes in his early study of Levinas (1967a: 95) – or it takes place from 'the heights of the soul' that Nietzsche describes in *Beyond Good and Evil*, 'from which even tragedy ceases to look tragic' (1882: 42). This fracture – of 'tragedy', of haunting 'otherness', of the 'name' *Death* (or 'woman', or 'Nietzsche', or 'Ariachne') – is part of deconstruction as a critique of the subject, of language, of history. All come together in the ethics of promising in which person, time, language and relations to other people are gathered together. 'Language promises,' Miller writes, 'but what it promises is itself [its own self-identical meanings]. This promise it can never keep. It is this fact of language, a necessity beyond the control of any user of language, which makes things happen as they do happen in the material world of history' (1987: 35). In *Memoires for Paul de Man* (1986) Derrida also examines the nature of promises.

> What is love, friendship, memory, from the moment two impossible promises are involved with them, sublimely, without any possible exchange . . .?
> These questions can be posed only after the death of a friend, and they are not limited to the question of mourning. What should we think of all of this, of love, of memory, of promise, of destination, of experience, since a promise, from the first moment that it pledges, and however possible it appears, pledges beyond death, beyond what we call, without knowing of what or of whom we speak, death. It involves, in reverse, the other, the dead *in us*, from the first moment, even if no one is *there* to respond to the promise or speak for the promise. (p. 149)

Derrida goes on to describe a promise as 'impossible' yet 'possible in its impossibility', to describe it as necessarily linked to death (it has 'meaning and gravity only on the condition of death'), and to describe it as an act made in the name of the other and an act making that name at the same time (1986: 150). Such promising, situated in the undecidability between ontological and linguistic necessity, takes its place among the various 'namings' – the genealogies of naming – we have been tracing in deconstructive critique. Moreover, it is always itself subject to the 'decision' of its undecidability, to the translation of promise to psychological intention, linguistic necessity, social contract. But even so, promise, in the 'logic' of deconstructive analysis, becomes critique in the unweaving of the assumptions inhabiting it. It becomes, as Shoshana Felman argues, the problematic inhabiting of literature by ethics. 'Like linguistics,' she writes, 'literature believes in meaning; like the philosophy of language, it deconstructs its own belief. Between the authority of the broken promise and the authority of the promise believed in . . . literature is precisely *the impossibility of choice*: the impossibility of keeping the promise of meaning, of consciousness; the impossibility of not continuing to make this promise and to believe in it' (1980: 68).

POST-STRUCTURALISM

The 'post-structuralist' work that has followed from (or at least along with) Derrida's work, such as Felman's reading of Molière and the British philosopher J.L. Austin against the work of Derrida and Lacan we have just quoted, takes in a large area of literary criticism. Psychoanalytic criticism, as we described it in Chapter 3, decentres the traditional Freudian version of the 'subject' and is distinctly deconstructive in its practice. Feminism, too, especially in the work of Hélène Cixous, Barbara Johnson, Jane Gallop and Patrocinio Schweickart, uses deconstructive strategies for displacing maleness and 'male' readings of literary texts. (Gayatri Spivak even uses deconstructive critique to displace the universalized 'female' in feminist criticism [see 1986].) Marxist critics, especially Louis Althusser, Fredric Jameson, John Ellis and Rosalind Coward, and Michael Ryan, have found deep affinities between the Marxist and deconstructive critiques of cultural production. All these critics have adopted what might be called (though not without contestation) a 'deconstructive' approach to literary texts. From different angles they have attempted to understand the forces that shape and 'rupture' those texts. In one sense, post-structuralism can be said to cover all post-Derridean developments in criticism (though it could be plausibly argued – Newton Garver and Richard Rorty have made this argument [see Garver 1973; Rorty 1982] – that Derrida is the latest example of a long tradition in philosophy which is quintessentially *rhetorical*). More conservatively, if the term 'post-structuralism' in literary studies arises from Derrida's critique of structuralism in the *Grammatology* and other essays, 'post-structural' definitions of literature and criticism have followed from Nietzschean ideas about 'truth', power and genealogy. In other words, such approaches might better be described as those of transformative critique in the constellation of which deconstruction takes its place.

If this is so, there is another sense in which 'post-structuralism' articulates a *critique* of deconstruction itself. For, as we have already suggested, the constant danger of deconstruction is that it falls into the same kinds of hierarchies it attempts to expose. Derrida himself is quite aware of this danger, and his response – which is really a *rhetorical* response – is, as we have seen, to multiply the 'names' under which 'deconstruction' traffics in order recurrently to present 'deconstruction' in relation to particular textual practices, those of Rousseau ('supplement') or Plato ('pharmakon') or Nietzsche ('woman'), and recurrently to articulate that practice in terminology specific to those contexts ('writing' in discussing Saussure, 'structure' in relation to Lévi-Strauss, 'iteration' in relation to Austin, etc.).

Nevertheless, as in both rhetoric and ethics, if deconstruction aims at situating seemingly universal concepts that are assumed in any discourses, then the focus on discourse in deconstruction can also be subject to examination. Michel Foucault advances the necessity of such a critique in *The Order of Discourse* in relation to the promissory 'ethics' of philosophy. This 'ethics', as we see it, resides precisely in Foucault's focusing on the *stake* of philosophy – on what matters, not in terms of 'ideas' or 'concepts' or 'words' – even in Derrida's deconstructive erasing of the hierarchy between concepts and words in his definition of *différance* as 'neither a word nor a concept' (1972: 3). Foucault directs his attention to traditional idealist philosophy of mind ('subjectivity'), beginning in Descartes but extending to all areas of 'intentional' meaning and psychological 'groundings', and on traditional materialist philosophy that grounds experience in the world ('empiricism'). But he also suggests that the seeming 'deconstruction' of this opposition between idealism and materialism, mind and world – which, in its seeming creation of a *genealogy* of 'concepts', appears to rediscover 'everywhere the movement [or 'mediation'] of a logos which elevates particularities to the status of concepts' (1970a: 65–66) – performs its deconstruction by continually avoiding the 'stake' and ethics of genealogy itself. 'Thus in a philosophy of the founding subject, in a philosophy of originary experience, and in a philosophy of universal mediation alike, discourse is no more than a play, of writing in the first case, of reading in the second, and of exchange in the third, and this exchange, this reading, this writing never put anything at stake except signs' (1970a: 66).

In 'What is an Author?' Foucault performs this 'post-structuralist' critique of philosophy itself. In that essay he examines the *function* of the author role as a social function, a 'position' (like the positions that structural analysis describes). It is not enough 'to repeat the empty affirmation that the author has disappeared', Foucault writes. 'Instead, we must locate the space left empty by the author's disappearance, follow the distribution of gaps and breaches, and watch for the openings that this disappearance uncovers' (1969: 105). In this way Foucault attempts to describe the social and political 'role' of the author, the ends it serves as a principle of unity, its links with juridical and institutional systems, its function within different classes, and, finally, its changing nature. He attempts to describe a genealogical 'ethics' of the 'author'.

Foucault's essay can be profitably contrasted to Roland Barthes's essay 'The Death of the Author' which is more conventionally a 'deconstructive' work. Barthes argues that in discourse 'it is language which speaks, not the author; to write is, through a prerequisite impersonality . . . to read that point where only language acts, "performs," and not "me"' (1968: 143). In this discussion Barthes hypothesizes 'language' rather than situating it. Instead of examining the 'death' of the author in situated terms which examines what Foucault calls the 'author function', Barthes reverses the opposition between author and reader and claims, in a deconstructive gesture of reversal, that it is in 'the place of the reader, not . . . the author' that writing exists: 'a text's unity lies not in its origin but in its destination' (1968: 148). And in the second phase of deconstruction Barthes explodes this opposition altogether by making the reader and the author equally unrecoverable. 'This destination,' he adds, 'cannot any longer be personal: the reader is without history, biography or psychology. He is simply that *someone* who holds together in a single field all the traces by which the written text is constituted' (1968: 148). But what Barthes fails to do is precisely what constitutes Foucault's implicit critique. He fails to show what situated function the role of author – or even Barthes's role of reader – serves: how it works within the confines of particular interpersonal discursive practices which are, also, practices of power, the confines of ethics.

Foucault is offering an implicit 'ethical' critique of deconstruction which is analogous to the critique of structuralism that Kristeva offers, which we described in the preceding chapter. Like deconstruction itself, Foucault's critique uses the categories of the object of critique to demonstrate its shortcomings. Yet Foucault – unlike Kristeva or Derrida – never makes that critique explicit. Instead, he offers a reading of a cultural and socially defined category, the 'author', which Barthes 'deconstructs' and both New Critical formalism and structuralism erase in their different ways (Eliot in his talk of the 'impersonality' of poetry, and Todorov in his discussion of genre without any regard for authorial intention), in order to show the relationship between discursive social 'categories' and practices and strategies of power within culture itself. This analysis, as we shall see in the next chapter, offers the possibility of reading philosophy against history in the study of literature and culture.

Before turning to that critique, however, we would like to return to Felman's more fully 'philosophical' critique of Derridean deconstruction in *The Literary Speech Act* to which we alluded at the end of the last section. Felman offers an *alternative* to Foucault's historicizing critique not in the terms, as Foucault says, of 'the philosophy of the event [that moves] in the at first sight paradoxical direction of a materialism of the incorporeal' (1970a: 69), but in terms of what she calls '*a new type of materialism . . .* [lying] *between* the materialism of psychoanalysis and that of atomic physics, since, like psychoanalysis, it is concerned with the speaking body, and since it displaces the notion of act in the same way that the physics of relativity displaces that of matter' (1980: 148). Like Foucault, Felman situates her critique between the mind and the world, between psychoanalysis and physics, not in 'history' but in the ('scandal', as she calls it, of the) 'speaking body'. The 'author' is not (or not only) a social function – which is to say (as Foucault in fact says) a locus of 'power' (see 1969: 117, 119); it is also a locus of 'pleasure'. Such 'pleasure', for Felman, falls *between* language and concepts not in order to fall into the ('historical') realm of 'events' Foucault describes. J.L. Austin, Felman writes, 'is in a way like Heraclitus, someone who thinks . . . about *the undecidability between things and events*' (1980: 107) in order to describe a new concept of history.

This 'new' concept is precisely the new type of materialism Felman speaks of. 'History,' she writes, 'only registers the theoretical acts or idea-events within the structure – always an ideological structure – of opposition or alternatives, but it is precisely what lies outside the alternative that makes an event, that makes an act, that makes history. Paradoxically, the things that have no history (like humor) are what make history'. (1980: 144): What lies outside the structure of oppositions or alternatives, in the terms we have been developing, is (and is not) transformative critique – the 'special cases' of ethics that substantiate and undermine the ethical universals that make the special cases 'cases' at all. In other words, critique always also falls back into universalizing structures. It does so, moreover, because pursuing the labour of the negative, the complexity of negativity always allows itself to be taken as simple negativity. Theories like 'psychoanalysis, the performative, Nietzschean philosophy' (1980: 139), Felman argues, attempt to articulate 'radical negativity' that cannot 'be reduced to a negative that is the simple – symmetrical – contrary of the "positive," to a reducible negative, caught up in a normative system' (1980: 139). Instead, radical negativity 'explodes' – or attempts, repeatedly, to explode – such normality and to remain complexly positive, fecund, 'affirmative' (1980: 141).

For Felman the 'special case' of Austin is especially instructive, not only in the 'history of philosophy,' but for 'history' itself. She writes (1980):

> That Austin may be *both* philosopher and linguist, and at the same time, properly speaking, quite *outside the alternative* – *neither* philosopher *nor* linguist (just as a psychoanalyst is *neither* a psychiatrist *nor* a psychologist) – this can scarcely satisfy the history of ideas, which in fact reproaches Austin for being too much a linguist for philosophy (at Rooyaumont), and at the same time too philosophical for linguistics (Benveniste . . .). What history always misunderstands, fails to recognize, or fails – actively – to retain, is the negative beyond the alternative, or radical negativity. (p. 143)

This 'negativity' is 'deconstruction' (or 'genealogy' or 'post-structuralism'), but only when deconstruction or whatever it is called never comes to rest in a particular 'concept' or 'word', when it never falls into its own 'seriousness' (as Foucault, in his way, falls into 'seriousness' – or Miller does, in his claim of the purity of slow reading, for instance).

Precisely in the 'special case' of Austin, in which Derrida critiques Austinian speech-act theory for grounding itself on the opposition between the serious and the non-serious, Felman argues that deconstruction fails to pursue its own 'affirmative' negativity by not 'hearing' (or, as Miller would say, by not 'responding to') the fact that Austin is not quite 'serious' when he makes this distinction. Neither, she argues, is Austin a defender of 'unseriousness'. She writes (1980):

> If Austin *dis-plays seriousness* it is not in order to *play an unserious role* but – in his own words – to *play the devil*. Is the devil 'serious' or 'unserious'? This is just what it is impossible to *decide*. Theory, which is by definition foreign to humor, is generally speaking in the habit, on the contrary, of playing God: of *underwriting*, by its authority of 'supposed knowledge,' the values or theses it proposes . . . .. The devil, in other words, does not take himself for God . . . .. That is the truly diabolical question inherent in joking, or in play: *Is* it a joke? *Is* it simply a game? (p. 131)

This is why, finally, Felman focuses on promises and the non-serious 'promise' of seduction in *The Literary Speech Act*. Felman notes (following Nietzsche's discussion of promising in the *Genealogy of Morals*) that 'the very logic of promising [is] a sign of a fundamental contradiction which is precisely the contradiction of the human' (1980: 10). This contradiction is 'the scandal (which is at once theoretical and empirical, historical) of the incongruous but indissoluble relation between language and the body; the scandal of the *seduction* of the human body insofar as it speaks – the scandal of the promise of love insofar as this promise is *par excellence* the promise that cannot be kept' (1980: 11–12).

Such a promise is also the 'promise' of meaning Miller speaks of, but Felman locates it in the body – unlike Miller, who locates it in discourse; or Derrida, who locates it in a 'word' like 'woman'; or Foucault, who locates it in the 'materialism of the incorporeal'; or even Nietzsche, who locates it in the 'method' of genealogy. Moreover, for Felman the promise of love is closely tied up with the promise of pleasure: 'speech is the true realm of eroticism', Felman writes, and 'to seduce is to produce language that enjoys . . . to prolong, within desiring speech, the pleasure-taking performance of the very production of that speech' (1980: 28). She asserts, as we have noted earlier, that *humour* is outside history: it remains 'outside' history the same way that the material (and gendered) subject does, punctuated by 'explosions' of pleasure or laughter, but finally outside the alternative of mind and body. In the 'scandal of the speaking body', then, Felman enacts the critique of the will to truth that Nietzsche called for. 'The history of ideas – seduced – believes in the "truth" taught by the master ("a stern master," said Freud, with regard to the humor of the superego), believes thus in the theory, not as a promise, but as an accomplishment, not as desire, but as satisfaction' (1980: 137).

Such a critique, as the title of her book suggests, is ultimately *literary*, but like criticism as philosophical critique, it is 'literary' (in quotation marks) also by being outside the alternative between literature and philosophy, neither literary nor non-literary. It is *literary* precisely in the ways that Nietzsche and Derrida are, in the ways (which we suggested in the contrast between the criticism of de Man and Miller) that the pleasures of literature breach and participate in the rigours of philosophical thought. In Felman, finally, the distinction we are pursuing among the 'fields' of psychoanalysis, linguistics and philosophy are both erased and maintained – in this they are transformed or deformed – without the great anxiety of de Man, the loquacity of Derrida, or the aestheticism of Miller. In Felman, transformative critique achieves a kind of ethical inquiry precisely by neither falling back into particularities nor asserting universalities. Instead it circumscribes our collective and cultural understanding of pleasure, recognized as both a universal and yet culturally instituted particularity of our time and place.

CHAPTER SIX
The Critique of Social Relations

I have very early memories of an absolutely threatening world [in World War II], which could crush us. To have lived as an adolescent in a situation that had to end, that had to lead to another world, for better or worse, was to have the impression of spending one's entire childhood in the night, waiting for dawn. That prospect of another world marked the people of my generation, and we have carried with us, perhaps to excess, a dream of Apocalypse.

Michel Foucault
Interview

GENEALOGY, HISTORY, AND PHILOLOGY

It will be tempting in this chapter (and we will discuss our own temptation in this regard) to collapse the species of critique we have discussed so far into versions of the critique of 'social relations', that is, the critique of the historical and socially constructed dimension of culture – the time and space with which we ended the preceding chapter. In a way, the concepts of culture we have examined in this book – those of Arnold and Tylor, Williams, and Geertz – suggest such a 'resolution' of the crises of common understanding we have explored under the headings of psychology, linguistics, philosophy and now history. In a manner parallel to our earlier chapters, this chapter addresses that moment of historical critique in which, as Raymond Williams says, 'the concepts . . . from which we begin . . . are suddenly seen to be not concepts but problems, not analytic problems either but historical movements that are still unresolved' (1977: 11). Williams's projection of the grand horizon of history as

184

encompassing the activity of critique is a gesture common to historical understanding and one with powerful explanatory power. However, such evocations of history in modern criticism and theory do not so much solve as deepen the dilemmas we have been discussing – in effect extending the problem of critique on to the stage of history and challenging the very possibility of the historical critique of culture. In the discussion of social relations, in other words, we will once again encounter criticism explicitly as critique, as a putting into crisis and a methodological losing of ground, this time within a historical dimension of understanding that implicates but still fails to contain the other moments of critique we have discussed.

Literary history has its own 'history', which itself is subject to the kinds of critique we have followed throughout this book. In the nineteenth century, the study of literature in situating literature and literary culture within history was closely linked to the positive 'science' of philology. This study had three main goals that were perhaps best articulated by Hippolyte Adolphe Taine's classic *History of English Literature* (1864). The first of these goals was to clarify the text itself, as in establishing the date of composition and the authoritative text (with regard to manuscripts or spurious editions) as well as identifying a text's references to history – specific allusions to actual people, political events, economic developments, and so on. This effort locates the text as a historical phenomenon, including the narrow 'source study' that Stephen Greenblatt describes in 'Shakespeare and the Exorcists' as 'the elephants' graveyard of [traditional] literary history' (1985: 163). The second goal was to describe the author as an artist in terms of a personal past including the predisposition to write in a certain manner. This element of historical criticism defined the goal of literary biography that tended to include a broad area of intellectual, cultural, and aesthetic concerns, including the 'symptomatic' (person-oriented) reading of literature. Such a goal not only dominated the aspects of biography and cultural 'background' in historical criticism, it also dominated the work of the later Freudian ego-psychology that we described in Chapter 3. In relation to this goal, the aim is history in the sense of being a single author's history as an author, or what is called 'life and work'. In his essays on Michelangelo (1914) and Dostoevsky (1928) Freud offers versions of this historical enterprise.

The third goal is to grasp a literary work as it reflects the historical forces that shaped it initially, to understand how a historical moment produced a particular work of literary art. This goal projects the historical process itself as a kind of ultimate author, both the origin and composer of any work. In his most philological work, *The Birth of Tragedy*, Nietzsche presents a powerfully sophisticated version of this mode of historical inquiry by describing the aesthetic and cultural forces manifest in the persons of Sophocles, Socrates and Wagner.

Even though Nietzsche was a trained philologist, however, the genealogy we described in the preceding chapter is an antithesis to nineteenth-century philology, which Mikhail Bakhtin described as concerned solely with 'the cadavers of written languages' and as lacking 'the range necessary for mastering living speech as actually and continuously generated' (1929: 71). In Bakhtin's understanding, philology *basically* rules out any social component in its positivistic sense of 'history'. Historical philology, he argues, 'is permeated through and through with the false notion of *passive understanding*, the kind of understanding of a word that excludes active response in advance and on principle' (1929: 73). As we have seen, Nietzchean genealogy opposes this sense of 'positive' history by responding to historical phenomena at every moment. Saussure also, as we have suggested, presents a critique of the philological project in his synchronic linguistics, and he presents what can only be taken to be a parody of philology's search for positive historical 'facts' in his lifelong research to discover anagrammatically coded names within late Latin poetry (the 'dead' language which Bakhtin contends is always the object of philology). And psychoanalysis, especially in what we called its critique of the subject in Chapter 3, resists the positivism of nineteenth-century philological conceptions of the author and linguistic authority. All the versions of critique we have examined, then, focus on issues of culture and social relations, so it would be a mistake, we think, to reduce all cultural critique too quickly to historical critique. Still, issues of culture and social relations are clearest in those critiques that most self-consciously focus on historical (as opposed to psychological, linguistic or conceptual) experience. It is for this reason that it remains tempting to see all cultural critique as historical critique.

MARX, HISTORY AND CRITIQUE

In *The German Ideology* Marx and Engels raise issues about social relations and culture within an explicitly historical context. The conception of history they describe, however, unlike the conception of positive history governing philology, is distinctly relational – that is, dialogical – in its operation. They present a foundation for understanding literary and cultural study in an analysis of social relations that calls into question, as does Williams, the positivistic conception of historical culture as 'the very product of rational institution and control . . . with laws [governing it] like the laws of the ("unchanging") physical world' (1846: 12). Marx and Engels attempt to think through the nature of culture and political economy in relation to the concept of social relations against the backdrop of history conceived as a totality of dynamic operations. They define a critical attitude towards history, for instance, when they argue that 'social relations' are constituted by 'four moments, four aspects of . . . fundamental historical relationships' (1846: 19).

They initially define social relations in two moments of human need and desire, beginning with the 'production of material life itself'. By 'material life' they mean, first, the basic satisfactions of supposedly universal human needs – eating, shelter, and so on. The second is the reiterative cycle of recurring human desires, the way that the exact form of the fulfilment of human needs for food and shelter is different at other, quite different moments. In these two moments they see the attempt to satisfy basic needs as an occurrence happening in accord with the immutable laws of an objective and unchanging 'physical world' that is otherwise characterized by shifting ratios of plenitude and scarcity (1846: 16–17). In making these distinctions, Marx and Engels clearly intend to outline a scientific project of observation and objective verification of the 'physical world' as manifesting the fixed laws that govern it.

But in a third 'moment' they complicate this 'scientific' accounting for human production within society by introducing the dimension of social relations. The primary needs people may have and the means they find for satisfying them together actually constitute a semi-autonomous mechanism for shaping 'life itself' not as a fully stable horizon of fixed needs and satisfactions but as a relative social construction continually being reproduced by social mechanisms. 'Life itself', at once seemingly a constant in their formulation, is in fact constructed provisionally in the interaction among and within groups of people whose collective and individual material interests diverge and coincide – among and within Marx's complex category of social classes. It is precisely this interaction that generates the space and ongoing potential of community within a social economy.

So while Marx and Engels attempt to define the social mechanism as an objective and scientifically verifiable set of conditions and activities, their working conception of social relations introduces an enormous area of freeplay of possible 'things' (including desires) to satsify cultural conditions and activities. Since they are not axiomatic about culture, they go on to critique the idea of the social relation itself in a manner that is neither naive nor uncritical. In their fourth 'moment', for instance, they assert that 'the multitude of productive forces accessible to men determines the nature of society' outside of any senses of agency or consciousness. Because 'the "history of humanity,"' they say (1846),

> must always be studied and treated in relation to the history of industry and exchange . . . it is quite obvious from the start that there exists a materialistic connection of men with one another, which is determined by their needs and their mode of production, and which is as old as men themselves. This connection is ever taking on new forms, and thus presents a 'history' independently of the existence of any political or religious nonsense which would hold men together on its own. (pp. 18–19)

They clearly reject the importance of either 'political or religious' ideas because so-called 'ideas' have a merely subordinate place as ephemera in the cultural superstructure arising out of the formative relations of a mode of production. Their argument is that the means of satisfying human needs structures society in certain of its manifestations, as, for example, in generating particular modes of social exchange, such as feudalism or capitalism. The economic origin of those modes ensures that the subsequent social relations will reflect their material origins through a 'materialistic connection', one discoverable as causal relations between the base of economic relations and the products (in the superstructure) of the culture. Social formation, in this way, is then a prominent factor in the redefinition of human needs and will. It decisively participates in creating the conditions that define and determine the means of satisfying future needs.

Foregrounded in this analysis are cultural productivity and invention as part of a global generative system and the replication of the system's operation in the reproducing of specific social relations. That is to say, economic conditions give rise to a mode of production, which enfranchises a complex of social relations, and the social relations then shape the communal context for defining new, or newly instituted, human needs or desires; these 'needs' and the social relations they shape, in turn, serve as the grounding for the further institution of a mode of production. The sum of the relations in a mode of production – in a feudal or a capitalistic economy – will then continually define new human needs. In this account of culture's genesis, social relation is at once an effect of the material satisfaction of human needs, a dimension of the 'materialistic connection' in the production of 'life itself', and a function within an already existent social system. Like the 'ego', which is a construct at once conscious and unconscious in psychoanalysis, or the phoneme, which is alternatively the base and product of the language system, or the 'self-evident' conceptions of philosophy, social relations are irreducibly complex, existing in the interface and interaction of human needs as defined by class formation. Social relations, in other words, are a dimension of the historical dialectic of need and institution, of the material conditions and instituted economic functions and structures.

In *Capital* Marx further refines the definition of the social relation. Here he puts the focus on 'value' to emphasize the apparent primacy of what he calls 'use value'. In the chapter called 'The Commodity' he defines use value as the relatively simple inherent value 'conditioned by the physical properties of the commodity [with] no existence apart from the latter' (1867: 126), suggesting a conception of inherent and even objective worth. In this analysis, use value is a fully independent characteristic of a commodity dependent only on 'the physical body of the commodity itself, for instance iron, corn, a diamond' (1867: 126). He is saying that iron is intrinsically valuable *as iron*, corn *as corn*, a diamond *as a diamond*, and so on. To emphasize the free standing nature of use value as an absolute calculation of worth, he even makes use value 'independent of the amount of labour required to appropriate its useful qualities' (1867: 126).

This definition, however, immediately creates conceptual difficulties in the relation of use value to what Marx calls 'exchange value', the 'commodity's simple form of value . . . contained in its value-relation [compared] with another commodity of a different kind, i.e. in its exchange relation with the latter' (1867: 152). The introduction of 'exchange value' as inherently a social practice reveals that the idea of value itself 'conceals' and had concealed all along 'a social relation' (1867: 149). One may posit, for example, the existence of inherent and objective use value, but it follows that any particular instance of use value, so called, will be discoverable precisely and only in the act of exchange for 'another commodity'. The value of a commodity, in other words, is discoverable exclusively within a social frame where some commodities are exchanged for others with different or potentially different degrees of use value. The exchange activity, during which use value makes its debut *as value*, constitutes a system of social exchange, in effect making use value not an absolute and isolated attribution – a positive 'fact' in relation to an object – but an attribution positioned, in any practical sense, within the social relation where 'exchange value' defines 'the necessary mode of expression, or form of appearance, of value' (1867: 128). The social relation inherent to the activity of exchange, in other words, defines the only context in which a particular use value may be postulated.

Gayatri Chakravorty Spivak notes this same theoretical priority of exchange value over use value as an absolute quality when, in 'Can the Subaltern Speak?', she argues that use value as described in *Capital* as an inherent and essential value can be taken best as a '"theoretical fiction" – as much of a potential oxymoron as "natural exchange"' (1988: 309). She reasons that use-value cannot be an absolute and objective quality in that it is known only, as we are arguing, within a social context. In this revised definition, use value is actually collapsed into exchange value and then distinguished as the special case of exchange value *separated or abstracted from the particular circumstances of actual exchange*. In this, Spivak is pursuing the 'phases' of deconstructive analysis we described in the preceding chapter. In other words, if use value is based, in the first instance of Marx's analysis, on 'the physical properties of the commodity [with] no existence apart from the latter' (1867: 126) in a binary opposition to 'social properties', then Spivak is questioning the very priority of such a 'positive' or 'natural' conception of the 'property' of use and, further, of the existence of 'basic human needs' outside of socially conditioned desire. Anyone must grant that basic needs do exist as do different forms of usefulness of material objects, but it is precisely whether the issue of 'natural properties' makes sense in relation to creatures as wholly social as human beings that Spivak wants to question.

Marx and Engels also raise this same question. That is, while they posit a scientific system of political economy, they also insist upon the difficulty and complexity they face, repeatedly emphasizing the instability of positing 'value', 'use', or any such reference in the critique of culture. Such definitions and references become problematic as Marx and Engels move from the potential activity of critique to the *practice* of criticism in different domains of the human sciences. The procedure of application, of practice, makes the definition of use value problematic insofar as the practice of critique exposes the social mechanisms that produce the supposedly objective references and axioms without which practice cannot advance. In this aspect of Marxist analysis, as we have seen so often before, the execution of critique erodes its own ground. The great difficulty in this instance is that of identifying and formulating the ethical ends that such an operation serves. To what ends does critique erode its own grounds and destroy itself? And towards what historical or ethical purpose does historical critique, ever disappearing, move? Critics of history and historical understanding throughout the twentieth century have tended to define themselves by the way they formulate and answer these very questions. Most notably the Frankfurt School and the New Historicists pose exactly these questions about the ethical and moral aims, even the practicality, of historical inquiry – ultimately a question about the deeply ambiguous functioning of critique itself.

HISTORICAL POSITIVISM AND DIALECTICAL HISTORICISM

One approach to these questions is to reframe them in relation to the positivism of philological and other forms of nineteenth-century historiography we have already discussed. If Nietzsche and Freud, as we suggested in earlier chapters, focus their critiques most forcefully on philosophical and psychological idealism (even if they both also want to counter simple positivism), so Marx, like Saussure, focuses the great energy of his critique on the reductive historicism of nineteenth-century positivism (even if he also loudly proclaims his opposition to Hegelian idealism). This resistance to positivism is perhaps most clear in relation to the work of Hippolyte Adolphe Taine, whose historical literary criticism parallels Marx and Engels' project and the modern tradition of critique they exemplify in a counter tradition of fierce positive pragmatism concerning the definition of social relations. In fact, Taine's approach to historical criticism is still a strong current in twentieth-century thought, evident in historical neo-pragmatism, in the historical but anti-theoretical critics of current culture, and in much historical writing by academic historians.

In *History of English Literature*, Taine frames social relations not within the recursive problematic of critique but in the wholly positive relations of historical events. Not taking the social relation to be in any way problematic, Taine advances the existence of 'spiritual forms' for different races and cultures as being what makes up the grand scenario of history's master narrative (1864: 10). Those races and cultures constitute the pure essences of history. 'Just as crystals in mineralogy, whatever their diversity, proceed from a few simple physical forms,' Taine writes, 'so do civilizations in history . . . proceed from a few spiritual forms' (1864: 9–10). 'In order to comprehend the entire group of mineralogical species,' he goes on,

191

'we must first study a regular solid . . . and observe in this abridged form the innumerable transformations of which it is susceptible.' The reliance here on such regular 'solids' – the cultures of the Aryan and Chinese peoples among other supposedly 'unmixed' races – signals an essentialist approach to race that is non-dialectical and certainly racist in its implications (1864: 9–10).

Drawing on the existence of pure 'spiritual forms', Taine further extrapolates 'general traits, certain characteristics of thought and feeling common to men belonging to a particular race, epoch, or country', what Taine calls the *faculté maitresse* (1864: 9). These generally unified characteristics of race show that culture is a homogeneous 'system in human ideas and sentiments' and appears otherwise only when we contemplate the diversity of essences (1864: 9). An institution such as 'literature', therefore, can be deduced to be a 'transcript of contemporary manners and customs and the sign of a particular state of intellect' (1864: 1). These precepts concerning human cultural and social relations provide the ground on which to advance three principles that guide all historical inquiry into cultural phenomena, such as literature or historical documents:

1. 'Historical documents serve only as a clue to reconstruct the visible individual. . . .'
2. 'The outer man is only a clue to study the inner, invisible man. . . .'
3. 'The state and the actions of the inner and invisible man have their causes in certain general ways of thought and feeling.'
(p. ix).

Here Taine posits a unique *origin* for social relations as an unambiguous and idealized reference in the fixed 'spiritual form' that constitutes positive ethnic identity as a given component of historical diversity. This spiritual form is at one remove from the Platonic 'form' of national character and the 'general ways of thought and feeling' that distinguish one culture from another. A further step back from the 'spiritual form' reveals the documents and historical 'clues' that will serve as the basis for reconstructing 'the [original] visible individual' who embodied the 'spiritual form' to begin with.

In other words, Taine's model of social relations has a secondary 'outer' and a primary 'inner' dimension constituting historical surface and depth. The surface consists of the literary documents and cultural systems that together comprise an imperfect and fragmented record, and at history's depth is the original person who serves as the core of national identity that enfranchises social relations. In Taine's historical criticism, the critic literally follows the trail of documents and reconstructions to the inner dimension of history so as finally to enable 'penetration into the soul itself', that is, into the 'invisible man' (1864: 6) in which the historical critic arrives closer to the actual 'spiritual form' of history. This discovery procedure, unlike Marx and Engels's critique of history, is advanced as non-problematic in that it has the supposed potential of arriving at unassailable conclusions about historical epochs, conclusions arrived at as rational deductions from reliable and stable premises about national identity. This conception of social relations as essential historical 'facts' bypasses the problematic of the dialectical definition of social relations within a constantly changing economy of new human needs and relative exchange values.

The historicisms of Taine and Marx contrast as sharply opposed versions of historical criticism and, in the process, signal two different versions of a subject of historical understanding. The first version positions a subject 'outside' of history as a viewpoint shaped by an axiomatic historical understanding. The second version positions the subject of historical understanding 'within' history questioning what constitutes the historical dimension of society and culture. Taine's subject 'outside' of history consists in what is left when the historical trail of 'clues' in behaviour and customs have been followed and discarded. At that point a pure immanation of historical form, a pure subject, still remains. This pure historical form is the constitutive logos, the actual content, of the historical panorama. Taine's conception of 'spiritual form' and the 'inner man' suggests that the subject's view of history and the subject outside of history are identical in that both are modelled on the Romantic conception of a completely unified perspective on the constitution of race, culture, and the very essence of history itself. Underlying this set of assumptions is the belief that the 'spiritual form' of history guides the pursuit of historical understanding, and the activity of historical criticism is then given shape by human 'experience' as the substance, or ultimate content, of history – hence the pragmatic appeal to 'experience' itself.

By contrast, the subject of dialectical critique is modelled not on the metaphor of the unified human form but according to the operation of a dialectical *contradiction*. It is a historical critique founded, that is, not on an essential figuration but on an ongoing activity. Marx and Engels's *The German Ideology* and Marx's *The Eighteenth Brumaire of Louis Bonaparte* (1852), for example, project the historical subject not as an essential human, or human form, but as a historical monstrosity founded on conflict as exemplified in the divided subjectivity of social class. In this view, the social relation exists precisely as a tension within history between what Marx called the representation of the social relation as *Darstellung* (trope) and *Vertretung* (persuasion). In 'Can the Subaltern Speak?' (1988) Spivak quotes *The Eighteenth Brumaire* and notes the contradictions between these two versions of representation in the social class of peasant proprietors in nineteenth-century France.

> The necessarily dislocated machine of history moves because 'the identity of the *interests*' of these [peasant] proprietors 'fails to produce a feeling of community, national links, or a political organization.' The event of representation as *Vertretung* (in the constellation of rhetoric-as-persuasion) behaves like a *Darstellung* (or rhetoric-as-trope), taking its place in the gap between the formation of (descriptive) class and the nonformation of a (transformative) class: 'In so far as millions of families live under economic conditions of existence that separate their mode of life . . . *they form a class*. In so far as . . . the identity of their interests fails to produce a feeling of community . . . *they do not form a class*.' The complicity of *Vertreten* and *Darstellen*, their identity-in-difference as the place of practice – since this complicity is precisely what Marxists must expose, as Marx does in *The Eighteenth Brumaire* – can only be appreciated if they are not conflated by a sleight of word. (p. 272)

For clarity's sake, Spivak focuses on the social relation in the French peasant class at a static moment of contradiction between *Vertreten* and *Darstellen*, persuasion and representation. In reality, that moment is part of the ongoing activity of history as the great nullifier of all substances and essences. In any case, Spivak argues that the 'subject' even at the level of class identity is an activity constituted not as a form, like a supposed racial essence, but as a site of competition for power circumscribing individual and class interests.

DIALECTICAL CRITICISM

The literary criticism that develops from Marx rather than Taine is distinctly dialectical in its methods. That is, it does not assume a stable historical frame of interpretation but a shifting set of complex dialectical relationships. By contrast, criticism developing in the essentialist manner of Taine, what Taine describes as the attempt to recover 'through literary monuments . . . the way in which men felt and thought many centuries ago' (1864: 1), defines literary interpretation on a *genetic* model, as an explanation of how a work's genesis in a historical situation (where specific causes are manifested) brings the work into being as a distinct aesthetic object. From this essentialist viewpoint the literary critic necessarily grasps non-textual historical 'truths' before interpreting actual texts, because 'history' contains the source of culture and social relations in the *faculté maitresse* that is the essential genius of all culture. Indeed, because history produces or determines literature, history is a kind of master text, a grand *faculté maitresse*, in that 'history' does not have the contingent ambiguity of mere texts. From this viewpoint, contrary to Aristotle's opinion, history is superior to literature in shaping and fixing its nature. 'In such a model' of historical essentialism, as Fredric Jameson interprets it, 'we are tempted to say, time can never run anywhere but down', by which he means that historical essentialism through time necessarily confronts the ineluctable deterioration of culture and social relations and will tend to posit, for example, the 'decline of the West' (1981: 325).

A crisis in the interpretation of historical dialectics and Western historiography has been evident since at least the 1950s, and currently historical criticism has veered away from the 'old' historicism to disrupt both the hierarchy of history as superior to literature and the division between history and literature. Instead of viewing 'history' as the master, extra-textual context for literature, dialectically oriented critics like Georg Lukács and Raymond Williams earlier in the twentieth century gradually began to reconceive of history as a field of discourse in which literature and criticism make their own impact as political forces and, in effect, participate directly in the historical dialectic. In this Marxist view of literary criticism, the engaged critic promotes and helps to effect cultural revolution through a political commitment in literary studies. Lukács fulfils a social commitment, for example, by attempting to 'lay bare' the 'devices' of literature that can lead us to see the ideological orientation of a work. In the case of modernist literature, particularly James Joyce's *Ulysses*, Lukács argues for the dehumanizing and fragmenting effect of capitalist culture and, further, shows how a modernist novel can promote the acceptance of underlying social principles and values. As Lukács writes of Franz Kafka, the 'nodal points of individual or social life . . . are cryptic symbols of an unfathomable transcendence,' and in this fiction is always an 'abyss,' a 'gap between meaning and existence' consonant with the modernist's world view with bourgeois ideology (1964: 78; see also Moretti 1983 for similar arguments about Joyce and Eliot).

The work of Raymond Williams typifies the temper of historical criticism through to mid–century in the investigation of interdisciplinary areas of modern culture in attempting to understand subtle coercion in the promotion of capitalist ideology. In his groundbreaking analysis of 'country and city' in English literature, he analyses ideological positions based on the polarization of pastoral and urban values, an 'opposition' governed above all by the 'contradictions' that inhabit all social life. In *Marxism and Literature*, Williams notes that 'it is one of the central propositions of Marx's sense of history that in actual development there are deep contradictions in the relationships of production and in the consequent social relationships' (1977: 82). The economic 'base' of a society, as manifested in the 'relations of production', he goes on, determines that society's 'superstructure' – its arts and ideology – as 'consequences' of the base (1977: 82). Here Williams articulates the central tenet of the Marxist dialectical critique: that literature and art are social practices not separate from other kinds of social practice and, to that degree, should neither be idealized as 'above' nor excluded from social relations. One may even risk being unappreciative of art, as Williams continues in *Marxism and Literature*, 'to put it above or below the social, when it is in fact the social in one of its most distinctive, durable, and total forms' (1977: 212). Literary texts and art works may have quite specific features as practices, but they cannot be separated from the general social process and do not, as Etienne Balibar and Pierre Macherey say, ' "fall from the heavens," the product of a mysterious "creation" '; rather, literature is 'inescapably part of a material process' (1978: 82).

In America since the 1960s, Fredric Jameson has attempted to pursue a dialectical critique of modern culture based, as Marx's critique is, on a perception of material historical forces independent of ideas or psychology or even linguistic forms, with minimal ideological prejudice that would automatically condemn modern literature and culture. In *The Political Unconscious* he modifies the prior Marxist view of inherently decadent modernism by isolating a 'Utopian compensation' in modernist discourse. He holds that while modernism creates 'waste products of capitalist rationalization', it also opens 'up a life space in which the opposite and the negation of such rationalization can be, at least imaginatively, experienced' (1981: 236). The great paradox of modernism, Jameson writes in discussing Joseph Conrad, is that it can project 'a unique sensorium of its own, a libidinal resonance no doubt historically determinate, yet whose ultimate ambiguity lies in its attempt to stand beyond [and, thus, to alter] history' (1981: 237). The relationship between art and society, that is, is thoroughly dialectical so that the very 'utopian' element inhabiting even a negative vision of social life remains an imaginative possibility of changing the world.

An example of a dialectical approach to modern culture generally is Jameson's analysis in *Marxism and Form* (1971) of the 'technological situation' after World War II when the United States and the Soviet Union continued German research in missile development:

> At that time, of course, the inequality was in the field of atomic power; and it was precisely toward reducing the size of the bomb and increasing its destructiveness that American experimentation aimed. The first Soviet bombs, several years later, were still relatively cumbersome affairs. Thus, in order to deliver these large and primitive devices, Soviet technology was obliged to develop missiles capable of orbiting enormous payloads, which were then used to put the first sputniks aloft. American superiority in weaponry, however, is translated into an American lag in missile development to the degree to which the missiles had been evolved for the purpose of conveying their own relatively small atomic warheads. In further development, of course, this situation is once again reversed: the Americans, precisely because their missiles are not so powerful, find themselves forced to develop smaller and more sophisticated packages of transistorized instruments for projection aloft; while the less refined machinery of the Soviets, who are under no such pressure, transmits back relatively smaller quantities of information. And so forth. (p. 310)

This analysis posits no sense of a *faculté maitresse* representing one culture or the other. At every step of his social and historical analysis, Jameson reflects the prior positioning of relations that, afterwards, constitute a new set of material conditions. The components of this dialectical analysis, as Jameson writes, 'stand in different and quite specific ratios to each other, so that as their proportions change, the nature of the whole process is transformed as well' (1971: 336).

Jameson shows the same dialectical strategy in his reading of several lines of Baudelaire's poem 'Correspondances':

> Il est de parfums frais comme des chairs d'enfants,
> Doux comme les hautbois, verts comme les prairies,
> – Et d'autres, corrompus, riches et triomphants,
>
> Ayant l'expansion des choses infinies,
> Comme l'ambre, le musc, le benjoin et l'encens,
> Qui chantent les transports de l'esprit et des sens.

Jameson comments that the lines 'establish two simultaneous but different sets of oppositions', one set delineated within the description of the various 'clear' senses, 'each sense making the other stand out sharply by the contrast'; and another, 'larger opposition of clear sensation itself to that rich, mingled corrupt sensory experience which is primarily odor and hallucinatory ecstasy' (1971: 317). From this base of effects he then generalizes further that 'all of Baudelaire's work, on a thematic and ethical level, can be seen as the reduplication on ever higher planes of this initial and paradoxical mingling of contraries in order to distinguish them: dandyism, sadomasochism, blasphemy: so many attempts, on the psychological plane, to flee the insipidity of pastel, of harmonic consonance or sentimental effusion, by soiling it with its dialectical opposite' (1971: 317). Again, this kind of dialectical analysis posits change in relation to prior change. Jameson reads lexical and rhetorical strategies as they perform rather than simply convey or tell the contents of a poem. In this analysis, despite its great sophistication, Jameson maintains the dialectical opposition between material social base and aesthetic or ideological superstructure. Here, clearly marked, is the opposition between the 'base' of material sensation and the 'superstructure' of phenomenal hallucinatory 'experience'.

Other Marxist critics similarly describe the dialectical forces shaping and working within art. One powerful instance is M.M. Bakhtin's insistence on the dialogical nature of linguistic, psychological, ideological, and artistic and social relations. There is, Bakhtin/Vološinov writes in 'Discourse in Life and Discourse in Art', a 'social essence of art' (1926: 97; for the relation between Bakhtin and works signed by Vološinov, see Clark and Holquist 1984). 'Verbal discourse, taken in the broader sense as a phenomenon of cultural communication,' Bakhtin writes, 'ceases to be something self-contained and can no longer be understood independently of the social situation that engenders it' (1926: 96). For this reason he argues that 'verbal discourse is a social event; it is not self-contained in the sense of some abstract linguistic quantity, nor can it be derived psychologically from the speaker's subjective consciousness taken in isolation' (1926: 105). The extra-verbal situation – the material/historical 'base' – enters into verbal discourse including literary discourse *as an essential constitutive part of the structure of its import*' (1926: 100). In this regard, Bakhtin argues, consciousness itself, insofar as it is a verbal phenomenon (of 'inner speech') 'is *not just a psychological phenomenon* but also, and above all, an *ideological phenomenon, a product of social intercourse*' (1926: 115). In other words, the phenomenon of private experience, meanings, feeling exists in dialectic relationships to public social foundations.

In *Freudianism: A Critical Sketch* (1927), Bakhtin/Vološinov makes this critique of psychologism even clearer.

What is the consciousness of an individual human being, if not the ideology of his behavior? In this respect we may certainly compare it with ideology in the strict sense – as the expression of class consciousness. But no ideology, whether of person or class, can be taken at its face value or at its word. An ideology will lead astray anyone who is incapable of penetrating beyond it into the hidden play of objective material forces that underlies it.   (p. 77)

In this passage Bakhtin critiques the psychological 'ground' of experience and understanding by marking the social constitution of consciousness (and, in *Freudianism*, of the 'unconscious' as well). But he also critiques the philosophical (or 'ideal') ground of experience and understanding by questioning the 'face value' of ideas. And a few years later, in *Marxism and the Philosophy of Language*, Bakhtin/Vološinov critiques the linguistic 'ground' of experience and understanding by arguing, as he does in 'Discourse in Life and Discourse in Art', that the essential function of language is social communication rather than the Saussurean 'articulation' of meaning. The difference between the abstract 'meanings' of linguistics and philology and the specific sense of discourse in its actual function is absolute: 'meaning', he says, 'in essence means nothing; it only possesses potentiality – the possibility of having a meaning within a concrete' and particular historical occurrence (1929: 101).

All of these critiques lead to Bakhtin's particular conception of literature (and especially the novel) as being essentially 'dialogic'. '*A poetic work*,' he says in 'Discourse in Life and Discourse in Art', '*is a powerful condenser of unarticulated social evaluations* – each word is saturated with them' (1926: 107). In *Marxism and the Philosophy of Language* he adds that '*any true understanding is dialogic in nature*' (1929: 102). This conception of the dialogic nature of discourse and literary discourse informs Bakhtin's strong readings of Dostoevsky and Rabelais in which, as he does throughout his career, he argues for the subtle and remarkable ways verbal art lends itself to social transmission by engaging particular historically situated people within the dialogue of its art. In Dostoevsky, Bakhtin (1935) finds

> the acute and intense interaction of another's words in two ways. In the first place in his characters' language there is a profound and unresolved conflict with another's word on the level of lived experience . . . on the level of ethical life . . . and finally on the level of ideology . . . What Dostoevsky's characters *say* constitutes an area of never-ending struggle with others' words, in all realms of life and creative ideological activity . . . In the second place, the works (the novels) in their entity, taken as utterances of their *author*, are the same neverending, internally unresolved dialogues among the characters . . . and between the author himself and his characters . . .   (p. 349)

Such never-ending conflict and interaction repeats, on the level of art, the never-ending interaction among language, consciousness and ideology – the elements, in Bakhtin's Marxist view, of the cultural superstructure – and the material base conditioning those cultural elements. Such 'conditioning' is not, of course, simple or positivistic. Rather, it itself is dialectical and dialogical and, as in Jameson's more formal reading of Baudelaire, the dialectic or dialogue itself 'produces' as well as responds to the material base in the ongoing production of discourse and literature.

In fact, as Terry Eagleton has argued following the theatrical practice of Bertolt Brecht, the rhetorical function of literature is precisely to *destabilize* seemingly stable 'material' positions – the positive 'facts' of philological historicism – to create what Brecht calls an 'alienation effect,' which, like the 'defamiliarization' of Russian Formalism, allows the reader or audience to reconceive his or her position as situated within a particular social structure. Alienation so conceived, Eagleton argues, 'hollows out the imaginary plenitude of everyday actions, deconstructing them into their social determinants and inscribing within them the conditions of their making' (1986: 168). Art, then, certainly as Brecht conceived it, can make one notice what is artificial in the seemingly 'natural', to ask the 'crude' question about what ends particular discursive practices serve rather than the 'refined' questions of criticism that assume the stability and permanence of those practices. This, Eagleton argues, is the significance of Brecht's slogan 'plumpes Denken' – think crudely.

In this way, contemporary Marxist thought situates criticism, like literature, as a social practice. In *Literary Theory*, Eagleton argues 'that critical discourse is power', a part of the political and ideological history of our epoch (1983: 203), and many contemporary critics – including Jameson, Williams, Eagleton, Spivak, Edward Said, and many of the feminist critics discussed here – share a strong sense of critique as a historically situated activity that deeply implicates the critic. Thus, Patricinio Schweickart describes 'a principal tenet of feminist criticism' as the fact that 'a literary work cannot be understood apart from the social, historical, and cultural context within which it was written' (1986: 46). The critic cannot stand apart from the text being read and interpreted and must account for his or her own effect on the critical process; the 'genuinely dialectical criticism', Jameson writes, 'must always include a commentary on its own intellectual instruments as part of its own working structure' (1971: 336). Any literary theory, Eagleton says, is either bound up with political beliefs and ideological values or is 'blind to power' (1983: 203).

Brecht's 'crude' thinking, finally, highlights performance and power rather than meaning and knowledge just as Bakhtin's dialogical readings do, and his 'crude' questions continually remind the reader that the 'superstructure' of knowledge and meaning has a 'crude' material base of prior economic relations. Such questions also remind the critic that even the most 'disinterested' contemplation of meaning and art – even the most esoteric criticism – is situated in a social and political world and, for that reason, is a more or less 'crude' activity with social and political consequences that can never achieve the purity of 'disinterestedness'.

It not surprising that Marxist approaches to literature in the late twentieth century have demanded that criticism become more overtly political, that it attempt, as Marx said, not simply to interpret but to change the world. This sense of the need for commitment (defined more expansively than Jean-Paul Sartre's idea of the subordination of literature to the 'higher' political commitment) and the political responsibility of the literary critic pervades the work of these critics and much of contemporary literary criticism carried out from a historical viewpoint. This stance was clear earlier in Williams' (implicitly 'utopian') assertion that human practices are 'inexhaustible' and consequently one can always imagine and work for a world better than we have. 'No mode of production,' he writes, 'and therefore no dominant society or order of society, and therefore no dominant culture, in reality exhausts the full range of human practice, human energy, human intention' (1977: 43).

This stance is evident in Eagleton's description of the function of rhetoric and in Frank Lentricchia's definition of criticism in *Criticism and Social Change* as 'the production of knowledge to the ends of power and, maybe, of social change' (1983: 11). 'The activity that a Marxist literary intellectual preeminently engages in – should engage in – ' Lentriccia goes on, 'is the activity of interpretation . . . which does not passively "see," as Burke put it, but constructs a point of view in its engagement with textual events, and in so constructing produces an image of history as social struggle, of, say, class struggle.' 'This sort of interpretation,' he concludes, 'will above all else attempt to displace traditional interpretations which cover up the political work of culture' (1983: 11). By emphasizing the political work of culture, Lentricchia is explicitly situating literary studies – even a literary historian like Taine – within the contested and interested terraine of politics. Even 'appreciation,' in this context, is a political act serving political ends.

In his literary criticism since *The Political Unconscious*, Jameson has consistently pursued such politically oriented cultural work – what he calls in 'The Politics of Theory' the disengagement of the 'seeds of the future' from the present 'both through analysis and through political praxis' (1984: 64). Jameson is distinguished by the range of his vision and his consistent attempts to discover the usefulness, in a Marxist sense of 'usefulness', of contemporary literary theory. For example, he uses Freudian, structuralist and post-structuralist concepts in his examination of the political work of culture. In his various discussions of 'post-modernism' Jameson brings the same range of methods and interests to bear as he attempts to present a sophisticated analysis of the relationship between base and superstructure regarding the specific cultural phenomenon of 'post-modernism'. Not dismissing post-modernism as an isolated cultural phenomenon, a mere symptom of the so-called 'post-industrial' society, Jameson tries to show in a number of essays how post-modernism serves the economic order, how 'what is most often conducted as an aesthetic debate' about the nature of 'post-modernism' defines 'political positions' (1984: 55; see also 1984a). Thus, the 'logical' positions on post-modernism 'can always be shown to articulate visions of history' and can, in fact, be related to 'moments of the capitalism from which it emerged' (1984: 53) – related, that is, to a material, economic base.

In all these examples of recent Marxist literary criticism, including, of course, Jameson's work on film and popular culture, we can see contemporary historical criticism moving even further away from the aestheticization of philological–historical criticism. This has happened, at least in part – as Eagleton suggests in his use of the term 'deconstruction' in his description of Brecht's rhetoric – under the sway of Continental philosopher-critics such as Michel Foucault and third-world critics such as Spivak who have begun to institute new boundaries for history as a discipline. Foucault, in particular, has been influential in his view of history as 'discursive practice', what it is possible to say in one era as opposed to another, claiming in 'What is an Author?' that 'the author's name manifests the appearance of a certain discursive set and indicates the status of this discourse within a society and a culture' (1969: 107). Such discursive practices are, as Williams says, 'hegemonic' in their effect, both creating and created by 'a whole body of practices and expectations' (1977: 38).

FOUCAULT, SUBJECT, POWER

Michel Foucault's work explores precisely this relationship between the hegemonic power of discourse and the subject of both language and history in a broad critique of social and historical relations in his major works from the *History of Madness* (1961) through *The Will to Knowledge* (1976, translated as Volume 1 of *The History of Sexuality*). But while Foucault focuses on disputes like that between Marx and Taine – the deployment of history as dialectic as opposed to history as positive value – rather than affirming generally that historical phenomena are dialectical and specifically that cultural critique should be pursued through the examination of the dialectical relationship between base and superstructure we have been describing, he sees historical phenomena as fundamentally relational and differential. (The contrast between opposition and difference discussed in the preceding chapter should clarify this distinction.) For this reason, then, he is not a Marxist. Foucault, in fact, rejects the Hegelian dialectic in a deliberate and obviously difficult stance taken by a French intellectual who consistently positioned himself on the left politically. 'It was Nietzsche,' as Foucault writes, 'who burned for us, even before we were born, the intermingled promises of the dialectic and anthropology' and, in so doing, made necessary the rejection of ultimately rational frames of interpretation, even the 'radical' rationalism of the historical dialectic (1970: 263).

Foucault chooses to define historical critique in his own way and, in effect, creates a new sense of crisis by rejecting philosophy and the rationalized critiques of strict dialectical argument – such as the historical episteme of the dialectic – that Marx advanced and situated himself in. Like others in the generation of French intellectuals after World War II – François Lyotard, Jacques Lacan, Jacques Derrida, Gilles Deleuze and Jean Wahl among them – Foucault challenged the 'stable forms' of all thoroughly rationalized thought underlying methodology. From such bases Marx, or even Taine, can make supposedly indisputable 'truth' claims about history, but these bases are themselves open to the most devastating critique (1970: 263). Any such claim to unassailable understanding, even the self-proclaimed radical (dialectical) 'truth' of Marxism, Foucault maintains, merely parades the familiar rationalizations of history in familiar representations. In other words, like other post-modern theorists in France, Foucault felt the immediate threat of a Hegelian rational and complete totalization of thought, and therefore attacked the schematizations that underlay totalizations such as dialectical thinking (see Descombes 1979: 136).

In pronouncing the end of such programmatic 'philosophy', Foucault even tried, as did Deleuze and Derrida, to proclaim the 'end of philosophy' itself, that is, the end of the regime of verifiable and stable 'truth' as a condition of inquiry. (This participates in the critique of philosophy we examined in the preceding chapter.) Thereafter, Foucault's explorations of the 'discursive formations' and institutions of Enlightenment and post-Enlightenment Western culture so thoroughly dissect the relations between the subject and power, so thoroughly undermine the subject's access to legitimate science, as to endanger all of Western philosophy's claims to 'truth'. In so doing, along with other post-structuralists (Foucault most immediately identified himself as a 'post-Nietzschean'), he initiates a distinctly post-modern discourse of cultural crisis.

The language of cultural crisis, a consistent and somewhat theatrical hallmark of Foucault's work, extends from his earliest theorizing about the classical *episteme* and subjectivity in the 1960s through his explicit discussions of power, subjectivity and body technology in *The Archaeology of Knowledge* and *Discipline and Punish* in the 1970s. A state of 'crisis' also describes the mode of Foucault's own discourse in that his thinking enacts a series of ruptures ranging from the epistemic view of culture, with its repressions of non-institutionalized thought, such as the 'experience' of 'madness', through his formulation later of 'discursive formations' and the deployment of technologies that have shaped and continue to shape the human body. In this range of discourse Foucault maps the extreme possibilities for a post-modern critique of culture, at once an instructive replaying of the Marx/Taine opposition and then a further venturing across utopian boundaries, as yet uncharted, of avant-garde theoretical practice and speculation – into the dimension of Foucault's work that Allan Megill calls a 'postanthropological future' (1985: 184). The shifts and ruptures of Foucault's discourse depict not only the changed focus and the eventual broader expanse of his critique but also preview, partly reflecting Foucault's own enormous influence, many of the institutional developments in cultural theory and criticism from the 1980s forward – in effect making Foucault a key figure in the enactment of post-Marxian cultural critique through the later twentieth century.

The Foucault of *Madness and Civilization* (1961; 1965) and *The Birth of the Clinic* (1963) investigates what he calls in *Histoire de la folie à l'âge classique* (1961) 'fundamental structures of experience' (1961: 633). Crucial to this version of Foucault's critique is the existence of a phenomenological reduction of experience that the institution of Freudian psychiatry suppressed as it failed, as Megill writes, 'to place itself at the center of the experience of mental illness, attempting, through intuition, to enter into the consciousness of the ill person' (1985: 201). In his early historical and cultural analysis of the psychiatric clinic and definitions of madness, Foucault tried to recover analytically the 'experience' of madness as a kind of genesis of cultural production existing prior to all institutional definitions of mental health and disease. (Ludwig Binswanger and R.D. Laing also attempt to articulate the phenomenology of psychological experience.)

Foucault's critical practice in these early works rests on the assumption of a hitherto concealed 'experience' that exists independently of cultural formulation or representations. In this vein, the goal of cultural critique is to make visible and audible this occluded 'experience' through a kind of excavation of that which existed prior to and still survives 'beneath', in the 'depth' of, institutional categories and bureaucratic tables of organization. The very act of tracing the history of the clinic and paradigms of madness foregrounds the cultural constructedness of such social institutions and hence the suppressed state of non-institutional speech, that is, irrational awareness. Evident in this programme for revolutionary liberation is the Rousseauean assumption of an original and purer, though currently shackled and restrained, version of 'experience' existing before cultural intrusion. Inimical to this Romantic precept is the assumption of an ever-present oppression by all dominant orders of a basic and intrinsically vital humanity, a notion of cultural crisis 'committed to the notion', as Megill writes, 'that the reigning order, whatever its nature, is degraded' and in practice works to diminish human potential (1985: 239).

In the late 1960s and early 1970s, Foucault abandoned this critique of power as a force inevitably working to suppress a 'natural' human subjectivity and instead, especially in *The Order of Things* (*Les Mots et les choses*, 1966; revised English edition 1970), rejects the belief of 'experience' existing prior to or apart from culturally instituted 'discourse'. Thereafter, in the manner of Derrida's claim that 'there is nothing outside of the text' (1967: 158), Foucault credits dominant discourses as frequently oppressive but also world-producing and enabling structures, or texts. Rather than oppressors of a natural humanity in the exercise of 'power' (*pouvoir*) in virtually all dimensions of cultural life, the dominant discourse is a prime agent in creating an essential scaffolding or staging for cultural exchange. No longer the apologist for pre-cultural, repressed human subjectivity, Foucault now posits the autonomous operation of cultural 'discourse' as power in the constitution of historical and social relations. In *The Order of Things*, in particular, he consistently equates language, ideological hierarchies, and the operation of social institutions as specific operations of 'power' in a positive sense as 'discursive formations'. In this version of critique, Foucault no longer envisions an activity of analytical liberation allowing 'madness' or other such pre-cultural experiences to speak in their own voice or on their own behalf.

In this consideration of power and 'the problem of the subject', Foucault distinguishes 'between the epistemological level of knowledge (or scientific consciousness) and the archaeological level of knowledge' – 'archaeological' in the sense of being structured and stratified but without a privileged perspective or subject who views it (1970: xiii). In this period, berating the 'tiny minds' that tried to connect his work with French Structuralism as understood by Claude Lévi-Strauss and Jean Piaget (1970: xiv), Foucault nevertheless frames social relations in structuralist terms as constructible in a paradigm of rules and transformations. History itself is then the succession of cultural epistemes, or dominant discourses, separated from each other by the deepest fissures and discontinuities. He then defines 'power' in this period as meaning structural 'relations, a more-or-less organized, hierarchical, co-ordinating cluster of relations' (1977: 198).

In this version of critique, cultural 'crisis' is now subsumed in the tyrannical rigours of what can and cannot be said or thought in a particular episteme or discourse of culture – in a particular historical cultural formation. Foucault believes that modernist discourse reveals, for example, 'not the sovereignty of a primal discourse, but the fact that we are already, before the very least of our words, [forever] governed and paralyzed by language' (1970: 298). In other words, in modernism's totalized discursive formation we are fixed in 'an order of representations' which by necessity appears to us as 'a manifestation of a language which has no other law than that of affirming . . . its own precipitous existence' (1970: 300). Granting modernism's view of language as a totalized world body, Foucault goes on, 'there is nothing for [discourse] to do but to curve back in a perpetual return upon itself'. Contemporary discourse, in this way, must always address 'itself to itself as a [recursive] writing subjectivity' (1970: 300). Cultural 'crisis' in this scenario is defined by the difficulty – at times Foucault says the 'impossibility' – of locating strategies that allow the movement either through or else 'beyond' the discursive formations that construct us as subjects of culture and history.

In the last phase of his work in the 1970s, Foucault went on to abandon the structuralist critique of culture as well. In the figure of an archaeology of the sciences, as was true of the structuralist project generally, Foucault had imagined by his own account a largely unmediated appraisal of the different strata of cultural production and interaction, as if there were no actual subject performing his critique. Critics often comment, and it is true, that the whole era of Foucault's work up until *The Order of Things* (1966/1970) was dominated by a structuralist reliance on the privileged metaphor of seeing and the unobstructed observation of culture – the structuralist penchant, as Derrida notes in *Writing and Difference* (1967a: 3), for deploying metaphorical derivatives of the 'gaze' as enhancements of the notion that structuralism allows the observation of discourse from a fully scientific or objective (God-like and unobstructed) view. (Roman Jakobson, as we have seen, participates throughout his career in such a scientific and passive rhetoric.) This tendency for deploying the visual metaphor is evident in Foucault's frequent postulation of the panopticon, the 'Medical Gaze', and his exploitation of other spatially situated metaphors to establish theoretical bases and critical strategies.

In place of 'gazing' upon a cultural stage, a stage set with properties found through the archaeological investigation of culture's 'depth', Foucault in the middle 1970s posited the technology of 'genealogy', the exploration of cultural association and groupings not connected through causal relations or defined by the construction of actual subjectivities as the products of culture. In this third version of cultural critique, Foucault no longer takes up the vantage of the panopticon in observing cultural production around him. Rather, he proposes investigating the genealogy of conditions, instead of 'causes', that have evolved into perspectives and subjectivities, as is suggested by the extreme example of Jeremy Bentham's masterful subjectivity defined by the panopticon plan for a prison. Such historical inquiry leads Foucault to make closer connections between the public and private spheres of culture, as in the postulation of a 'technology' of the body in which the body is actually constructed within the limits of a socially constructed subjectivity. In the volumes of *Histoire de la sexualité* he likewise investigates, without any pretensions to a scientific foundation or objective mode, the local constraints that have shaped the human body in the West as a locus of 'personal' concern, what in Volume 3 of the *Histoire* he calls antiquity's institution of the 'cultivation of the self' (1984: 43). In this critique, 'genealogy', as a replacement for the structuralist 'archaeology', carries with it no warranty of accuracy or significance, and genealogical critique certainly presupposes no privileged perspective for cultural observation or intervention. For Foucault's purposes, in other words, genealogy is not a science and not a methodology but a loose (non-scientific) set of strategies. As a method of critique, however, genealogy is potentially efficacious as a practice of intervention

207

precisely for its lack of ideological and methodological prescription, for the fact that it leaves open, to be determined *in situo*, the particular relation and responsibility of an actual cultural intervention. The genealogist is a kind of poststructuralist version of the *bricoleur* that Lévi-Strauss describes, the 'tinkerer' as opposed to the scientist or the highly rational engineer. Furthermore, the concept of 'intervention' itself is finely calculated to evoke a relation other than the aesthetic distance of 'observation' and other than the isolated category of an 'event'. 'Intervention', rather, presupposes the deploying of a prior strategy in an instance of cultural practice and situatedness, the activity not of an observer but of a participant already located on the field of action.

In no longer maintaining the pose of disinterestedness in theory or practice, Foucault has now nearly collapsed critique into practice, a move giving the critic no privileged position as an investigator studying culture, but instead erasing, in effect, the concept of 'theory' and leaving 'practice' in its stead. While Foucault destroys 'theory', his genealogical critique, as a variable strategy, has the potential to escape the fixity and blindness of institutionalized criticism and, in this way, is potentially responsive to the vicissitudes of cultural transformation. In this version of critique, in which the social relation is defined as *practice*, the situated intervention that responds to and observes culture also *creates* culture within a micro-sphere of influence in which responsibilities are local and immediate. In this new analytical/participatory posture, Foucault has withdrawn from the grand interventions that previously aimed to go behind and supervene the technologies of culture. He seeks through genealogical investigation to describe the formulation and impact of those technologies at the site of an actual subject's cultural engagement and participation. Cultural critique in the mode of genealogy is none other than Foucault's definition of a post-modern cultural and political activism, a post-structuralist recasting of the ancient science of applied knowledge – *techne*.

CULTURAL CRITIQUE AND COMPLICITY

In our own genealogy of the deployment of critique, it is perhaps fitting to say now that Foucault's final claim to a mode of cultural criticism adequate to the radical potential of critique does not go unchallenged. His genealogical critique, in fact, has not escaped serious scrutiny concerning, in turn, its failure as critique insofar as it substantifies itself into criticism. Gayatri Spivak, for example, reads Foucault's mode of intervention in the micro-sphere, despite his protestations, as a form of unacknowledged complicity, of collaboration, with reigning imperialist ideologies. Her critique of Foucault on the issue of complicity, moreover, is important for understanding not just Foucault's notion of critique but also for understanding his influence on and place in literary and cultural studies in the Anglo-American academy since the 1960s. Whereas the encounter we staged between Marx and Taine defined the controversy over the nature of social relations in an earlier era of historical criticism, the scene of Spivak reading Foucault – which we will consider briefly – serves a similar purpose by defining the problematic of the social relation as well as historical criticism in the late twentieth century.

In 'Can the Subaltern Speak?', which we discussed earlier, Spivak examines Foucault's position in relation to the issues of representation and ideology. Representation, which she casts in its functions as knowledge and power, can never imply a purely structural or purely 'representational' (*Darstellung*) version of culture. Culture and social relations are never purely an aesthetic spectacle or a structural formulation in that representation is always simultaneously a specific implementation of power (*Vertretung*, or persuasion) as well as a tropological articulation of knowledge (*Darstellung*). In this complexity, representation is never idealizable as a universal view or picture that does not change. Foucault does name the micro-sphere as identifying the *interest* of his genealogical approach, but, Spivak argues, he consistently evokes the 'unnamed Subject' of pervasive cultural power without caring to act in relation to this power in local spheres (1988: 274). The theoretical point is that he continues to keep the 'subject' of the investigator out of his analytical frame and never overcomes his own 'resistance' to the '"mere" ideological critique' that is appropriate to a claim for intervention (1988: 273).

By contrast, Spivak holds that cultural critique must 'consider the relations between desire, power, and subjectivity' in order for analysis to be sufficiently grounded in a historical locality. Such historical grounding provides a basis for any version of intervention that can be distinguished from (structuralist) reflection (1988: 273). Certainly it is Foucault's intention in his later work to descend from the panoramic and Olympian heights of discursive matrices to locate critique in a reading of micro-spheres. However, his view of the 'pervasive heterogeneity of power' actually leads him at times 'to conflate "individual" and "subject"' (1988: 274) and, in so doing, undermine all of his claims to be responsible for action in a micro-sphere of intervention.

The crucial lack in Foucault's critique, even at this late stage of genealogical critique, is what Derrida calls in 'Force and Signification' the lack of a strategic recognition of 'force' that can never be deleted from theories of cultural representation (1967a: 26–7). Representation-as-*Darstellung*, or mere troping, may give an accounting of the pervasive (that is, 'global') effects of 'power' in culture, but it tells nothing about the 'force' that raises one structure and the interests that accompany it over others that conceivably could come forward instead. This failure to consider the actual effects of power, what Derrida calls a failed recognition of 'force' in structuralism's cultural theory, is exactly Spivak's point about Foucault's 'disavowal of the role of ideology in reproducing the social relations of production' (1988: 274). Insofar as 'force' and 'ideology' together designate value and the social and economic relations that impel one value, or complex of values, over others, the critique of the subject in social relations can never escape the issues of alignment and commitment in relation to one's own analysis.

Because Foucault consistently fails to see that force exists as complexly 'representational' as well as in its most abstract ('global') sense, his claims for genealogy as intervention must be rejected as a further aestheticizing of social relations. Social relations in Foucault, it turns out, are 'represented' (*Darstellung*) within the incidental staging of what he calls the 'micro-sphere', but this 'representation' does not attempt to account for the 'force' of representation, the political dimension, present in every instance. The particular situated instance of power at work in historically unique situations – in particular instances of 'ideological' activity and representation – must be clearly distinguished from the 'pervasive heterogeneity of power' that Foucault seems willing to represent in his genealogical discourse. Spivak's view of Foucault's genealogical critique – and we think she is correct – is that Foucault seems unaware 'that the intellectual within socialized capital, brandishing concrete experience, can help consolidate the international division of labor' (1988: 275). That is, the intellectual is always a participant with particular, if unacknowledged, ideological commitments and, in any case, acts – whether he or she acknowledges them or not – in relation to those commitments. Foucault's theory of 'power', therefore, is a theory not of power as constitutive of social relations in a dynamic operation of cultural production but a blanket rationale for the aesthetic representation of the *forms* of power in cultural discourse in which the 'base' of material force is erased through generalization. In this sense, again and perhaps most radically, critique becomes criticism precisely because the representational *force* of critique necessarily assumes the form of the representation of *knowledge* – its very force inhabits 'knowledge' and leads to the very 'disinterested' contemplation critique seeks to resist.

HISTORY AFTER FOUCAULT

It is this sense of the textual and subtly aestheticizing nature of the study of history and the historicity of texts in Foucault that marks the movement in literary criticism that has come to be called the 'New Historicism'. In such historical inquiry, as in Foucault, the opposition between base and superstructure is abandoned or 'deconstructed'. However, Stephen Greenblatt first coined the label 'New Historicism' in relation to the 'old' philological historicism of Taine rather than against Marxist dialectical historicism. In his argument, the dominant historical scholarship of the 'old' positivist historiography practised throughout the nineteenth century and into much of the twentieth in literary studies is opposed by a 'new' historicism that shares with semiotics, post-structuralism and even psychoanalysis a sense of the *textual* nature of 'experience' – a sense of how experience, as a condition of being experience, has to be encoded in manners that are closely linked to textual encoding. In the 'Introduction' to *The Forms of Power and the Power of Forms in the Renaissance*, Greenblatt says that the 'old' kind 'tends to be monological – concerned with discovering a single political vision, usually identical to that said to be held by the entire literate class or indeed the entire population' (1982: 5).

This is the approach we have designated as 'criticism' in the narrowest sense. As such, Greenblatt argues, 'this vision can serve as a stable point of reference, beyond contingency, to which literary interpretation can securely refer'. The result of this process is that 'literature is conceived to mirror the period's beliefs, but to mirror them, as it were, from a safe distance' (1982: 5). Greenblatt refers specifically to traditional literary scholarship but is also describing a certain doctrinaire Marxism regarding the absolute division and overly linear relationship between the 'historical' economic base of relationships – the mode of production at a given historical moment – and the superstructure of ideology, beliefs and assumptions embodied in art, intellectual 'world views' and other consciously or unconsciously held 'ideas'. Joined by the work of Jonathan Goldberg, Louis

Montrose, Leonard Tennenhouse and others, Greenblatt has produced a significant re-reading of Renaissance literature in terms of a sense that, in Tennenhouse's words, 'the history of a culture is a history of all its products, literature being just one such product, social organization another, the legal apparatus yet another, and so on' (1982: 141). Tennenhouse argues, further, that 'one is forced to make an artificial distinction among cultural texts between those which are literary and those which are political in the effort to demonstrate how, in sharing common themes and a common teleology, they actually comprised a seamless discourse' (1982: 141).

In claiming that the contemporary practice of 'history cannot be divorced from textuality, and all texts can be compelled to confront the crisis of undecidability revealed in the literary text' (1985: 164), however, Greenblatt and the New Historicists are also erasing the opposition between base and superstructure that governs the Marxist dialectical criticism we examined earlier. In general, this conception of literary history abandons any notion of history as direct mimesis, any belief in history as a mere imitation of events in the world – history as a reflection of an activity happening 'out there'. Hayden White, especially, tends to view history as itself a narrative, a narrated sequence marked by inexplicable gaps or ruptures. The sequence of history itself elaborates relationships that belong to what Foucault calls an *episteme*, not a mode of thought that characterizes an age (as in the 'old' historicism), but the discursive limits on what can be thought or 'discursivized' at any particular moment, so that history as a discipline necessarily traces ruptures rather than continuities and empty spaces of thought within and between epistemes. This definition of history would hold true for the immediate sense we have of history as reality, even its personal impact as well as for the histories we write. Thus, the new textual sense of history has done much to encourage literary critics both to view history as a species of language and to look beyond formalist aesthetics (as in Spivak's reading of Foucault) in order to read literature in the context of power relations and practice.

The current view of history as a discourse, indeed, reverses the hierarchy of history over literature. Now history, like literature, is seen as structured textually, like a language, and both are represented as formed in a sequence of gaps, as a narrative discourse. If in this way fundamentally a breached narrative, history in its constitution is virtually indistinguishable from literature. This is not to say that history is 'made up' – 'fictitious' or 'mythical' in the derogatory sense – and, thus, rendered trivial. On the contrary, the reality of history in this new view is as 'real' (as intractable and even as potentially 'hurtful') as it ever was. The new awareness, rather, is that history, like a fictional narrative, exists in a dialogue with something 'foreign' or 'other' to it that can never be contained or controlled by the historian. Instead of being a more or less accurate story about something that already exists, history is now a knowing that is a making that never quite makes what was intended. Alternatively, we can try to make of history a process of repetition, as T.S. Eliot imagined, so that what was valuable in the past is continually regained ('made new') through poetry in a kind of cultural retrieval mechanism. Or we can make of history an apocalyptic promise to be fulfilled in time, as Northrop Frye in *Anatomy of Criticism* – and, indeed, the Bible – envisioned it. And history can be projected as the genealogy of a series of irrational ruptures, as Nietzsche and Foucault imagined it. But whether as repetition, apocalypse or rupture, history is not an order in the world that simply is copied but an order of practice in the world, a conception of making and participating with the world all at once.

In any case, it is evident that the controversies characteristic of the interest in New Historicism are, in fact, controversies about the nature of critique – not just about the nature of historical criticism but the broader perspective on critique that we have discussed in this book. When Greenblatt, for instance, quite recently wrote that 'methodological self-consciousness is one of the distinguishing marks of the new historicism in cultural studies as opposed to a historicism based upon faith in the transparency of signs and interpretive procedures', the scope of his commentary extended to a theory of signs, discourse, and culture itself (1989: 12). His comment manifests, moreover, an awareness and interest in the possibility of critique, of criticism in 'crisis', as opposed to an activity that legitimizes reigning ideologies.

Likewise, Stanley Fish, in assessing New Historicism, is quite clear that his concern goes beyond that immediate task. Fish characterizes New Historicism as believing fundamentally in ' "wall to wall" textuality' and as denying 'that the writing of history could find its foundation in a substratum of unmediated fact' (1989: 303). But, largely unsympathetic with New Historicism, Fish goes on, 'the fact that the textualist views of the New Historicists do not prevent them from making specific and polemic points means that those points will be made just as everyone else's are' (1989: 309). 'In the end,' he concludes about New Historicism, 'you can't "defy categorization"[;] you can only categorize in a different way. (Itself no small accomplishment.)' (1989: 309). In a similar negative assessment of cultural studies, Fish advances bluntly his fundamental belief that 'we cannot achieve an "authentic critique"' of history or anything else, that is, a final and apocalyptic exposition of analytical grounds and assumptions. From this observation regarding the dynamic function and ultimate incompleteness of any particular critique, he then draws the conclusion that 'the impossibility of authentic critique is the impossibility of the interdisciplinary project' (1989a: 21). In these assessments Fish has succeeded only in describing the ongoing, rather than the apocalyptic, nature of change, the reconstitutive rather than the ideal nature of academic disciplines, and the temporal as opposed to the transcendent status of knowledge. These are commonplace tenets of ancient and modern epistemology, and certainly of current discourse; Fish deploys them, however, as strategic counters to his own construction of ideal and transcendent version of cultural studies and New Historicism. The question of whether he is *ultimately* right or wrong about critique goes to the heart of what Geertz calls the essentially incomplete nature of cultural analysis.

The strongest refutation of such scepticism about critique and cultural studies can be found in critical practices that operate either in the name of or in support of feminism. Many such practices attempt to expose cultural institutions previously termed 'natural' and inevitable as, in reality, culture-specific and, thus, functioning in the service of a reigning ideology. When Annette Kuhn discusses the 'ways in which sexual difference is constructed' in *Pumping Iron II – the Women*, her interest is explicitly the 'spectator-text relations' produced as women watch other women mimic male bodybuilders. Her critique, in other words, focuses on the way 'representation . . . sets in play certain relations of power through which, among other things, discourses around sexual difference and subjects in and for those discourses are ongoingly produced' (1988: 20). The ultimate goal of such feminist historical critique is to situate the gendered subject at a certain cultural time and place in order to explore the possibility, in this instance, of feminism as an oppositional strategy in relation to a certain moment in the deployment of cinema as a technology of male power. The situating of the gendered subject could then create 'the possibility that feminist critical practice may constitute not only a resistance to the power of visual representation, but also an attempt to bridge the gap between woman as spectacle, as object of the look, and wom*en* as historical subjects' (1988: 22).

Kuhn, like many other feminists with a historical orientation, effects a critique that aims not to assume the preconstitution of the category of 'woman' but to interrogate the historical forces that create such a category and its endless subcategories in the first place. Many productive feminist critiques of this sort, understandably, focus on the powerful and formative texts of commercial and mass media that alter and shape contemporary culture and the disempowered subject positions of women.

The argument against the possibility of 'authentic critique', as we saw it in Fish, is often evoked to undermine the feminist critique of history. Tania Modleski argues that influential male critics from Marx and Jacques Ellul to Roland Barthes and Fredric Jameson have categorically denied the very subject matter, the *interests*, that will empower and situate the feminist critique of contemporary culture. In 'The Terror of Pleasure', for example, Modleski shows that the cultural fear manifested in film criticism and many American films of 'the "feminization" of American culture is synonymous with the rise of mass culture' (1986: 163). In David Cronenberg's *Videodrome*, for instance, she argues that 'the openness and vulnerability of the [electronic] media recipient are made to seem loathsome and fearful through the use of feminine imagery (the vaginal wound in the stomach) and feminine positioning'. Accordingly, the feminized television viewer is finally 'raped with a video cassette' (1986: 163).

Such historically grounded critical practices attempt to account for the appearance in specific historical instances of certain kinds of gendered subjects. The goal of such feminist critique, as Irene Diamond and Lee Quinby argue, is to situate and critique male definitions and framings of culture as historically bounded and specific, and to demonstrate 'the ways in which Western humanism has privileged the experience of the Western masculine elite as it proclaims universals about truth, freedom, and human nature' (1988: x). What ultimately turns out to be a feminist critique of Western history, thus, consistently turns to Western humanism and perennial verities about 'human nature', the very issue of natural and material-ism with which we began in our discussion of Taine and Marx. To the degree that such critiques – the accomplishments of feminist criticism in literature and popular culture – are now resetting the stage for all critiques of contemporary culture, they are indeed 'authentic' critiques of contemporary culture that are creating the direction and future of literary and cultural studies with methods that are conspic-uously interdisciplinary in orientation.

HISTORY AND CRITIQUE

We mentioned earlier our own temptation to collapse *all* versions of critique, wholesale, into a historical perspective and create a kind of master critique, a gesture, in fact, common to much contemporary criticism. Such a temptation is embodied in the theme of genealogy – and the transformative mode of critique that genealogy allows – that runs throughout this book. The temptation to do this amounts to designating *history* once and for all as the 'last instance' of an otherwise ungovernable proliferation of futures for which we as yet have no models, a genealogy of one critique overlapping and melding into another and then giving way to yet another, and so on, until the last one marked 'History' is reached. This prospect, with its evident promise of control and finality, cannot fail to be tempting, but clearly in the context of our discussion it is not an open choice. Such a conception denies the revolutions of transformative critique by leaving out the complexity of representations and the *institutional* power and knowledge that genealogy and critique alternatively promote. One might view history as the 'last instance' in a privileged and exclusive sense, but then 'history' becomes none other than a global sign for a cloudy mass or constellation of practices that advance too many different values and technologies under the misleading sign of one practice – as if these practices were not *practices* at all but derivatives of a single, spectacular truth.

Our own commitment after Marx, after Foucault and after Spivak is to remain within the logic of representation and ideology informing this book – to take the notion of history, even 'History' itself, as always a particular practice that by definition is not and cannot be the last instance in a series – even if that particularity is culturally *instituted* and thus neither random nor unintelligible. Insofar as one might wish to collapse all possibilities of critique into one, we believe that there is no 'History' as such, only – as Foucault believed – historical institutions and practices and the quite different ends that they might achieve. In this conception, history itself is subject to transformation even as its intellectual practices are subject to institutional critique. Language is also such an institution which is subject to transformation, yet *alternatively* – in another use and apprehension – it 'grounds' cultural institutions and, thus, never changes. In the same way, the subject and agent of knowledge in psychoanalysis constitute such a complex cultural 'institution', as do the grounding concepts of philosophy and, as we have discussed in this chapter, the ideological 'representations' of history. In our presentation of all of these cases –

which we have examined in tracing the operations of twentieth-century literary and cultural studies – institution and transformation define and delimit the practice and understanding of critique.

And yet, as Fish notes sceptically, the notion of 'complexity' we are foregrounding and valorizing in our genealogy of critique as idea and practice should not automatically be constitutive of a new understanding of critical practices. Our own discussion of the practice of historical criticism is a socially bounded practice too, and bears traces of the social relations and material conditions that construct us as subjects (that is, occupying subject positions) within our own culture. However, we do not deny the historical and social dimension of our own practice in this chapter but wish to avoid the vacuous designation of the 'historical' as if it were not a *practice* but a 'transparency', as Greenblatt said, 'of signs and interpretive procedures'. We are *interested* in history, in other words, but unlike Taine do not attempt to stand outside of it. From this position in the conclusion to this book, by foregrounding our own concluding *interests* – as Nietzsche and Marx would describe them – we will identify our own practice and situation as best we can. To do this, we return to feminist studies and cultural studies as historically informed practices traversing the various focuses we have pursued in examining literary studies. We believe that such practices, in important and powerful ways, are shaping possibilities and enhancing the prospects for pedagogically effective cultural critique.

CHAPTER SEVEN

Notes Towards a Definition of Cultural Studies

The alternatives – either calling culture as a whole into question from outside under the general notion of ideology, or confronting it with the norms which it itself has crystallized – cannot be accepted by critical theory. To insist on the choice between immanence and transcendence is to revert to the traditional logic criticized in Hegel's polemic against Kant. . . . [I]f stubbornly immanent contemplation threatens to revert to idealism, to the illusion of the self-suffcent mind in command of both itself and of reality, transcendent contemplation threatens to forget the effort of conceptualization required. . . . The dialectical critic of culture must both participate in culture and not participate. Only then does he do justice to his object and to himself.

Theodor Adorno
Prisms

The path of this book goes from eighteenth-century attempts to define the nature of critique through the institution of literary criticism in the twentieth century in the Anglo-American academy in response to a number of cultural texts and forces. We have explored the various ways in which critical practice in modern literary studies over the last thirty years has functioned fundamentally as the practice of critique within the contexts of Romantic and post-Romantic conceptions of subjectivity and language, and we have attempted to mark this exploration with commitments to particular culturally instituted values and social aims. Within historical and intellectual developments, we have examined the issue of ethical responsibility in criticism, which has moved to the centre of literary studies so that literary critics have turned generally from what they may *know* to what they may *do* in the context of the cultures they inhabit. The study of literature has come to address this reconception or reorientation in many different guises – all of them, we believe, movements towards *critique* – as shown in the polemical debates Edward W. Said describes as the conflict between 'the new subculture of theoretical opposition' and the 'old traditions' now fighting against 'theory' with 'appeals to humanism, tact, good sense, and the like' (1983: 167). These are the very appeals Matthew Arnold used in response to the 'terrible learning' of philology he opposed in 1862.

A hallmark of the 'old tradition' is what Lillian Robinson has called its 'apparently systematic neglect of women's experience in the literary canon', a silence about gender and an inability to reconsider 'whether the great monuments are really so great, after all' (1983: 106, 108). For the Arnoldian tradition of humanism the rationale for inclusion in the canon – what makes a literary work 'great' – is presented as self-evident and without need of discussion, the promotion of the self-evident drawing generally from the four basic assumptions about modes of inquiry in the 'human sciences' that have governed our discussions in this book. These assumptions, and the 'grounds' they form, make certain kinds of understanding possible by organizing the play of discourses in the human sciences, discourses that correspond to various focuses of cultural critique in psychology, linguistics, philosophy and history. Our point in this book, like that of Said, Graff, Spivak and many others writing today about cultural studies and social institutions, is to test these critical modes against the tasks they set for themselves to perform. Most immediately, the test is of 'literature' itself, as Miller says, against the 'entire body of traditional inquiries in the human sciences' that the Arnoldians load on to literary study. To this end, we have challenged the 'imperialism' of each of the grounds, their tendency to reduce and dismiss all other explanations and to make each ground, in turn, a kind of 'base' for the superstructure and epiphenomena of other discursive formations. This tendency is at the heart of the blind and yet fierce resistance among contemporary versions of these grounds – Marxist, structuralist, psychoanalytic and deconstructive – to the institution of alternative modes of literary criticism and pedagogy. It is resistance to the rigours of unending critique.

Each of the grounds of criticism we explore tends to situate itself as a self-evident explanation for 'everything' and then dismiss further inquiry. The study of literature reduced to the study of language, accordingly, becomes 'scientific' in relation to other cultural formations, often refusing to traffic in the discussion of cultural values and constantly returning to the supposed objective nature of linguistic conditions. Limited to psychological study, criticism becomes a guide to the 'inevitable' symptomatics of the text, diagnosing particular

219

authors or even particular eras in terms of 'health' or 'disease', in a model of understanding based upon more or less autonomous subjects (or what Deleuze and Guattari describe in the broadest sense as the Western Oedipus). Based on religious and deconstructive concerns, literary criticism, in Stephen Greenblatt's words, often leads fairly directly 'and predictably to the void', or at least to reifications of the 'void' in various manifestations of the sublime (1985: 164). Finally, scaled to the study of history and society, criticism becomes a programme for social action – what Lentricchia calls 'the production of knowledge to the ends of power' (1983: 11) – in which case the study of literature recognizes cultural values defined collectively and socially as power. This grounding gesture 'marginalizes' (as 'false consciousness', 'ideology' or 'self interest') what it cannot describe as belonging to the base of historical formation in the global historical explanation we discussed in the preceding chapter.

In each case, the tendency towards imperialism and resistance constitutes the slide of critique into 'criticism' based on particular and often exclusive assumptions that often, as we mentioned earlier, appropriate all phenomena as *examples* of the 'basic' mechanisms. These grounds account for particular discourses while claiming, in Raymond Williams's terms, 'to exhaust the full range of human practice, human energy, human intention (. . . that extraordinary range of variations, both practiced and imagined, of which human beings are and have shown themselves to be capable)' (1977: 43). In each case there is a dimension, at least implicitly, of ethics which deals, in John Dewey's terms, 'with conduct in its entirety, with reference . . . to what makes its conduct, its *ends*, its real meaning' (1891: 241). The definition of ethics as the ends of conduct even encompasses Julia Kristeva's description of contemporary social control in which the 'coercive, customary manner of ensuring the cohesiveness of a particular group' is less evident. Instead, Kristeva argues in a definition compatible with Dewey's, that 'ethics crops up wherever a code (mores, social contract) must be shattered in order to give way to the free play of negativity, need, desire, pleasure, and jouissance, before being put together again' (1980: 23). For Kristeva, ethics inhabits the work of negative critique, and for her, as for Dewey, the relationships between knowledge and power, the universal and the particular, are realized in the provisional descriptions of the ends of conduct made by institutional and transformational critique.

CRITIQUE AND LEARNING

The potential of critique in literary studies has ethical implications for the understanding of 'culture', and those implications are perhaps clearest in the institutional conduct of the study of literature. In 'The Function of Criticism at the Present Time' Frye complains that the apparent arbitrary and unsystematic nature of the institutionalization of literary studies in Anglo-American higher education did 'not . . . make any sense at all' (1949: 257). Earlier, Kenneth Burke had attempted to breach the interested complacency of 'those persons who take the division of faculties in our universities to be an exact replica of the way in which God himself divided up the universe' (1937: 303) with a rhetorical and 'sociological' understanding of literature. Recently, in *Professing Literature*, Gerald Graff traced the institutionalization of English studies in America and described how its structuring into chronological periods has served institutional, 'departmental' interests rather than the ends of critique by avoiding the view of literary study and literature 'as social products with a history that [readers] might have a personal and critical stake in' (1987: 258). The result is that professors have no need to critique their professional activity or their intellectual and social practice. 'The notions of institution, genre, and language,' as Robert Scholes has said, are examples of 'powerful tools of thought . . . whose interrelatedness has only recently become apparent.' 'This new perception,' he goes on, 'is leading many scholars to reconsider the dimension of their academic disciplines, as they rediscover the very objects of their study' (1985: 3).

If critique calls into question the institutional structures that transmit knowledge (just as Nietzsche questioned the concept of 'knowledge' itself), then it also questions the concepts of teaching and education. Shoshana Felman argues, for instance, that 'teaching, like psychoanalysis, does not deal so much with *lack* of knowledge as with *resistances* to knowledge' (1987: 79); the critique of pedagogy, therefore, needs to situate pedagogy in relation to the relationships of power that discourse coordinates along with its 'knowledge'. She attempts to explore and analyse the relationships between knowledge and ignorance – between teacher and student – in a way suggestive of structuralism's reconsideration of language-effects as opposed to the unconscious structures which allow language to function. Parallel to both is post-structuralism's reconsideration of the 'constative' and 'performative' forces of discourse, and behind these – Foucault's caution about dialectical critique notwithstanding – is the Marxist relationship of base and superstructure, the relationship between supposedly transcendent, timeless ideas, beliefs and feelings about the world and the modes of cultural production – psychological, linguistic, philosophical and social modes – that give rise to those ideas.

Felman traces the relationship between knowledge and ignorance in teaching and psychoanalysis in ways that shed light on the rethinking of the profession and discipline of English studies more generally. Teaching, psychoanalysis teaches us, must learn to learn from ignorance, 'ignorance' not simply as the absence of knowledge but as an orientation to knowledge as power and the situating of power that '*itself can teach us something*' (1987: 79), the aim of teaching being 'not the transmission of ready-made knowledge; it is rather the creation of a new *condition* of knowledge' (1987: 80), or what could be called a new condition for the production of knowledge. The teacher's and the analyst's 'competence, insists Lacan, lies in "what I would call *textual knowledge*"', which is, Felman says, 'the very stuff the literature teacher is supposed to deal in . . . knowledge of the functioning of language, of symbolic structures, of the signifier, knowledge at once derived from – and directed towards – interpretation' (1987: 81).

Felman's description of the teacher using rather than 'exchanging' knowledge also suggests a reorientation in English studies from a model of transmitting great works of art and the 'tradition' which engenders or is constituted by these works, to the study of literature as a form of cultural critique that examines the conditions and realization of discourse in its various groundings. Teaching uncovers the conditions of knowledge, functioning through performative 'utterances' as well as constative statements. 'Misinterpretations of the psychoanalytical critique of pedagogy,' Felman says, 'refer exclusively to Lacan's or Freud's explicit *statements* about pedagogy, and thus fail to see the illocutionary force, the didactic function of the *utterance* as opposed to the mere content of the statement' (1987: 72–3). If it 'is not a purely cognitive, informative experience', she says, but also an emotional, 'transferential' one, then literary study must expand and re-structure itself to emphasize the functioning of language, of symbolic structures, of signification – knowledge at once derived from and directed towards the ongoing activity, the doing, of interpretation. This reorientation of literary studies, then, is an orientation towards cultural studies as a kind of activism in its various modes, as we have been suggesting throughout this book.

Such institutional 'reorientation', of course, can be subject to its own critique. It's all well and good, one could object, to describe but not to make ethical choices, to define teaching as both cognitive and emotional, to say there are many ways to organize the discipline of English studies, but the fact is that such a 'pluralism' simply demonstrates 'complicity' with a repressive social order (Lentricchia 1983: 65), or an 'inability to look into things all the way down to the bottom' (Miller 1985: 23). Such 'pluralism' could also be 'mystified' apprehension of the effects that linguistic relationships occasion as substantialized 'objects' in the world (Greimas 1966: 65). Pluralism may also embody the psychological resistance to the truth, as Freud often implies. The fact is, as each of these positions argues, sooner or later critique requires ethical and political choices.

In teaching, a 'political' choice is made each time texts are ordered for a course. Lillian Robinson makes this point in describing the 'turn from the construction of pantheons, which have no *prescribed* number of places, to the construction of course syllabi, [when] something does have to be eliminated each time something else is added, and here ideologies, aesthetic and extra-aesthetic, do necessarily come into play' (1983: 112). What does the teacher do? What is to be taught? What is the object of literary studies? Robinson argues that, in one way or another, the feminist critique answering these questions 'humanize' male critical theory and that such 'humanity' provides a basis for informed choice.

Underlying the self-evident opposition between 'aesthetic' and 'extra-aesthetic' considerations, as we have suggested, is the self-evident 'truth' in need of further critique. The site of this opposition is where *literary* criticism becomes *cultural* criticism, where the four 'grounds' we have been examining come together in constant competition. Sandra Gilbert stages such a competition between literary history and operative concepts from psychoanalysis in rewriting a feminist literary history in 'Life's Empty Pack: Notes Toward a Literary Daughteronomy' (1985), and Henry Louis Gates Jr follows structuralist and post-structuralist 'signifying' and 'signification' in situating traditions in African–American literature in relation to itself and to a critical canon in 'The Blackness of Blackness: A Critique of the Sign and the Signifying Monkey' (1984) – both critics arguing for restructuring and expansion of the literary canon. Gates situates himself and the object of literary study 'in this space between two linguistic domains', standard American English and 'American Negro usage' (1984: 293) and suggests that the use of '*signifying* as the slave's trope, the trope of tropes . . . a trope that subsumes other rhetorical tropes, including metaphor, metonymy, synecdoche and irony' (1984: 286) in contemporary black literature and criticism defines the themes and techniques of post-modern literary practice – much the way New

Criticism used modernist texts to define and justify its critical formulations.

In this way, the practice of literary study itself is always forming canons, is always a *cultural* activity. Stanley Fish and others have argued that interpretive strategies condition and determine the so-called 'facts' of discourse (1980: 165–66), the practices of criticism determining the objects of study. Criticism becomes critique, though, only when it becomes self-consciously framed in this activity. When it does so, *critique* itself necessarily becomes *cultural critique* – that is, the 'signify'n' Gates describes, like the critical practice that allows him to see its significance, produces, as he says, 'a critique of traditional notions of closure in interpretation' (1984: 304). The strongest of those notions for the *institution* of literary studies, like the 'restrictive institution' we are hardly aware of 'until we come into conflict with it', Robinson describes, is the very construction of objects of knowledge, the literary canon itself. Critique in the sense we have been discussing, therefore, is constitutive of literary and cultural study at the most basic level in the formation of the objects of study.

FEMINIST CRITIQUES

Throughout this book we have consistently returned to various feminist critiques of gender formation for their productive engagement with the institutional and transformative concerns of cultural study. If critique entails a rethinking of the object of knowledge, it also means a rethinking of the subject of knowledge in ways that question the 'grounds' of dominant critical activities. This challenge is foregrounded most dramatically in the cultural critique of gender, in which the diversity of approaches has developed with remarkable intensity, suggesting a development characteristic of a significant critical reorientation in the practices of criticism and in the potential for critique.

Evident in this reorientation is the urgency to understand literature *subjectively*, from the viewpoint of a *culturally* gendered subject, the project that has already led many to rethink their assumptions and practices. When Elaine Showalter cites Irving Howe's description of Michael Henchard's selling of his wife and daughter at the beginning of *The Mayor of Casterbridge* and Howe's assertion that to 'shake loose from' and 'discard' his wife 'through the public sale of her body to a stranger' wrings a 'second change out of life', she notes that 'a woman . . . will have a different experience of this scene' (1979: 129) and that only the training in 'androcentric' reading has obscured this difference. As Patrocinio Schweickart adds, 'the feminist inquiry into the activity of reading begins with the realization that the literary canon is androcentric, and this has a profoundly damaging effect on women readers' (1986: 40). The reorientation effected by the inquiry into reading in relation to gender suggests that all readings are not the same and that 'texts' are not endowed with transcendent ('constative') meanings but are historically and socially situated through gender markings – as well as, for example, class issues.

This situation is clear if we contrast the survey of feminist literary criticism Showalter presents in 'Feminist Criticism in the Wilderness' with the 'grounds' for literary study we have been exploring. Showalter isolates four approaches for feminist inquiry parallel to our four grounds. She, too, describes 'theories of women's writing [which] presently make use of four models of difference: biological, linguistic, psychoanalytic, and cultural' (1981: 249). Three of the four categories coincide with ours, even though the order of their presentation is different. But the category in our discussion occupied by the philosophical approach to literature is Showalter's category of biology and gender difference, that is, the 'natural' materiality of gendered existence. If, in part at least, philosophy is taken to be ontology, where we are most abstract, Showalter is at this point most concrete; where we explore post-structuralism as a language which can address the 'situation' of humankind, as Hillis Miller says, as 'something encountered in our relations to other people, especially relations involving love, betrayal, and the ultimate betrayal by the other of our love for him or her, the death of the other' (1985: 22), Showalter surveys literal and metaphorical articulations of the physical difference between men and women in 'feminist criticism which itself tries to be biological, to write from the critic's body, . . . [criticism which is] intimate, confessional, often innovative in style and form' (1981: 251). She posits not abstract 'grounds' but concrete models for difference, an approach that situates the act of reading and criticism in particular gendered contexts for culture.

Showalter's taxonomy for feminism, drawing from at least four areas of contemporary critical thought, indicates not just the interdisciplinary nature of feminist critiques but their explicitly critical orientation. An example is Hélène Cixous's drawing on both biology and psychoanalysis in her description of Little Red Riding Hood as 'a little clitoris' in her psychoanalytically informed discussion in 'Castration or Decapitation?' Cixous also relies on the opposition between nature and culture introduced by Lévi-Strauss (and critiqued, from the vantage of the gendered subject, by Kristeva) and examines the relations between female silence – the loss of speech – and female decapitation. Schweickart also examines the linguistic strategies of literature from a viewpoint that encompasses biological, psychological and cultural concerns with rhetoric, as do many other critics of gender and culture (1986).

Feminist critiques of culture *as critiques*, however, have proven ultimately not to be confinable to the grounding of biological, or 'natural', gender differences, suggesting the resituated dimension of critique that has emerged strongly in feminist cultural criticism. Under pressure – that is, tested under the weight of numerous literary and social texts – the biological grounding of gender inquiry has given way, probably decisively, to other approaches to culture and ideology. The ideology of 'natural' *men* and *women* with essential 'sexual difference [merely] functions', Monique Wittig warns, 'as censorship in our culture by masking, on the ground of nature, the social opposition between men and women'. The ground of 'masculine/feminine, male/female are the categories', she goes on, 'which serve to conceal the fact that social differences always belong to an economic, political, ideological order' (1982: 64). In other words, the *idea* that there is a human nature structured irremediably within the categories of heterosexual opposition as situated and known within a particular culture 'is only an *idea*' (1981: 47). In Wittig's and others' challenges to gender as a 'natural' ground of cultural inquiry there is a reinstitution of Simone de Beauvoir's critique of 'natural' gender in *The Second Sex* where she argued that 'no biological, psychological, or economic fate determines the figure that the human female presents in society; it is civilization as a whole that produces this creature, intermediate between male and eunuch, which is described as feminine' (1952: 249).

Wittig's critique of the biological grounding of gender difference – and her consistent articulation of a lesbian critique in regard to the decidedly male underpinnings of the whole heterosexual order of Western culture – is a powerful formulation, at the very least, of the social construction of gender, a position that Wittig has advanced in other provocative critiques such as 'On the Social Contract' (1989) and 'Homo Sum' (1990). Her critique of gender breaks through the implicit biological 'grounding' of many other feminist inquiries and mandates that no social practice or text can be naturalized, or removed from the contest with other social practices, based on the supposedly natural and unassailable categories of sexual difference. Henceforth, according to this critique, all social institutions must be understood as the management of power as marked by gender in the social construction of class and gender.

Wittig's position continues the critique of gender differences that we discussed in Freud, Lacan, and psychoanalysis generally in Chapter 3. There we also highlighted questions of sexual difference in relation to linguistic strategies and cultural understanding. Also in the critique of structuralism in Chapter 4 we followed Kristeva's weaving together of different discourses in 'Stabat Mater' – a discourse of the maternal body and a discourse of cultural history – to articulate the multi-faceted relationship between an 'experience' of womanhood that seemed, scandalously, impersonal and collective in relation to biology, language, psychology and cultural order. In Chapter 5 we examined Felman's Austinian critique of Derridean deconstruction and Derrida's and Spivak's genealogical critique of the concept of 'woman'. In the preceding chapter on social relations we examined Spivak's social critique of the historicization of Foucault from the vantage of the historical position of the (female) subaltern, and juxtaposed the claims of New Historicism with the particularities of feminist readings of cultural artifacts. In other words, we have drawn out the elements of several feminist critiques in our own critical practice in this book to expose our own interests and simultaneously to facilitate the further shifting of grounds, even the grounds we necessarily assume in arguing our position. We have attempted to adopt the double gesture of critique in interrogating the suppositions of a narrative and its derivative modes of analysis, as suggested in Nietzsche's aphoristic style and Derrida's multiplication of analytic frames in philosophic critiques as well as Marx's attempt constantly to make contradiction both an object and a method of understanding.

In examining the ways in which contemporary literary and cultural criticism have become species of cultural critique by reorienting its inquiry in relation to a gendered subject of knowledge, we have followed feminist critiques that challenge literary theory to confront the difficult task of assimilating the findings of an expanding sphere of cultural inquiry. To the degree that this challenge has already been accepted in literary and cultural studies, we believe that a significant shifting of ground is already taking place, a decisive reorientation. It may well be that the future of literary studies is being decided as current feminist theory and cultural criticism are being formulated.

If this is so, it is because feminist critiques, more explicitly than other forms of cultural critique, call for social, linguistic and ideological interrogations of their own premises. In 'Imperialism and Sexual Difference' Spivak tries to situate feminist criticism as it is practised within the context of middle-class academic life in the West, placing some modes of feminist practice within the context of New Critical formalism and structuralist and post-structuralist economies. She also enlarges that context to articulate feminism in relation to imperialism and the colonial tendency to universalize a particular situation into the human condition. She writes, 'even as we feminist critics discover the troping error of the masculist truth-claim to universality or academic objectivity, we perform the lie of constituting a truth of global sisterhood where the model remains male and female sparring partners of generalizable or universalizable sexuality who are the chief protagonists in that European context' (1986: 226). She notes, in particular, the 'post-romantic concept of irony' which springs 'from the imposition of her own historical and voluntarist' position with 'U.S. academic feminism as a "universal" model of the "natural" reactions of the female psyche' (1986: 235). Such a practice, she argues, carries with it the '*structural* effect' specifically colonialist and imperialist in origin.

Like Wittig, Spivak articulates a critique of feminism informed by the advances that psychoanalysis, structuralism, post-structuralism and Marxism have brought to the examination of discourse in general. She reads literary texts in such a way that 'discourses' – personal discourse, political discourse, and philosophic discourse – are seen to be *cultural* discursive practices. Together, in specific practices of literary and cultural critique, Spivak and also Wittig delineate the outlines of feminist practices in particular as part of a larger effort to demonstrate the reconception and reorientation of literary studies in the twentieth century as cultural critique.

Irigaray, Deleuze and Guattari, Spivak, and Wittig, among others, all redefine social behaviour that was previously unexamined or vaguely conceived as existing outside of an analytical frame in order to locate it in relation to cultural institutions and possibilities of transforming those institutions. They expose social behaviour in its cultural dimension as an instituted practice occurring at a particular historical moment. The force of this generalizing critique, consistent with the particularities of Annette Kuhn's and Tania Modleski's critiques of gender differences in popular culture within a larger ethics of cultural studies, has the potential to dislocate countless critical practices that have silently ignored the operations of power in supposedly neutral zones of gender (and genital) organization. It is for this transformative potential, and the opportunity not merely to understand but to change culture, that we have consistently high-lighted feminist critiques of cultural understanding.

THE INSTITUTED SUBJECT OF CULTURAL STUDIES

In the challenge of feminist critiques we see the instance of cultural critique as a pedagogical mode – an exemplary instance of cultural studies. Our strategy for cultural studies in the broadest sense is derived precisely from the critical reformulation of the four groundings of criticism in this book. Fundamental to that working model is the 'instituted subjectivity' within cultural inquiry. Such instituted subjectivity is the complex interrelationship between the subject and object of cultural studies. As such, it is outside the opposition between subject and object of inquiry. By subjectivity we do not mean non-'objective' or non-rigorous and do not intend simply to denote the concept of culture implied in Raymond Williams' 'structure of feeling', the common human 'experience' as the absolute 'ground' of all cultural elaboration and formations – an essentialist construction of 'experience' as the irreducible 'terrain of the lived' (quoted in Hall 1980: 66). From Williams' perspective, 'culture' is the outgrowth of 'experience' in the sense that 'experience', as Stuart Hall says, is where 'all the different practices [of culture] intersect' (Hall 1980: 63).

Rather, we have positioned the subjective nature of cultural studies according to what Hall calls the 'structuralist' understanding of culture (1980: 64), which suggests that 'experience', so called, is no ground of culture at all but, in its substantiated form, is the instituted 'effect' of a specific cultural text and practice. That is, a particular culture at a particular moment produces 'experience' in a specific configuration: in effect, first culture and then 'experience'. In this perspective, in which 'experience' is not the natural foundation of culture, it becomes necessary to define and situate the critical viewpoint, or 'subject', that constitutes any instance of experience being investigated. Analysis of the 'subject' as a construction within a cultural frame then begins with the critic's own 'subjective' historical placement, the investigator's own insertion into a historically and ideologically specific moment. The investigator then represents him- or herself in the activity of cultural discourse. Never simply personal, the subjective moment – the situating and constructing of a subject at a historical juncture – is a crucial reference for cultural studies in that it is the rigour of critique that this model has instead of 'disinterestedness' or 'objectivity'. We have ended our discussion with feminism and a provisional definition of cultural studies precisely to mark our own 'subjective' sense, our own placement in relation to intellectual and ethical practices.

Such placement, asserting some version of universality in conjunction with the particular, makes cultural inquiry an ethical activity. It is just this ethical activity that Derrida describes in 'The Principle of Reason: The University in the Eyes of its Pupils' (1983). Derrida argues that institutional knowledge as produced in the Western university is a product of the eighteenth-century separation of pure knowledge from the practicality of ethics as it was expressed by Kant. In this scenario, aesthetics and art are the mediating terms between knowledge and ethics. Rigorously extending Kant's logic, Derrida projects social and cultural experience as texts with textual and aesthetic dimensions. He then situates the object of cultural studies in precisely that mediating position – constituted simultaneously by knowledge and power. This organization of 'disciplines' creates a sense of what it means to be *interested*. In this view, the cultural studies critic, for example, will not seek to perform a strictly 'disinterested' inquiry but will always be enacting a participatory relation within the discourse of inquiry. The critic, in other words, cannot be an innocent observer passively recording an 'other' world, as we discussed in relation to Foucault and Spivak, but is defined as a subject position in relation to knowledge and power. The resultant activity of a performative 'knowing' grounds one's 'interest' both as awareness but also as ethical responsibility for the discourse of inquiry itself. It follows that intellectual scrutiny must always be ethical engagement. Again, in that there is rigour but not disinterested objectivity from this viewpoint, it is important to acknowledge the roles the participant/observer may *and* may not occupy – that is, may *actually* occupy and be responsible for in ethical and ideological terms.

By 'participants', further, we mean those subject to the particular constraints in a sphere of possibility in terms of what is thinkable and doable, what Foucault means by *pouvoir*, which not only describes the ideal of Power but also, as a verb, means 'to be able', designating what is possible in the world as we know it – the limit of what can be done as it consistently constrains action posing a fair working definition of ideology. On this important point we think, for example, of Gulliver's situationally imposed limits in *Gulliver's Travels*. In Lilliput, or in any of the 'other' worlds into which Gulliver is inserted, there is an outlandish asymmetry between his subjective intentions and the material conditions that constrain him. The tale's frequent and satiric reversals as Gulliver encounters enormously large and tiny people suggest the fundamental lack of any natural isomorphism between Gulliver as a culturally instituted subject and the social and material discourses in which he operates. That is, the narrative reversals mark Gulliver's own capability in every instance in relation to the possibilities of knowledge and power. His mediate distance between knowledge and power is, above all, textual in the psychological, linguistic, philosophical, and historical conceptions of text and marking we have explored throughout this book. Gulliver, gullibly situated like the rest of us, never quite understands this textuality; he never understands, *ideologically*, the mediated relationship between knowledge and power.

This misrecognition of ideology is the constitutional instability, the inevitable misrecognition, of ideology apprehended as a merely cognitive awareness of a text. Such cognition mistakes perception for unmediated apprehension, just as, at another extreme, Paulo Freire describes a kind of anti-Gulliver, an impossible ideal of a person who recognizes perfectly the implications of ideological and class struggle and who has the unerring ethical and critical 'ability', as Freire says, 'to perceive social, political, and economic contradictions' in society and culture (1968: 19). Such perfect recognition fails to take fully into account the instituted and limited subjectivity always necessary for the work of negativity – the work of critique – to continue within culture.

THE TRANSFORMED OBJECT OF CULTURAL STUDIES

These notes towards a definition of cultural studies suggest something quite different from 'disinterested' observation and indicate what we think of as a post-modern and post-structuralist *activism* – a cultural and political position wagered on an always to be enacted interpretation of a social text interwoven by social relations. The possibility of success for such a practice must continually be resituated within historical change as a virtual rather than an actual text – hence the need for ongoing contest and struggle to achieve cultural knowledge and change, and the necessity to reject the concept of the 'last instance' of critique. The subjective and ideologically motivated 'interest' of cultural studies derives from a commitment to a continual resituating within multiple contextual frames that include, and perhaps begin with, the local situation in institutions in which we can act as teachers and intellectuals and, in so doing, discover our mutual interests in a collectivity.

The critique of the subject is a key to cultural studies and formulates a critique of 'culture' itself. In this critique, critics read the discourses and texts of contemporary culture to expose crucial oppositions and contradictions that govern the exercise of power, to expose what Homi K. Bhabha calls at one extreme 'the political "rationality" of the nation as a form of narrative – textual strategies, metaphoric displacements, sub-texts and figurative stratagems' (1990: 2). Through such critiques Bhabha, Stuart Hall, Gayatri Spivak and other cultural critics work, in effect, continually to manoeuvre themselves into strategic conflicts with cultural practices in the interventionist style of one working from within an institution – as theorists and teachers in the academy – to change and transform culture. Such interventions must always be repeated in that they always succumb to the ideality of 'reading' and the monumentality of 'practice'.

It is to underline the necessity of this repetition that Clifford Geertz describes cultural analysis as 'intrinsically incomplete'. He writes (1973) that the deeper cultural analysis 'goes',

> the less complete it is. It is a strange science whose most telling assertions are its most tremulously based, in which to get somewhere with the matter at hand is to intensify the suspicion, both your own and that of others, that you are not quite getting it right. But that, along with plaguing subtle people with obtuse questions, is what being an ethnographer is like.
>
> There are a number of ways to escape this – turning culture into folklore and collecting it, turning it into traits and counting it, turning it into institutions and classifying it, turning it into structures and toying with it. But they *are* escapes. The fact is that to commit oneself to a semiotic concept of culture and an interpretive approach to the study of it is to commit oneself to a view of ethnographic assertion as . . . 'essentially contestable'. (p. 29)

Such contestation defines culture as well as cultural studies. The four examples of 'escape' that Geertz presents offer four different definitions of culture: the collection of folklore which, like the Arnoldian canonization of literature and art we examined in Chapter 2, attempts to encompass a self-evident cultural tradition. The enumeration of cultural traits, as in scientifically modelled social sciences critiqued by structural linguistics and Marxism, attempts to define culture positivistically. The apprehension of intellectual structures, like the linguistically modelled analyses critiqued by post-structuralism and historicism, attempts to understand culture in terms of its hermetic and idealistic logic of signification. In this chapter we are foregrounding the last of these definitions of culture, the description of social institutions, in an attempt to see culture in terms of relationships of power. Two of these definitions – those of intellect and language – encompass what Raymond Williams calls the '"inner" process' of culture. The others, scientific positivism and historical institutionalism, encompass what he calls the 'general process' of culture.

As we saw in Chapter 1, Williams specifically describes the 'complexity of the concept of "culture"' we are trying to describe here as both 'a noun of "inner" process, specialized to its presumed agencies in "intellectual life" and "the arts"' and 'a noun of general process, specialized to its presumed configurations in "whole ways of life"' (1977: 17). For Williams, 'culture' encompasses an individual subject's 'inner' world and a society of individuals conceived as a whole greater than the sum of its parts. For him, both definitions of culture are thoroughly historical. Throughout *Culture and Society*, for instance, he argues that the 'idea' of culture in each of these senses responds to the growing industrialism of Britain, and more specifically to the fragmented individualism of laissez-faire capitalism. In his definition of culture, Williams above all wants to demonstrate that 'culture', as both an inner process and a general process, can be subject to a transformational critique.

The historical and intellectual complexity of culture is subject to institutional critique. In his attempt to understand culture, Geertz develops what he calls the 'essentially semiotic' conception of culture as textual (1973: 5), and he seeks to rescue social discourse 'from its perishing occasions and fix it in perusable terms' (1973: 20). That is, this conception of culture attempts to avoid imprisonment 'in the immediacy of its own detail' without falling into vacuously abstract generalizations (1973: 24). The collections of folklore or of the 'facts' of positive science present the danger of detail. The abstractions of structuralism or of grand institutional histories present the danger of unsubstantial universals. Against these dangers, Geertz suggests that the 'thick descriptions' of cultural institutions, seeking 'a stratified hierarchy of meaningful structures' (1973: 7), can be achieved only by situating the events we call culture within the particularities of historical understanding. For Geertz within cultural analysis 'the essential task of theory building . . . is not to codify abstract regularities but to make thick description possible, not to generalize across cases but to generalize within them' (1973: 26).

Williams pursues and achieves such an analysis in his tracing of the great nineteenth-century articulations of 'culture' as a concept in *Culture and Society*, even if, unlike Geertz, his aim is the transformation rather than the understanding of culture. In this pursuit, however, Williams demonstrates the problem and danger of the strict separation between knowledge and power, institutional and transformational critique, and the object and subject of cultural studies. 'A culture,' Williams writes, 'while it is being lived, is always in part unknown, in part unrealized. The making of a community is always an exploration, for consciousness cannot precede creation, and there is no formula for unknown experience' (1958: 334). This definition of culture substantiates Geertz's description of cultural studies as 'essentially contestable' (1973: 29). It also substantiates the complex relationship between criticism and critique we have delineated in this book that describes the historicity of cultural studies as neither the prisoner of positive detail nor the working out of transhistorical destinies. Bakhtin's dialogical aesthetics attempts a similar complex historiography, as do Derrida's conceptual grammatologies. Lacanian psychoanalysis and the scientific semiotics of Jakobson attempt parallel synchronic critiques. In this definition Williams is attempting to *situate* historically what seems, in the Arnoldian tradition, to be a universal and transcendental idea. Both Williams and Geertz locate the contest in the word 'culture' to define it not in terms of transcendent meaning nor in terms of local dialect, but within what Geertz calls 'the flow of social discourse' (1973: 20).

Williams, as we have seen, pursues this contest historically, in the genealogy of 'culture' which, as Foucault says, attempts to 'record the singularity of events outside any monotonous finality; it must seek them in the most unpromising places, in what we tend to feel is without history – in sentiments, love, conscience, instinct [– in order] to isolate the different scenes where they engaged in different roles' (1971: 139–40). In this approach, culture itself, 'what we tend to feel is without history', is realized within historical consciousness. This is the approach of critique – specifically the critiques of psychological, linguistic, conceptual and social formations we have traced in this book.

In creating the possibility of the realization and transformation of culture, Williams achieves what Geertz describes as the achievement of cultural studies at its best, the possibility of bringing 'us in touch with the lives of strangers' (1973: 16). That those strangers are often ourselves – this, after all, is the discovery of contemporary feminism – is the promise of understanding and power of transformation that cultural studies offer. These are precisely the complex ends of making the familiar 'odd', 'peculiar', 'unpleasant', 'ignoble' – all that Arnold describes under the label of 'terrible learning' (1862: 184–5). In such learning – the 'terrible' learning of critique – the distinctions between inner and general processes, private responses and public responsibilities, break down. In it aesthetics and ethics, literary and cultural studies, are reoriented in relation to one another.

Bibliography

Note: Works cited are noted by the date of original publication. The editions or translations used are subsequently identified.

Adorno, Theodor (1967), *Prisms*, trans. Samuel and Shierry Weber. Cambridge: MIT Press, 1981.

Armstrong, Nancy (1987), *Desire and Domestic Fiction: A Political History of the Novel*. New York: Oxford University Press.

Arnold, Matthew (1853) 'Preface' to *Poems*, in *Complete Prose Works of Matthew Arnold*, ed. R.H. Super, 11 vols. Ann Arbor: University of Michigan Press, 1960–77.

—— (1862), 'On Translating Homer: Last Words' in *On the Classical Tradition*, ed. R.H. Super. Ann Arbor: The University of Michigan Press, 1960, 168–216.

—— (1865), 'The Function of Criticism at the Present Time' in *Selected Prose*, ed. P.J. Keating. New York: Penguin Books, 1970, 130–56.

—— (1869), *Culture and Anarchy* in *Selected Prose*, ed. P.J. Keating, New York: Penguin Books, 1970, 202–301.

Attridge, Derek (1988), *Peculiar Language*. Ithaca: Cornell University Press.

Babbitt, Irving (1919), *Rousseau and Romanticism*, Boston and New York: Houghton Mifflin.

Bakhtin, M.M. [V.N. Vološinov] (1926), 'Discourse in Life and Discourse in Art (Concerning Sociological Poetics)' in *Freudianism: A Critical Sketch*, Trans. I.R. Titunik. Bloomington: Indiana University Press, 1987, 93–116.

—— [V.N. Vološinov] (1927), *Freudianism: A Critical Sketch*, trans. I.R. Titunik. Bloomington: Indiana University Press, 1987.

—— [V.N. Vološinov] (1929), *Marxism and the Philosophy of Language*, trans. Ladislav Matejka and I.R. Titunik. Cambridge: Harvard University Press, 1986.

—— (1935), 'Discourse in the Novel', in *The Dialogic Imagination*, trans. Caryl Emerson and Michael Holquist. Austin: University of Texas Press, 1981, 259–422.

—— (1976), 'The Problem of the Text in Linguistics, Philology, and the Human Sciences', in *Speech Genres and Other Later Essays*, trans. Vern McGee. Austin: University of Texas Press, 1986, 103–31.

Baldick, Chris (1987), *The Social Mission of English Criticism: 1848–1932*. Oxford: Clarendon Press.

Balibar, Etienne and Pierre Macherey (1978) 'On Literature as an Ideological Form: Some Marxist Propositions', trans. Ian McLeod, John Whitehead and Ann Wordsworth, in *Untying the Text*, ed. Robert Young. London: Routledge and Kegan Paul, 1981, 79–99.

Barrett, William (1983), 'Writers and Madness' in *Literature and Psychoanalysis*, ed. Edith Kurzweil and William Phillips. New York: Columbia University Press, 85–100.

Barthes, Roland (1963), 'The Structuralist Activity', in *Critical Essays*, trans. Richard Howard. Evanston: Northwestern University Press, 1972, 213–20.

—— (1964), *Elements of Semiology*, trans. Annette Lavers and Colin Smith. New York: Hill and Wang, 1968.

—— (1968), 'The Death of the Author', in *Image-Music-Text,*' trans. Stephen Heath. London: Fontana, 1977, 142–8.

—— (1970), *S/Z*, trans. Richard Miller. New York: Hill and Wang, 1974.

Baudrillard, Jean (1976), *Simulations*, trans. Paul Foss, Paul Patton, and Philip Beitchman. New York: Semiotext(e), 1983.

Belsey, Catherine (1980), *Critical Practice*. New York: Methuen.

Benhabib, Seyla (1986), *Critique, Norm, and Utopia: A Study of the Foundations of Critical Theory*. New York: Columbia University Press.

Benveniste, Emile (1966), *Problems in General Linguistics*, trans. Mary Elizabeth Meek. Coral Gables: University of Miami Press, 1971.

Berman, Marshall (1982), *All That is Solid Melts into Air: The Experience of Modernity*. New York: Touchstone Books.

Berman, Art (1988), *From the New Criticism to Deconstruction: The Reception of Structuralism and Post-Structuralism*. Champaign: University of Illinois Press.

Bhabha, Homi K. (ed.) (1990), *Nation and Narration*. London and New York: Routledge.

Blanchot, Maurice (1980) *The Writing of the Disaster*. trans. Ann Smock, Lincoln: University of Nebraska Press, 1986.

Bremond, Claude (1973), *Logique du récit*. Paris: Seuil.

Brooks, Cleanth (1947), 'The Language of Paradox', in *The Well-Wrought Urn*. New York: Harcourt Brace Jovanovich, 1975, 3–21.

Brooks, Peter (1977), 'Freud's Masterplot', *Yale French Studies* **55/56**: 280–300.

Burke, Kenneth (1937), 'Literature as Equipment for Living', in *The Philosophy of Literary Form*. Berkeley and Los Angeles: The University of California Press, 1973.

Cavell, Stanley (1976), *Must We Mean What We Say?*. Cambridge: Cambridge University Press.

Cixous, Hélène (1975), 'The Laugh of the Medusa', *Critical Theory Since 1965*, ed. Hazard Adams and Leroy Searle. Tallahassee: Florida State University Press, 1986, 309–20.

——, 'Castration or Decapitation,' *Signs* 7, 11, (1981): 41–55.

Clark, Katerina and Michael Holquist (1984), *Mikhail Bakhtin*. Cambridge: Harvard University Press.

Conley, Verena Andermatt (1984), *Hélène Cixous: Writing the Feminine*. Lincoln: University of Nebraska Press.

Connerton, Paul (1980), *The Tragedy of Enlightenment: An Essay on the Frankfurt School*. Cambridge: Cambridge University Press.

Culler, Jonathan (1981), *The Pursuit of Signs*. Ithaca: Cornell University Press.

—— (1982), *On Deconstruction*. Ithaca: Cornell University Press.

De Beauvoir, Simone (1952), *The Second Sex*, trans. H.M. Parshley. New York: Bantam Books.

De Man, Paul (1979), *Allegories of Reading*. New Haven: Yale University Press.

—— (1984), 'Phenomenality and Materiality in Kant' in *Hermeneutics: Questions and Prospects*, ed. Gary Shapiro and Alan Sica. Amherst: University of Massachusetts Press, 139–53.

—— (1984a), *The Rhetoric of Romanticism*. New York: Columbia University Press.

Deleuze, Gilles (1962), *Nietzsche and Philosophy*, trans. Hugh Tomlinson. New York: Columbia University Press, 1983.

—— (1963), *Kant's Critical Philosophy: The Doctrine of the Faculties*, trans. Hugh Tomlinson and Barbara Habberjam. Minneapolis: University of Minnesota Press, 1984.

—— and Felix Guattari (1972), *Anti-Oedipus: Capitalism and Schizophrenia*, trans. Robert Hurley, Mark Seem, and Helen R. Lane. Minneapolis: University of Minneapolis Press, 1983.

—— and Felix Guattari (1980), *A Thousand Plateaus*, trans. Brian Massumi. Minneapolis: University of Minnesota Press, 1987.

Derrida, Jacques (1966), 'Structure, Sign, and Play in the Discourse of the Human Sciences' in *The Structuralist Controversy*, ed. Richard Macksey and Eurenio Donato. Baltimore, Johns Hopkins University Press, 247–72.

—— (1967), *Of Grammatology*, trans. Gayatri Chakravorty Spivak. Baltimore: Johns Hopkins University Press, 1976.

—— (1967a), *Writing and Difference*, trans. Alan Bass. Chicago: University of Chicago Press, 1978.

—— (1967b), *Speech and Phenomena*, trans. David Allison. Evanston: Northwestern University Press, 1973.

—— (1972), *Margins of Philosophy*, trans. Alan Bass. Chicago: University of Chicago Press, 1982.

—— (1972a), *Positions*, trans. Alan Bass. Chicago: University of Chicago Press, 1981.

—— (1977), 'Limited Inc.', trans. Samuel Weber, *Glyph* **2**: 162–254.

—— (1978), *Spurs: Nietzsche's Style*, trans. Barbara Harlow. Chicago: University of Chicago Press, 1979.

—— (1982), 'Choreographies,' interview with Christie McDonald, *Diacritics* **12** (no. 2): 66–76.

—— (1983), 'The Principle of Reason: The University in the Eyes of its Pupils,' trans. Catherine Porter and Edward Morris, *Diacritics*, **13**: 3–20.

—— (1984), *Signponge*, trans. Richard Rand. New York: Columbia University Press.

—— (1985), *The Ear of the Other*, trans. Peggy Kamuf *et al.* New York: Schoken Books.

—— (1986), *Memoires for Paul de Man*, trans. Cecile Lindsay, Jonathan Culler, and Eduardo Cadava. New York: Cambridge University Press.

Descombes, Vincent (1979), *Modern French Philosophy*, trans. L. Scott-Fox and J.M. Harding. Cambridge: Cambridge University Press.

Dewey, John (1891), *Outlines of a Critical Theory of Ethics*, in *Early Works, Volume 3, 1889–1892*, ed. Jo Ann Boydston. Corbondale: Southern Illinois University Press, 1969, 239–388.

Diamond, Irene and Quinby, Lee (1988), Introduction to *Feminism and Foucault: Reflections on Resistance*, eds Irene Diamond and Lee Quinby. Boston: Northeastern University Press, ix–xx.

Eagleton, Terry (1983), *Literary Theory: An Introduction*. Minneapolis: University of Minnesota Press.

Bibliography

—— (1984), *The Function of Criticism: From 'The Spectator' to Post-Structuralism*. London: Verso Books.

—— (1986), 'Brecht and Rhetoric', in *Against the Grain*. London: Verso Books, 167–72.

—— (1990) *The Ideology of the Aesthetic*. Oxford: Basil Blackwell.

Eliot, George (1855), 'Margaret Fuller and Mary Wollstonecraft', in *The Norton Anthology of English Literature*, fourth edition, ed. M.H. Abrams *et al*. New York: Norton, 1979, 1655–61.

Eliot, T.S. (1919), 'Tradition and the Individual Talent', in *Selected Prose*, ed. Frank Kermode. New York: Harcourt Brace, 1975, 37–44.

—— (1923), 'The Function of Criticism', in *Selected Prose*, ed. Frank Kermode. New York: Harcourt Brace, 1975, 68–76.

—— (1933), 'Matthew Arnold', in *The Use of Poetry and the Use of Criticism*. London: Faber & Faber, 1964, 103–19.

Ellmann, Richard, and Feidelson, Charles Jr (1965), *The Modern Tradition*. New York: Oxford University Press.

Felman, Shoshana (1980), *The Literary Speech Act: Don Juan with J.L. Austin, or Seduction in Two Languages*, trans. Catherine Porter. Ithaca: Cornell University Press, 1983.

—— (1987), *Jacques Lacan and the Adventure of Insight*. Cambridge: Harvard University Press.

Fenollosa, Ernest (1919), *The Chinese Written Character as a Medium of Poetry*. Washington: Square Dollar Series, 1956.

Fish, Stanley (1980) *Is There a Text in this Class*. Cambridge: Harvard University Press.

—— (1989), 'The Young and the Restless', in *The New Historicism*, ed. H. Aram Veeser. New York: Routledge, 303–16.

—— (1989a), 'Being Interdisciplinary Is So Very Hard to Do', in *Profession* **89**. New York: the Modern Language Association, 3–20.

Foucault, Michel (1961), *Histoire de la folie à l'âge classique*. Paris: Gallimard, 1972.

—— (1961), *Madness and Civilization: A History of Insanity in the Age of Reason*, trans. Richard Howard. New York: Random House, Pantheon Books, 1965.

—— (1963), *The Birth of the Clinic: An Archaeology of Medical Perception*, trans. Alan Sheridan. New York: Random House, Pantheon Books, 1973.

—— (1969), 'What is an Author?' in *Language, Counter-Memory, Practice*, trans. Donald Bouchard and Sherry Simon. Ithaca: Cornell University Press, 1977, 101–20.

—— (1970), *The Order of Things: An Archaeology of the Human Sciences.* New York: Vintage/Random House, trans. and revision of *Les Mots et les Choses*, 1966.

—— (1970a), 'The Order of Discourse', trans. Ian McLeod, in *Untying the Text: A Post-Structuralist Reader*, ed. Robert Young. London: Routledge & Kegan Paul, 1981 48–78. This essay is also translated as 'The Discourse on Language'.

—— (1971), 'Nietzsche, Genealogy, History', in *Language, Counter-Memory, Practice*, trans. Donald Bouchard and Sherry Simon. Ithaca: Cornell University Press, 1977, 139–64.

—— (1977), 'The Confessions of the Flesh', in *Power/Knowledge: Selected Interviews and Other Writings, 1972–1977*, ed. Colin Gordon, trans. Colin Gordon, Leo Marshall, John Mepham, and Kate Soper. New York: Random House/Pantheon Books, 1980.

—— (1984), *The History of Sexuality, Volume 3: The Care of the Self*, trans. Robert Hurley. New York: Pantheon Books, 1986.

Frank, Joseph (1945), 'Spatial Form in Modern Literature', in *The Widening Gyre: Crisis and Mastery in Modern Literature*. New Brunswick: Rutgers University Press, 1963, 3–62.

Freire, Paulo (1968), *Pedagogy of the Oppressed*, trans. Myra Berman Ramos. New York: Continuum.

Freud, Sigmund (1893), 'Studies on Hysteria', *Standard Edition of the Complete Psychological Works of Sigmund Freud*, trans. and ed. James Strachey. London: Hogarth (24 vols, 1953–74), vol. 2, 1–307.

—— (1897), Letter of 27 October 1897, *Standard Edition*, Vol. 1, 266–67.

—— (1900), *Interpretation of Dreams*, *Standard Edition*, Vols. 4–5, 1–627.

—— (1905), 'On Psychotherapy', *Standard Edition*, Vol. 7, 55–268.

—— (1910), 'Wild Psycho-Analysis', *Standard Edition*, Vol. 11, 221–227.

—— (1913), 'Claims of Psycho-analysis to Scientific Interest', *Standard Edition*, Vol. 13, 165–190.

—— (1915), 'Instincts and Their Vicissitudes', *Standard Edition*, Vol. 14, 109–40.

—— (1920), *Beyond the Pleasure Principle*, *Standard Edition*, Vol. 18, 7–64.

—— (1925), 'A Note on the Mystic Writing Pad', *Standard Edition*, Vol. 19, 227–32.

—— (1933) *New Introductory Lectures On Psychoanalysis*, *Standard Edition*, Vol. 22, 7–182.

—— (1937), 'Analysis Terminable and Interminable', *Standard Edition*, Vol. 23, 216–53.

Frye, Northrop (1949) 'The Function of Criticism at the Present Time' in *Our Sense of Identity*, ed. Malcolm Ross, 1954, 247–65.

—— (1957), *Anatomy of Criticism*. Princeton: Princeton University Press.

Galan, F.W. (1985), *Historical Structures: The Prague School Project, 1928–1946*. Austin: University of Texas Press.

Garver, Newton (1973), Preface in Derrida 1967b pp. ix–xxix.

Gates, Henry Louis (1984) 'The 'Blackness of Blackness': A Critique of the Sign and the Signifying Monkey', in *Black Literature and Literary Theory*. New York: Oxford University Press, 285–321.

Geertz, Clifford (1973), *The Interpretation of Cultures*. New York: Basic Books.

Gilbert, Sandra (1985) 'Life's Empty Pack: Notes Toward a Literary Daughteronomy,' *Critical Inquiry*, **11**: 355–84.

Graff, Gerald (1979), *Literature Against Itself*. Chicago: University of Chicago Press.

—— (1987), *Professing Literature: An Institutional History*. Chicago and London: University of Chicago Press.

Greenblatt, Stephen, ed. (1982), 'Introduction' in *The Power of Forms and the Forms of Power in the Renaissance, Genre*, **15**: 3–6.

—— (1985), 'Shakespeare and the Exorcists', *Shakespeare and the Question of Theory*, eds Patricia Parker and Geoffrey Hartman. New York: Methuen, 163–87.

—— (1989) 'Toward a Poetics of Culture,' in *The New Historicism*, ed. H. Aram Veeser. New York: Routledge, 1–14.

Greimas, A.J. (1966) *Structural Semantics*, trans. Daniele McDowell, Ronald Schleifer, Alan Velie. Lincoln: University of Nebraska Press, 1983.

—— (1976), *Maupassant: The Semiotics of Text. Practical Exercises*, trans. Paul Perron. Amsterdam/Philadelphia: John Benjamins Publishing Co., 1988.

—— and Joseph Courtés (1979), *Semiotics and Language: An Analytical Dictionary*, trans. Larry Crist and Daniel Patte *et al*. Bloomington: Indiana University Press, 1982.

—— (1983), *Du Sens*, Vol. 2. Paris: Seuil.

—— (1987), *On Meaning: Selected Writings in Semiotic Theory*, trans. Paul Perron and Frank Collins. Minneapolis: University of Minnesota Press.

Hall, Stuart (1980), 'Cultural Studies: Two Paradigms', *Media, Culture and Society* **2**: 57–72.

Hartman, Geoffrey (1980), *Criticism in the Wilderness: The Study of Literature Today*. New Haven and London: Yale University Press.

—— (1978), 'Psychoanalysis: The French Connection' in *Psychoanalysis and the Question of the Text*. Baltimore: Johns Hopkins University Press.

Hayman, Ronald (1976), *Leavis*. London: Heinemann.

Hegel, G.W.F. (1807), *The Phenomenology of Mind*, trans. J.B. Baille. New York: Harper Torchbooks, 1967.

Holenstein, Elmar (1974), *Roman Jakobson's Approach to Language*, trans. Catherine Schelbert and Tarcisius Schelbert. Bloomington: Indiana University Press, 1976.

Holland, Norman (1975), *Five Readers Reading*. New Haven: Yale University Press.

—— (1980), 'Re-Covering the "Purloined Letter": Reading as a Personal Transaction', in *The Reader in the Text*, eds. Susan R. Suleiman and Inge Crosman. Princeton: Princeton University Press, 350–70.

Hjelmslev, Louis (1943), *Prolegomena to a Theory of Language*, trans. Francis Whitfield. Madison: University of Wisconsin Press, 1961.

Hulme, T.E. (1924), *Speculations*. London: K. Paul, Trench, Trubner, and Co.

Irigaray, Luce (1974), *Speculum of the Other Woman*, trans. Gillian C. Gill. Ithaca: Cornell University Press, 1985.

—— (1977), *This Sex Which Is Not One*, trans. Catherine Porter. Ithaca: Cornell University Press, 1985.

Jaeger, Werner (1933), *Paideia: The Ideals of Greek Culture*, vol. 1: *Archaic Greece, The Mind of Athens*, trans. Gilbert Highet. New York: Oxford University Press, 1974.

Jakobson, Roman (1929), 'Romantic Panslavism – New Slavic Studies' in *Selected Writings*, Vol. 2, *Word and Language*. The Hague: Mouton, 1971, 711–12.

—— (1932), 'Is the Film in Decline?' in Jakobson (1987), 458–65.

—— (1934), 'What is Poetry?' trans. M. Heim, in Jakobson (1987), 368–78.

—— (1935), 'The Dominant', trans. Herbert Eagle, in Jakobson (1987), 41–49.

—— (1936), 'Signum et Signatum', trans. M. Heim, in *Semiotics of Art: Prague School Contributions*, ed. Ladislav Matejka and Irwin R. Titunik, Cambridge: Harvard University Press, 1976, 176–87.

—— (1956), with Morris Halle, *Fundamentals of Language*, The Hague: Mouton.

—— (1960), 'Linguistics and Poetics', in Jakobson (1987), 62–94.

—— (1968), 'Poetry of Grammar and Grammar of Poetry', in *ibid.*, 121–44.

Bibliography

—— (1987), *Language and Literature*, eds. Krystyna Pomorska and Stephen Rudy. Cambridge: Harvard University Press.

James, Henry (1881), *The Portrait of a Lady*. Harmondsworth: Penguin, 1971.

Jameson, Fredric (1971), *Marxism and Form: Twentieth-Century Dialectical Theories of Literature*. Princeton: Princeton University Press.

—— (1981), *The Political Unconscious*. Ithaca: Cornell University Press.

—— (1984) 'The Politics of Theory: Ideological Positions in the Postmodernism Debate,' in *New German Critique*, **33**: 53–65.

Janik, Alan and Stephen Toulmin (1973), *Wittgenstein's Vienna*. New York: Touchstone Books.

Jay, Martin (1984), *Theodor Adorno*. Cambridge: Harvard University Press.

Johnson, Barbara (1980), *The Critical Difference: Essays in the Contemporary Rhetoric of Reading*. Baltimore and London: Johns Hopkins University Press.

—— (1982), 'Teaching as a Literary Genre', *Yale French Studies* **63**: iii–vii.

Kant, Immanuel (1781), *Critique of Pure Reason*, trans. Norman Kemp Smith. New York: Modern Library, 1958.

Karcevskij, Sergej (1929), 'The Asymmetric Dualism of the Linguistic Sign', trans. Wendy Steiner, in *The Prague School: Selected Writings, 1929–1946*, ed. Peter Steiner. Austin: University of Texas Press, 1982, 47–54.

Kermode, Frank (1957), *Romantic Image*. New York: Chilmark Press.

—— (1973), Introduction to *Modern British Literature*, ed. Frank Kermode and John Hollander. New York: Oxford University Press.

—— (1979), *The Genesis of Secrecy*. Cambridge: Harvard University Press.

Kristeva, Julia (1969), 'Semiotics: A Critical Science and/or a Critique of Science', trans. Sean Hand, in *The Kristeva Reader*, ed. Toril Moi. New York: Columbia University Press, 1986, 74–88. (This first appeared in *Séméiotiké: recherches pour une sémanalyse*).

—— (1973), 'The System and the Speaking Subject', trans. Sean Hand, in *The Kristeva Reader*, ed. Toril Moi. New York: Columbia University Press, 1986, 24–33.

—— (1974), *Revolution in Poetic Language*, trans. Margaret Waller, New York: Columbia University Press, 1984.

—— (1976), 'Stabat Mater', in *Tales of Love*, trans. Leon S. Roudiez. New York: Columbia University Press, 1986, 234–63.

244

Bibliography

—— (1980) *Desire in Language*, trans. Thomas Gora, Alice Jardine, Leon Roudiez. New York: Columbia University Press.

—— (1980a), *Powers of Horror*, trans. Leon S. Roudiez. New York: Columbia University Press. Originally published in 1980.

Kuhn, Annette (1988), 'The Body and Cinema: Some Problems for Feminism', in *Grafts: Feminist Cultural Criticism*, ed. Susan Sheridan. London and New York: Verso Books, 11–23.

Lacan, Jacques (1966), *Écrits: A Selection*, trans. Alan Sheridan. New York: Norton, 1977.

—— (1966a), 'Seminar on "The Purloined Letter",' trans. Jeffrey Mehlman, *Yale French Studies* (1972) **48**: 38–72.

—— (1973), *The Four Fundamental Concepts of Psycho-Analysis*, trans. Alan Sheridan. New York: W.W. Norton and Co., 1978.

Leavis, F. R., and Denys Thompson (1933), *Culture and Environment: The Training of Critical Awareness*. London: Chatto and Windus, 1937.

—— (1943), *Education and the University: A Sketch for an 'English School'*. London: Chatto and Windus.

—— (1963), '*Scrutiny*: A Retrospect', in *Valuation in Criticism and Other Essays*. Cambridge: Cambridge University Press, 1986, 218–43.

Leach, Edmund (1970), *Claude Lévi-Strauss*. New York: Viking Press.

Lentricchia, Frank (1980), *After the New Criticism*, Chicago: University of Chicago Press.

—— (1983), *Criticism and Social Change*. Chicago and London: University of Chicago Press.

Leibniz, Gottfried Wilhelm von (1714), *Mondology and Other Philosophical Essays*, trans. Paul Schrecker and Anne Schrecker. Indianapolis: Bobbs-Merrill, 1965.

Levinas, Emmanuel (1986) *Face to Face with Levinas*, ed R.A. Cohen. Albany: State University of New York Press.

Lévi-Strauss, Claude (1949), *The Elementary Structures of Kinship*, trans. J. Belle and J. von Sturmer. London: Jonathan Cape, 1969.

—— (1955), 'The Structural Study of Myth' in *Structural Anthropology*, trans. Clair Jacobson and Brooke Schoepf. New York: Basic Books, 1963, 206–32. Originally published in 1958.

—— (1960), 'Structure and Form: Reflections on a Work by Vladimir Propp', trans. Monique Layton, rev. Anatoly Liberman, in Vladimir Propp, *Theory and History of Folklore*. Minneapolis: University of Minnesota Press, 1984, 167–89.

—— (1962), *The Savage Mind* (no translator named). Chicago: University of Chicago Press, 1966.

—— (1964), *The Raw and the Cooked*, trans. John and Doreen Weightman. New York: Harper and Row, 1974.

Lowenfeld, Henry (1983), 'Psychic Trauma and Productive Experience in the Artist' in *Literature and Psychoanalysis*, eds Edith Kurzweil and William Phillips. New York: Columbia University Press, 55–66.

Lukàcs, Georg (1964), *Realism in Our Time: Literature and the Class Struggle*, preface by George Steiner. New York: Harper and Row.

Lyotard, Jean François (1970), 'The Jewish Oedipus', trans. Susan Hanson, *Genre*, **10** (1977): 395–411.

MacDonald, Henry (1986) *The Normative Basis of Culture*. Baton Rouge: Louisiana State University Press.

Mailloux, Steven (1977), 'Reader-Response Criticism?' *Genre* **10**: 413–31.

Marx, Karl and Friedrich Engels (1846), *The German Ideology*, ed. R. Pascal. New York: International Publishers, 1947.

—— and Friedrich Engels (1848), *Manifesto of the Communist Party*, in *Marx and Engels: Basic Writings on Politics and Philosophy*, ed. Lewis Feuer. New York: Doubleday, 1959, 1–41.

—— (1867), *Capital: A Critique of Political Economy* (vol. 1), trans. Ben Fowkes. New York: Vintage Books, 1976.

Megill, Allan (1985), *Prophets of Extremity: Nietzsche, Heidegger, Foucault, Derrida*. Berkeley: University of California Press.

Miller, J. Hillis (1976), 'Stevens' Rock and Criticism as Cure', *Georgia Review*, **30**: 5–33, 330–48.

—— (1976a), 'Ariadne's Thread: Repetition and the Narrative Line', *Critical Inquiry*, **3**: 57–77.

—— (1977), 'Ariachne's Broken Woof', *Georgia Review*, **31**: 44–60.

—— (1985), 'The Search for Grounds in Literary Study' in *Rhetoric and Form: Deconstruction at Yale*, ed. Robert Con Davis and Ronald Schleifer. Norman: University of Oklahoma Press, 19–36.

—— (1987), *The Ethics of Reading: Kant, de Man, Eliot, Trollope, James, and Benjamin*. New York: Columbia University Press.

—— (1990), *Versions of Pygmalion*. Cambridge: Harvard University Press.

Modleski, Tania (1986), 'The Terror of Pleasure' in *Studies in Entertainment*, ed. Tania Modleski. Bloomington: Indiana University Press, 155–66.

Moi, Toril (1986), Introduction to *The Kristeva Reader*, ed. Toril Moi. New York: Columbia University Press, 1–22.

Moretti, Franco (1983) *Signs Taken for Wonders*, trans. Susan Fischer, David Forgacs, and David Miller. London: Verso Books.

Neumann, Erich (1954), *The Origins and History of Consciousness*, Trans. R.F.C. Hull. Princeton: Princeton University Press.

—— (1955), *The Great Mother: An Analysis of the Archetype*. Princeton: Princeton University Press.

Nietzsche, Friedrich (1873), *On the Use and Abuse of History*, trans. Adrian Collins. Indianapolis: Bobbs–Merrill, 1957.

—— (1882), *The Gay Science*, trans. Walter Kaufmann. New York: Vintage Books, 1974.

—— (1886), *Beyond Good and Evil*, trans. Walter Kaufmann. New York: Vintage Books, 1973.

—— (1887), *On the Genealogy of Moral* and *Ecce Homo*, trans. Walter Kaufmann and R.J. Hollingdale. New York: Vintage Books, 1967.

—— (1889), *Twilight of the Idols*, trans. Walter Kaufmann, in *The Portable Nietzsche*, ed. Walter Kaufmann. New York: Viking Press, 1954, 463–565.

—— (1901), *The Will to Power*, trans. Walter Kaufmann and R.J. Hollingdale. New York: Vintage Books, 1968.

Norris, Christopher (1987), *Derrida*. Cambridge: Harvard University Press.

—— (1988), *Paul De Man: Deconstruction and the Critique of Aesthetic Ideology*. New York: Routledge.

Propp, Vladimir (1959), *Morphology of the Folktale* (English translation), trans. Rev. Laurence Scott. Austin and London: University of Texas Press, 1968. Originally published in 1928.

Rapaport, Herman (1985), 'Geoffrey Hartman and the Spell of Sound' in *Rhetoric and Form: Deconstruction at Yale*, ed. Robert Con Davis and Ronald Schleifer. Norman: University of Oklahoma Press, 159–77.

—— (1989), *Heidegger and Derrida: Reflections on Time and Language*. Lincoln: University of Nebraska Press.

Richards, I.A. (1925), *Principles of Literary Criticism*. New York: Harcourt Brace.

—— (1929), *Practical Criticism*, New York: Harcourt Brace.

Robinson, Lillian S. (1983) 'Treason our Text: Feminist Challenges to the Literary Canon', in *Feminist Criticism*, ed. Elaine Showalter. New York: Pantheon, 1985, 105–21.

Rorty, Richard (1982), *Consequences of Pragmatism*. Minneapolis: University of Minnesota Press.

Said, Edward W. (1983), *The World, the Text, and the Critic*. Cambridge: Harvard University Press.

Saussure, Ferdinand de (1916), *Course in General Linguistics*, trans. Wade Baskin. New York: McGraw–Hill, 1959.

Schleifer, Ronald (1987), *A.J. Greimas and the Nature of Meaning: Linguistics, Semiotics, and Discourse Theory*. Lincoln: University of Nebraska Press.

—— (1987a), 'Deconstruction and Linguistic Analysis', *College English* **49**: 381–95.

—— (1990), *Rhetoric and Death: The Language of Modernism and Postmodern Discourse Theory*. Urbana: University of Illinois Press.

Scholes, Robert (1985) *Textual Power*. New Haven: Yale University Press.

Schweichkart, Patrocinio (1986) 'Reading Ourselves: Toward a Feminist Theory of Reading', in *Gender and Reading*, ed. Elizabeth Flynn and Patrocinio Schweichkart. Baltimore: Johns Hopkins University Press, 31–62.

Shapiro, Karl (ed.) (1962), *Prose Keys to Modern Poetry*. New York: Harper and Row.

Shklovsky, Viktor (1917), 'Art as Technique' in *Russian Formalist Criticism: Four Essays*, trans. Lee Lemon and Marion Reis. Lincoln: University of Nebraska Press, 1965, 3–24.

Showalter, Elaine (1979) 'Toward a Feminist Poetics', in *Feminist Criticism*, ed. Elaine Showalter. New York: Pantheon, 1985, 125–43.

—— (1981) 'Feminist Criticism in the Wilderness', in *Feminist Criticism*, ed. Elaine Showalter. New York: Pantheon, 1985, 243–70.

Spivak, Gayatri Chakravorty (1984), 'Love Me, Love My Ombre, Elle' in *Diacritics* **14** (no. 4): 19–36.

—— (1986), 'Imperialism and Sexual Difference' in *Oxford Literary Review* **8**: 225–40.

—— (1988), 'Can the Subaltern Speak?' in *Marxism and the Interpretation of Culture*, eds Cary Nelson and Lawrence Grossberg. Urbana and Chicago: University of Illinois Press, 271–313.

Stambaugh, Joan (1972), *Nietzsche's Thought of Eternal Return*. Baltimore: Johns Hopkins University Press.

Starobinski, Jean (1971), *Words Upon Words: The Anagrams of Ferdinand de Saussure*, trans. O. Emmit. New Haven: Yale University Press, 1979.

Steiner, George (1978), 'On Difficulty' in *On Difficulty and Other Essays*. New York: Oxford University Press, 18–47.

Steiner, Peter (1982), 'To Enter the Circle: The Functionalist Structuralism of the Prague School' in *The Prague School: Selected Writings, 1929–1946*, ed. Peter Steiner. Austin: University of Texas Press, ix–xii.

—— (1984), *Russian Formalism: A Metapoetics*. Ithaca: Cornell University Press.

Stocking, George (1968), *Race, Culture, and Evolution*. New York: Free Press.

Striedter, Jurij (1989), *Literary Structure, Evolution, and Value: Russian Formalism and Czech Structuralism Reconsidered*. Cambridge: Harvard University Press.

Taine, Hippolyte Adolphe (1864), *History of English Literature*, trans. Henry Van Laun. New York: P.F. Collier, 1900.

Tate, Allen (1941), 'The Present Function of Criticism' in *Reason in Madness: Critical Essays*. New York: Putnam's, 3–19.

Tennenhouse, Leonard (1982) 'Representing Power: *Measure for Measure* in its Time,' in *The Power of Forms and the Forms of Power in the Renaissance*, *Genre*, **15**: 139–56.

Todorov, Tzvetan (1970), *The Fantastic: A Structural Approach to a Literary Genre*, trans. Richard Howard. Ithaca: Cornell University Press, 1975.

—— (1971), *The Poetics of Prose*, trans. Richard Howard. Ithaca: Cornell University Press. Originally published in 1971.

Weiskel, Thomas (1986), *The Romantic Sublime*. Baltimore: Johns Hopkins University Press.

Wellek, René (1986), *A History of Modern Criticism: 1750–1950*, Volume 5. New Haven: Yale University Press.

West, Cornel (1988), 'Historicizing the Postmodern Debate: Arnold, Eliot, Trilling, and Fannon on the Crisis in Modern Culture', unpublished lecture presented at the University of Oklahoma, 2 November 1988. Videotape available.

Williams, Raymond (1958), *Culture and Society: 1780–1950*. New York: Columbia University Press.

—— (1961), *The Long Revolution*. Harmondsworth: Penguin Books.

—— (1976), *Keywords*. New York: Oxford University Press.

—— (1977), *Marxism and Literature*. New York: Oxford University Press.

Wimsatt, W. K., Jr. and Monroe C. Beardsley (1946), 'The Intentional Fallacy' in *The Verbal Icon*. Lexington: University of Kentucky Press, 1967, 3–18.

—— (1949), 'The Affective Fallacy' in *The Verbal Icon*. Lexington: Univ. of Kentucky Press, 1967, 21–39.

Winters, Yvor (1943), 'The Morality of Poetry' in *In Defense of Reason*. Denver: Alan Swallow, 1968.

Wittig, Monique (1981), 'One is Not Born A Woman' in *Feminist Issues* **1**, 2 (Winter): 47–54.

Bibliography

—— (1982), 'The Category of Sex' in *Feminist Issues*, **2**, 1 (Fall): 63–8.
—— (1989), 'On the Social Contract' in *Feminist Issues* **9**, 1 (Spring): 3–12.
—— (1990), 'Homo Sum' in *Feminist Issues* **10**, 1 (Spring): 3–11.
Yeats, W.B. (1956), *Collected Poems*. New York: Macmillan.

Index

Index

alienation effect, 200
Brooks, Cleanth, 81, 94, 131–2
'The Language of Paradox', 79, 131
Brooks, Peter, 107
Burke, Kenneth, 36, 130, 135, 201, 221
Byron, George Gordon, Lord, 61–2

Cassirer, Ernst, 122
Cavell, Stanley, 15
Chaucer, Geoffrey, *The Canterbury Tales*, 52
Chomsky, Noam, 23–4
Cixous, Hélène, 108–10, 178
'Castration or Decapitation?', 225–6
'The Laugh of the Medusa', 109
The Newly-Born Woman, 109
classicism, 71–2, 81
Clement, Catherine, 109
Coleridge, Samuel
definition of fancy, 71
and imagination, 79
Connerton, Paul, 3–5, 23–4, 26
critique as reconstruction and 'criticism', 23–4
Conrad, Joseph, 73, 196
'Secret Sharer', 104
constative, 26, 107, 162–3, 221, 222, 225
and irony, 165–6
Continental linguistics, 120
contradiction
principle of, 4
See also Leibniz
Coward, Rosalind, 178
criticism, 211, 219–20
canny, 20–1
compared with critique, 6, 7, 12, 21, 118, 220
as cultural critique, 18, 26
uncanny, 20–1
See also archetypal criticism
critique
'authentic', 215
classical usage, 3
compared with criticism, 6, 7, 12, 21, 82, 98, 118, 220
cultural, 2–3, 7, 30, 40–1, 46, 49, 57–8, 224
cultural critique of gender, 224–9
cultural critique as pedagogical mode, 229
defined, 3
and reason, 4, 17–18
and the signifier, 17
significance in the Renaissance, 3
term appropriate for the Enlightenment, 3

See also institutional critique; transformative critique
Cronenberg, David
Videodrome, 215
Culler, Jonathan, 127, 145, 151, 163
Structuralist Poetics, 141
culture, 36
Lévi-Strauss's definition of, 8

Darwin, Charles, 30
Origin of Species, 52
deconstruction, 152, 159–167, 177–9, 182, 202, 219, 220
two strategic phases of, 164–5
See also undecidability
defamiliarization, 130–1, 200
Deleuze, Gilles, 13–14, 31, 109, 113–17, 153, 158, 162, 168, 203, 228
Nietzsche and Philosophy, 151, 169
A Thousand Plateaus, 113, 116
definition of genealogy, 169
description of the Western Oedipus, 220
Empirisisme et subjectivité, 113
and Felix Guattari: *Anti-Oedipus*, 113
Kant's Critical Philosophy, 113
De Man, Paul, 22, 36, 52, 54, 66, 67, 157, 160, 162–7, 176, 183
Allegories of Reading, 165
aporia, 163–4
definition of teaching, 70
opposition between rhetoric and grammar, 165
'Semiology and Rhetoric', 161, 165
Derrida, Jacques, 14, 19–21, 25, 28, 33, 126, 146–8, 151–2, 159–78, 180, 183, 203, 205, 227, 234
active and reactive, 169
criticism of Freudian subject, 104–6
critique of Lévi-Strauss, 146, 160–1
critique of speech-act theory, 182
and deconstruction, 159–67, 181
definition of grammatology, 168–9
description of the Nietzschean affirmation, 164, 168
différance, 179
discussion of Kant, 49
Elementary Structures, 146
'Force and Signification', 210
'Limited Inc.', 170
Memoires for Paul de Man, 177
Of Grammatology, 146, 160, 178
and the reserve of language, 27
Signponge, 172
Spurs, 162–4, 166, 166, 168–71

Index